African History and Culture

African History and Culture

**Edited by
Richard Olaniyan**

Longman Nigeria

Longman Nigeria Limited,
P.M.B. 21036
52 Oba Akran Avenue,
Ikeja, Lagos, Nigeria

Longman Group Limited,
Longman House, Burnt Mill,
Harlow, Essex CM20 2JE

First published 1982
Second impression 1982
ISBN 0 582 64369 4

Printed in Hong Kong by
Wilture Enterprises (International) Ltd.

Contents

List of illustrations

List of maps

Preface

This book is intended for those pursuing a general studies course in African history and culture in universities and post-secondary institutions. The need for a book of this kind has become urgent and imperative in our institutions of higher learning where a deeper appreciation and consciousness of the African past has become part and parcel of our educational and national commitment. We do not claim that the result of our efforts assembled here is comprehensive or definitive, but we have tried to give prominence to the important issues in a thematic fashion comprehensible to the university student or to the general reader who seeks a reliable panoramic view before venturing upon the more specialised studies suggested at the end of each chapter. References and notes have been kept to the minimum, and readers are referred to the relevant sources in the suggestions for further reading. We have also included questions to stimulate discussion.

By its very nature as an edited interdisciplinary work, the book does not claim to have that uniformity of style which would be expected in a volume written by a single author. Perhaps, in a way, this seeming weakness may in fact prove to be a strength, for each contributor brings to his chapter his own insights and perspectives; thus a variety of academic interests and points of view is found within a reasonably compact volume. Inevitably, overlapping occurs here and there in the book, and we have therefore provided a cross-reference system through the notes placed at the end of each chapter. As much as possible, we have tried to maintain a continental outlook, because we believe that in spite (or because) of diversity, there has been, and still is, much contact and interaction between the many African peoples and regions.

For many reasons the completion of this work has taken much longer than was anticipated, but its completion is a testimony to the commitment and co-operation of the contributors. Of these ten contributors, six are from the University of Ife in Nigeria: S. O. Arifalo, Toyin Falola and Richard Olaniyan of the Department of History; Professor Adebisi Afolayan, Head of the Department of English Language; Professor Wole Soyinka, Head of the Department of Dramatic Arts; and J. R. O. Ojo, Senior Lecturer and Acting Head, Department of Fine Arts. The others are: Professor Akin Euba, Director of the Centre for Cultural Studies, University of Lagos, Nigeria, and formerly Acting Head of the Department of Music, University of Ife; Jolayemi Solanke, resident in Washington, D.C., U.S.A., who has degrees in the Social Sciences; Professor John S. Mbiti, formerly of the Religious Studies Department, Makerere University, Kampala, Uganda; and finally, Oluwole Omoni, a former colleague in the Department of History, at Ife, who is now on the staff of the Oyo State College of Education, Ilesa, Nigeria. The editor is grateful to them all for their co-operation. He also owes a special debt of gratitude to William Heinemann, Ltd. for permission to make use in Chapter 11 of material first published by them.

Our indebtedness to many others is considerable: to the authors and colleagues whose ideas have been useful to us we offer our unalloyed gratitude; to the co-operative librarians at Ife, the World Bank, the Library of Congress, and Georgetown University, Washington, D.C., we give our thanks; special thanks go to Elizabeth Paren, Ann Price and A. Akinyemi who offered us invaluable comments and assistance. We also thank F. E. Ogunsakin for typing the first draft. However, each of us gladly accepts responsibility for whatever faults remain in our individual contributions.

Finally, without the incalculable assistance to the editor during his sabbatical leave in the United States in 1977–78 of the Rev. Francis Colgan, F.S.C., J. L. Stanley and Sister Jeannette F. Ryan, who removed from him much of the anxiety of living in Washington without benefit of a grant, the editorial work would have taken much longer to complete. The editor is also appreciative of the kindnesses of the Rev. Richard F. Ryan, S.J., Mr and Mrs R. B. Potter, Mr and Mrs Arnold Ordman, Mr and Mrs Frank Lattanzi, the late Mrs Mary Peck, and the families of Daniel Akande and Samuel Olayinka.

Richard Olaniyan
Oshogbo, Nigeria
December 1980

Acknowledgements

We are grateful to the following for permission to reproduce copyright material:
Heinemann Educational Books for an extract from 'African Views of the Universe' by J. S. Mbiti in *Introduction to African Religion*.
The publishers are grateful to the following for permission to reproduce photographs in the text:
Associated Press Ltd. for page 108; BBC Hulton Picture Library for pages 46, 63 and 130 bottom; British Museum for page 21; Camera Press Ltd. for pages 102, 139, 152 top left, 152 top right, 152 bottom left and 152 bottom right; Clarendon Press for page 89; Basil Davidson for page 15; Department of Information, Salisbury, Zimbabwe, for page 24; Werner Forman Archive for page 59; Ife Museum for page 209; Keystone Press Agency Ltd. for page 92 bottom left; Keith Nicklin/Jill Salmon for page 211; Popperfoto for pages 92 top left and 92 bottom right; Royal Geographical Society for page 73.
The publishers are unable to trace the copyright holders of the following photographs and apologise for any infringement of copyright caused: pages 43, 86, 91, 92 top right and 130 top.
The cover photograph was kindly supplied by the National Museum, Lagos.

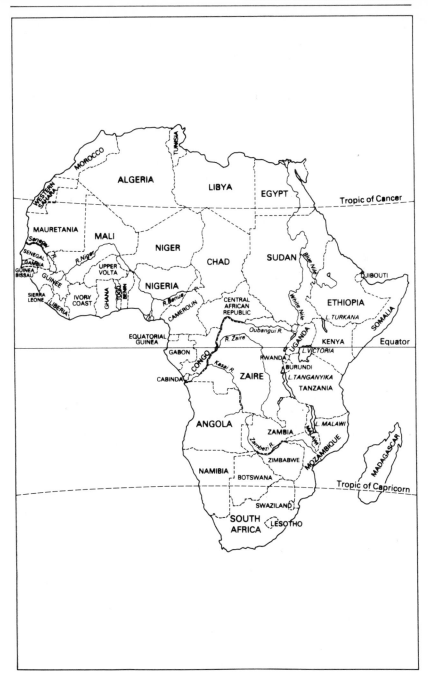

Map 1   *The countries of Africa*

1 African history and culture: an overview

Richard Olaniyan

With an area of 11·7 million square miles (30·3 million square kilometres) and amounting to a fifth of the Earth's land mass, Africa is the second-largest continent in the world. It contains more than fifty independent countries, has a population of 436 million people (mid-1978 estimate) with almost a thousand separate language groups, a variety of climatic regions and greatly different levels of social and economic development. Africa is a continent of bewildering diversity and extraordinary dynamism, and is the theatre of constant social and political change.

This brief introductory chapter focuses on themes that will provide the setting for an appreciation of what this book is all about – the history and cultures of the African peoples. Three topics will come into our purview, namely: the African's sense of history, the sources of African history and the African's relation to his environment. The significance of these themes will become ever more clear as we consider the topics dealt with in the succeeding chapters of this book. Inevitably, we shall make generalisations in our discussion of these themes, but this should not be construed as meaning that there are no exceptions or differences from one culture area to another.

African peoples' sense of history

The peoples of Africa, like all other peoples of the world, are inseparable from their history and culture, for their history is the record of what they did, thought and said; and their culture is the totality of the ideas, concepts and values that characterise their societies.[1] These cultural elements are manifested in their literatures (oral as well as written), religions, social, economic and political institutions, music and dance, arts and drama, and their languages – all these in turn have been and still are profoundly influenced by their environments.

A generation ago, it might have been necessary to 'prove' that Africa's history did not start with the coming of the Europeans. Today, that is no longer in question. The efforts of the growing community of scholars – international in its make-up and interdisciplinary in its approaches – to unearth the facts about the African past have yielded and continue to yield impressive harvests. The study of African history and culture has now become part and parcel of the academic curricula in universities all over the world. Recent archaeological findings by the Leakey family point to Africa as the birthplace of man. It is from Africa that man may have moved to the other continents and because of his remarkable capacity to adapt himself to the demands of various environments, man can now be found in all parts of the world where human habitation is possible. Thus, we can no longer deny that we all are products of what Leakey calls the same 'genetic heritage'.[2] And, as the illustrious black nationalist and scholar, Edward Wilmot Blyden, put it in 1880, 'Africa is no vast island . . . Africa has been connected, both as source and nourisher, with some of the most potent influences which have affected for good the history of the world.'[3] But how does the African view his history? What is his consciousness of his past? What is the role of history in his universe?

The African views history as a continuum consisting of a past, a present and a future – all inseparably linked together. The sequence is crucial in that the past has a significant role to play in the evolution of the present, and in turn the present can affect the turns and twistings of the future. The stuff of history includes migrations, wars, triumphs and tragedies, the extinction and the emergence of city-states and kingdoms, and much else. This historical consciousness recognises continuity and change, order and purpose within the framework of man and his environment, man and the gods, man and his ancestors.

In the African historical tradition, myth and symbolism are often employed to explain origins of peoples, historical causation, migrations, and relationships among various communities. The present is never wholly liberated from the past in that through rituals, the credibility of old verities and institutions is constantly being re-enacted and validated. This dependence on the past can be explained in terms of the reverence accorded to the ancestors, the founders of the clan, the progenitor of the ethnic group or the kingdom, who may often indeed be elevated in the group's historical consciousness to the level of gods;[4] being gods, their influence on the living becomes even more important as their spirits and memories are invoked from generation to generation. This helps the process of historical awareness in the youth who sees that his behaviour and that of his elders is praiseworthy only when it is in conformity with the traditions of the group. To offend the moral laws of the society as laid down in distant times by the ancestors is to offend the ancestral spirits. To do this would be foolhardy. In that sense, history could be and was indeed used as a weapon of social control and group cohesion and solidarity. For such purposes and in its capacity to grasp the past, tradition is more interested in what we may call the historical sweep, the larger issues, than in the details or even strict chronology of the past.

This African historical tradition suffered a set-back when it confronted invading colonial values, technology, racial pride and prejudice. The pernicious contention that the African had no past worth preserving was a strategy concocted (though often unconsciously) by the colonial invaders so that their ideas, values and institutions could have pride of place; it was also the product of a European intellectual milieu under the influence of the Darwinian theory of the survival of the fittest. However, the resilience of African institutions prevented a sharp break with the past for, during this colonial period, a substantial proportion of the population remained relatively untouched by the new cultural infusion. There were also many who adhered to Islam. However, even those who accepted the new values and the white man's religion resorted for solace during moments of stress and anxiety to the faith of their forefathers. There were those among the literate who, motivated by the need to preserve their culture, produced books and pamphlets on their local history and customs: men like Samuel Johnson and Jacob Egharevba in Nigeria, Apolo Kagwa in Uganda, Hamphate Ba in Mali, and Boubou Hama in Niger, to name just a few. Nevertheless, colonialism took a painful toll among the emerging indigenous elite who, in the cultural and intellectual enslavement, became estranged and alienated from their cultural heritage. This process varied from one colonial people to another; the impact of this on the contemporary African scene is pervasive and will receive further consideration in later chapters of this book.

Reconstructing African history

The task of reconstructing African history has been a challenging one. The greater part of the challenge springs from the fact that many parts of Africa until recently remained pre-literate and therefore lacked records of their past. However, it would be misleading to contend that all parts of the continent suffered from this limitation. Egypt had evolved its hieroglyphics some three thousand years before the beginning of the Christian era; in Ethiopia, there was Ge'ez, the language of ancient Axum, which had been committed to writing before A.D. 400. In addition, external contacts long enriched the continent. Islam brought not only the Arabic language but also a tradition of scholarship and historiography which to this day remains a source of information and inspiration to students of African history. This tradition created such centres of learning as Timbuktu, Jenne and Sokoto in the western Sudan* and Harar in the Horn of Africa. Contact with the classical civilisations of Greece and Rome helped to introduce their languages and literatures to Mediterranean Africa. In East Africa Swahili developed, becoming a language of commerce. There were other places in Africa where, for example, Arabic script was used to write indigenous languages. Finally, the Europeans, explorers, missionaries and colonial officers, who came to tropical Africa from the fifteenth century onwards – the Portuguese, Dutch, English, French, Danes and Germans – kept records of their contact and activities. All these are valuable sources of African history but, like all historical sources, must be used with proper care and circumspection.

*Here we need to define the term 'the Sudan' in order to avoid confusion. It comes from the Arabic expression *bilā al-Sūdān*, 'the land of the blacks', and was applied to the whole of Africa south of the Sahara by the early Muslim writers. In its restricted modern sense, however, it refers to the savannah belt stretching from the Atlantic to the Red Sea between the Sahara and the tropical forest regions, and it is in this sense that we refer to the western and eastern Sudan. At other places in this book references are made specifically to the modern Republic of Sudan.

It is nevertheless significant to stress that vast areas in Africa south of the Sahara remained without written sources for their past before the advent of the colonial era. In such situations, the use of oral tradition – a body of knowledge pertaining to the origin and history of a people transmitted orally from generation to generation – has great value. In many of these pre-literate areas there are still old men and women who are versed in the ancient lore of their people. These and the traditional court historians whose job it is to memorise and recite on occasions their traditions are the custodians of this heritage. Again, it is necessary to issue a warning about the limitations which apply to all kinds of historical evidence, since there are many pitfalls in the use of oral tradition. Yet as a source of historical information in the pre-literate, colonial and, indeed, even contemporary African communities where written sources cannot be taken as sufficiently comprehensive or reliable, oral tradition must be given special consideration. It is no longer disputable that various African countries preserve aspects of their traditions in their myths, proverbs, poetry, rituals, tales and music; when used with proper care and according to rigorous standards, these are legitimate and reliable sources of information. With increasing usage and improvements in method, the usual problems associated with oral tradition – problems of collection, chronology, documentation and interpretation – are being solved. What is essential to the use of oral tradition is that the researcher be familiar with the culture, the social and political structure, and thought systems of the community in which he is working.[5] There are now a number of admirable volumes on how to collect and use oral history materials.

As we have pointed out elsewhere, the multi-disciplinary approach to the study of African history and cultures is imperative because each discipline has a unique contribution to make to the process of reconstructing the African past.

The significance of archaeology to the study of African history is increasingly realised. Through excavations and painstaking study of artefacts collected from sites, archaeology can lend the needed credence to, or induce scepticism about, the claims of oral tradition regarding, for example, the locations and patterns of old settlements. Even more encouraging is the increasing competence of archaeologists, through the use of radio carbon-dating and other techniques, to provide some relatively firm chronological basis in place of the 'long ago' of oral traditions. Through the pioneering work of Dr Louis Leakey and others in the Olduvai Gorge in East Africa, contemporary man has gained a deeper insight into the intricacies of human evolution and has come to appreciate that Africa may in fact be the birthplace of the human race. Furthermore, archaeological research and excavations in other parts of Africa have revealed a high level of artistic achievements – Nok, Ife and Benin in Nigeria, and the civilisation of Zimbabwe in Central Africa, to name only the more familiar archaeological success stories, in the continent. Archaeology can tell us about Africa's early material culture, level and variety of technology, and even early types of economic activities. It is therefore necessary for the student of African history to equip himself with the knowledge that would make the cross-fertilisation between history and archaeology a productive venture, and thus enrich our understanding of the African past.

Anthropology is another discipline that can aid the use of oral tradition to reconstruct the African past. The anthropologist is concerned with the scientific study of man, his mind, body and society. He is interested in understanding a society's material culture, social and political institutions, social groups, social change, values among the various groups, as well as religious and philosophical beliefs. The anthropologist's method of collecting information and his interest in the past of the society he studies can prove useful to the historian in his effort to unravel the early history of Africa.

Another source of benefit to the historian in his quest to gain insight into the past of Africa is linguistics. As a discipline, linguistics is the study of the origins, history, use, structures and other aspects of particular languages or of languages in general. Language is an essential aspect of a people's culture. How did a particular language develop? What relationship did it have with other languages? What measure of interaction among language groups has taken place? These questions are vital to the interests of the discipline of linguistics. Thus linguistics can indicate changes that have occurred in a language either through contact or interaction with other linguistic groups and can, by employing approaches such as lexico-statistics and glottochronology, suggest answers to the historian's probing questions about where, when and how changes have taken place.

Again, the zoologists and the botanists can offer clues as to the origins and dispersion of animals and plants and explain how they came to be where they now are, and can give some insight about the flora and fauna of a given area in the past. It is possible for the historian using the leads suggested by these sources to attempt a sketch of probable patterns of diffusion of ideas, institutions and objects, migrations and trade routes.

Indubitably, these and other ancillary disciplines can be used to shed further light on the African past in its many facets.[6] Obviously, there are problems arising from limited resources, human as well as material; there are not enough anthropologists or linguists or botanists, and there are even fewer archaeologists to uncover the African past in their special ways. But the promise is there as we have begun to see if experts in the related and allied disciplines continue to co-operate in this exciting and rewarding enterprise. Not only could their co-operation contribute to building a more complete picture of the African past but indeed may also lead us to ask more searching questions whose answers might further illuminate the history of man's common heritage.

Man in the African environment

In our quest for the past we need to study the geography of Africa, for it is only thus that we can comprehend the various aspects of the continent's history and cultures. Perhaps more than in any other continent the physical environment – the climate, the nature of the landscape, the vegetation, the quality of the soil, the precipitation factor or distribution of rainfall, the flora and fauna – has played (and, of course, still plays) a crucial role in the activities and affairs of man in Africa. There is a great need for caution here otherwise we may fall into the error of environmental determinism – that is, of claiming that man's activities are wholly determined by environmental factors. There were, of course, external forces that also contributed to the pattern and direction of development, for example, imperial interests and the impact of the slave trade. Yet the most pervasive culture trait of traditional Africa was the inextricable relationship between man and his environment. Indeed, the African saw himself as being part of the environment, hence his almost instinctive adaptation to its varied imperatives. Because there was such a great variety of climatic environments and because he sought to function as part of the natural world, inevitably his culture developed in part from the nature of the demands made on him by the physical environment and his own adaptive response to it. It then follows that differences in climatic regions would, again in part, account for the diversity of cultures all over the continent. It is also important to appreciate that climate has been a crucial factor in the distribution of people and, to a very large extent, has dictated their occupational activities. This environmental diversity explains not only cultural pluralism but also, at least indirectly, the existence of the observable differences of physical type ranging, for example, from the shortest in stature (the Mbuti Pygmy hunter-gatherers of the Ituri, the equatorial rain forest in eastern Zaire) to the tallest (the Tutsi of Rwanda). Other factors which could explain differences of physical type include isolation of a group, which impeded interaction with other peoples and thereby affected their genetic make-up; and hybridisation – a phenomenon that was inevitable during migrations and inter-group contacts.[7] There are other physical characteristics which may set one group apart from others, such as skin pigmentation. There is more to it than this as we shall see when we come to correlate the environmental imperatives with man's activities and to understand how these are enhanced or hindered.

In the meantime, let us take a look at some of the geographical or climatic realities with which man had to come to terms in his efforts to maximise his opportunities for progress in his environment. Africa is a massive, compact land mass with relatively straight coasts and few natural harbours. Much of the area is desert (the Sahara and the Kalahari, for example); more than half of tropical Africa has little or only rare and irregular precipitation, while the tropical rainy regions receive too much rainfall, certainly more than the prevailing capacity to utilise it; and with few exceptions, African soils are poor and unproductive.

The problem of communications all over the continent can be traced to the physical environment; its sheer size, the comparative lack of navigable inland waterways, the dearth of facilities along the desert tracks, the lack of major harbours. In consequence, much of the hinterland has remained culturally remote from the coasts. In their wisdom, the imperial powers partitioned the continent without much consideration for these physical features; the effect today is that more than a dozen African countries are landlocked and therefore have to bear high transportation costs for their exports and imports.

Although we may admit that most African societies produced enough food to satisfy their needs, it could hardly be seriously maintained that whatever surpluses remained were enough to cater for that section of the population that was involved in pursuits other than the three principal occupations of traditional Africa: hunting – gathering, pastoralism and agriculture. We are here speaking about the men and women of skill engaged in woodwork, metalwork, weaving and so on. We are, of course, generalising widely here and allowance must be made for some prominent exceptions; there were, for example, communities in Africa where technicians and craftsmen reached a high level of mastery and artistic accomplishment; communities with complex social organisations, intricate centralised political systems and a high level of technology. Even in the midst of their relative poverty and environmental limitations, African societies developed their oral literature, and in places where writing was part of the culture, we find that they were not idle.

However, the question still remains: why did the African culture fail to reach a level of technology comparable to that of Euro-America? Here the facts of the African past and environment will guide us. In the first place, the soils and water resources of Africa were poor and could hardly be compared with the large areas of Europe and America where agriculturists with better technology could produce enough, and often far more than enough, to feed their populations. There can be no denying that these continents have an environmental advantage over Africa. Secondly, contact which could make ideas and knowledge and application of new inventions and technologies spread quickly over a wider area was hampered in Africa. Without contact with the new ways and challenges coming from other societies where the new techniques had been evolved, it was impossible to effect any transformation in the traditional methods of solving problems posed even by environmental constraints. Thirdly, we must take account of the prevalence of disease and sickness, partly due to poor or inadequate diet and partly due to disease-carriers present in the natural environment like the mosquito which transmits malaria, the tsetse fly which brings trypanosomiasis or sleeping sickness to man and cattle, and so on. These sap man's energy and affect his productive capability. There are also many pests which annually cause great havoc to his crops and thus reduce his food supply.

There was another factor which contributed to the technological underdevelopment of pre-colonial Africa, that is, the lack of large political entities. On the eve of the partition of Africa, except for such older states as Egypt, Morocco, Tunis, Liberia and Ethiopia, and the states that were at the height of their power at this time in sub-Saharan Africa, there were no large political entities; and those which did exist could not be compared with England, France or Germany which had achieved a higher level of political integration, demographic homogeneity and national outlook. African states such as Asante, Buganda, Zulu and Sokoto lacked the natural resources and the fairly heavy populations that could be commanded by the large political organisations of Europe or Asia. In Europe, moreover, cultural homogeneity and the Christian religion served as agents of national integration and consolidation. In Africa, on the other hand, cultural heterogeneity and low population concentrations contributed to the maintenance of a mosaic of small nationalities not strong enough to effect the kind of technological transformation we are speaking about.

Certainly, environmental factors and cultural heterogeneity alone are inadequate to explain the phenomenon of African under-development. In addition, the Atlantic slave trade caused a massive depopulation amounting to more than the 11 million suggested by Professor Curtin in his recent study.[8] Those millions who were captured and were ultimately carried away as slaves to the Americas represented a virile, productive segment of the population: healthy men and women in their prime. It must be borne in mind that millions more also died or were maimed during the slave raids, slave wars and the 'Middle Passage' or the Atlantic crossing. The number of people forcibly removed from Africa becomes even more staggering when we consider the consequences of the East African slave trade where African captives were taken to work on plantations owned by Europeans in such places as Mauritius, the Seychelles and Reunion. Arab slavers were so prominently involved in the East African slave trade that the trade is sometimes referred to as the Arab slave trade. For very much longer than in the Atlantic trade, Africans were sent from here as slaves to the Arab countries of North Africa and the Middle East, and then later, through what we may call the 'southern passage', by way of the Cape of Good Hope, also to the Americas.

Certain consequences follow from this: a massive loss of population, especially of the type pointed out above, which meant loss of productive labour forces; the possibility of increasing agricultural interests and harvests was considerably hampered; and other economic activities also suffered. The harmful effects of the methods employed in securing slaves must also be considered: slave raiding caused social dislocation and insecurity; the preoccupation with the slave trade distracted Africans from creative interests and ideas which could have enriched their technological arsenal; disruption and stagnation also resulted in weakness in domestic and inter-regional trade and economies because of the preoccupation with the foreign trade in slaves. In sum, the slave trade created socio-political instability, depleted the labour force, encouraged a dependence mentality, truncated the evolution of indigenous African technology, and discouraged the introduction of European technology – all of which were inconsistent with what Walter Rodney defines as the 'capacity for self-sustaining growth'.[9] Africa's contact with Europe for centuries under these inauspicious circumstances made Africans an unwilling subordinate, abused and exploited, for the enrichment and development of Europe. The exploitation of Africa's resources, human as well as natural, meant impoverishment, decline and disintegration to the African states.[10]

But if the African lagged behind in the development of large political entities and technological advancement, he nevertheless came to grips with the problems of his environment in ways which affected the development of his religion, his world view, his music, dance and art. In general, the African believed that the universe was created by God, but the details of this belief in a divine creation differed from one culture area to another. There existed two conceptions of the universe: the earthly one (man's home) and the heavenly (the home of the Creator), the visible and the invisible. The heavenly world was seen as being populated by other spiritual beings whose function was to serve as intermediaries or messengers of God; in some African cultures, these were identified with the ancestors. Even though man was at the centre of the universe, there were other beings besides man, invisible or immanent but all related to the world of nature. The reality of the spirits was fully incorporated into African cosmology, and religion permeated man's everyday life, moulding the morals of the society and keeping man in harmony with his environment.

Music and dance were inseparable from religion. They were essential aspects of religious worship and observances. The costumes, the songs, the steps, when not for mere entertainment, represented the same religious symbolism, indicating and sustaining the myths and beliefs and invoking ancestral memories according to the occasions. But music and dance also served non-religious purposes in the community as well. African traditional art was another dimension in the expression of the people's world view: it reflected the inimitable and animating spiritual force of the peoples. There was no indulgence in art for art's sake, it was a functional art. There was diversity, but the essential and underlying unifying factor in African art in general was spiritual. It was a mirror of the society, and in each society the artist found his motifs to include religion, man, God, nature, and the ancestral spirits in a creative balance.

There is, then, a fundamental trait that is common to the African cultures, and by extension, to most extra-continental black culture: that is, the duality in the African perception of the universe as between the visible and the invisible world, the natural and the divine, this world and the world of the gods and the ancestors, man in his eco-system and God. It is this duality that defines the African's cultural manifestations. Yet, there is unity and mutuality in this duality, harmony as opposed to antagonism, rationalisable order as opposed to disorder in the universe. Perhaps it is in the African cultures that religion, art, music, dance and drama are best fused, maintaining in their inescapable repetition a constancy and harmony rarely encountered elsewhere in the world.

Environment has also affected the evolution of states and the various social and political institutions that emerged in each of the climatic regions. These themes will be dealt with at greater length in the chapters that follow, and we need not examine them further here other than to emphasise that the key to understanding all these cultural manifestations in Africa is that they evolved as part of man's responses to the rigours of his environment and his creative functional adaptation to it.

The traditional balance between man and nature has been complicated by the intrusion of a third factor into the equation, that is, science and technology. Although technology gives man greater control of his environment, its potential is double-edged: technology ill-applied, can as easily upset the delicate balance as it can, when carefully applied, lend itself to solving man's problems. The preoccupation of contemporary African governments to develop their countries through industrialisation has meant an unfortunate neglect of the agricultural sector. This unbalanced emphasis on industrialisation has turned out to be a chimera in spite of some modest successes scored in a few African countries. A more realistic appraisal should have made it clear from the start that manufacturing would not transform the African economies as if with a magic wand. For several reasons agriculture deserves more attention than it has so far been given by the 'developing' countries. In spite of neglect, it remains the leading economic sector in which the bulk of the population (between 70 and 90 per cent) in most African countries is still engaged. It is the chief source of food supply, and ought to be so protected and developed as to prevent total dependence on food imports to meet the rapidly expanding population. For that reason, it is now imperative to embark upon mechanisation of agriculture not only to improve the yield but also to increase the quality and variety of agricultural products. There is also need for a more rational policy on rural development which will provide attractive living alternatives to the filth and squalor in the urban areas. It is shameful that many governments have still not realised that the congestion and frustration present in the cities and high rates of urban unemployment are partly due to neglect of the rural areas. Unfortunately, the lopsided development policies which favour the urban areas have created rising hopes and diminishing fulfilment, contributing to the mass movement of population into the cities and the unprecedented increase in the seemingly intractable urban crime rate.

There are remarkable contrasts among the various African countries which stem from the nature of the national leaderships, different stages of political integration and stability, and natural resources. Many face heavy difficulties in their efforts to improve their economic and social conditions. It is now clear that all African governments are committed to the goals of social and economic development. There can be no doubt about the urgency for qualitative change in all sectors of the society. Much is at stake for the cause is human, and delay, indecision, ineptitude, lack of vision, parochial and limited approaches to the perennial social and economic problems may bring disappointments and disasters.

Perhaps the African governments should address themselves more to meeting basic human needs and encouraging the development or transfer of appropriate technology than to attempting to modernise with the primary objective of 'catching up' with the developed countries. There is, as more and more policy planners and development strategists are learning, a world of difference between increasing the GNP and improving the quality of life of the citizens: in simple terms, the former is of statistical importance, the latter is about hope or despair, education or ignorance, good health or suffering and misery.

The chapters which follow all deal with broad themes. From the nature of the material with which we are dealing, it is difficult to establish a division, but, broadly, the chapters cover socio-political themes in the pre-colonial era, the colonial era and the era of independence. The last five chapters deal with what could be collectively referred to as cultural studies. Rather than attempt a synopsis of each chapter here, it seems better to apply the adage that 'the proof of the pudding is in the eating'. Opinions have been expressed, positions taken, especially on some important contemporary issues, such as military rule or development, which are not easily categorised or distilled into dogmas. As may be expected in a dynamic setting like Africa, social, economic and political changes are taking place fast and at times furiously. The contributors to this symposium have brought to their analyses of such matters caution, maturity, objectivity and a modicum of boldness.

Finally, the vastness of our subject – African history and culture – is in itself intimidating; the variety of expertise needed in the writing of an introductory work of this nature no less so. To accept our limitations, however, is no demonstration of timidity but rather an act of realism in the face of an almost overwhelming array of sources and of conflicting interpretations. Furthermore, such admission of limitations may well be considered as peculiarly inseparable from the very nature of the historian's craft. Perhaps the best encouragement has been provided by Robin Hallett whose modesty fortifies us:

> No historical work is ever absolutely authoritative, ever completely definitive. Basically, it is no more than temporary framework fated to be superseded sooner or later by the work of other scholars. But if for a time it can provide new insight to the past and contribute to a better understanding of the present, it will have served a worthwhile purpose.[11]

We have no other justification for our present effort.

Notes

1   Clyde Kluckhohn, 'The Study of Culture', in Daniel Larner and Harold D. Lasswell (eds), *The policy sciences,* Stanford University Press, 1951, p. 86

2   Drs Louis and Mary Leakey and their son Richard. See Richard E. Leakey and Roger Lewin, *Origins: What new discoveries reveal about the emergence of our species and its possible future,* E. P. Dutton, 1977, p. 8; also J. Desmond Clark, 'African beginnings', in *The horizon history of Africa,* A. M. Josephy, Jr. (ed), American Heritage Publishing Co., 1971, pp17–32

3   Quoted in Basil Davidson, *A history of West Africa to the nineteenth century,* Anchor Press, 1966, p. 312

4   See Section One, Legends of Origin, in T. Hodgkin, *Nigerian perspectives: an historical anthology,* 2nd ed., Oxford University Press, 1975, pp. 74–86; J. S. Boston, 'Oral tradition and the history of Igala', *Journal of African history,* 10(1), 1969, pp. 29–43; Igor Kopytoff, 'Ancestors as elders in Africa', *Africa,* 41(2), 1971, 129–42

5   E. J. Alagoa, 'Oral tradition and history in Africa', *Kiabàrà, Journal of the humanities,* University of Port Harcourt, I, Rains issue, 1978, 8–25

6   Robert G. Armstrong, 'The use of linguistics and ethnographic data in the study of Idoma and Yoruba history', *The historian in Tropical Africa,* J. Vansina, R. Mauny, L. V. Thomas (eds), London, pubd. for the International African Institute, Oxford University Press, 1964, 127–44; I. M. Lewis (ed), *History and social anthropology,* New York: Tavistock Publications, 1968; S. O. Biobaku (ed), *Sources of Yoruba history,* Oxford, 1973

7   Colin M. Turnbull, *Man in Africa,* Anchor Press, 1976, pp. xii–xx, 3–9, *passim*

8   Philip D. Curtin, *The Atlantic slave trade: a census,* University of Wisconsin Press, 1969

9   Walter Rodney, *How Europe underdeveloped Africa,* Dar es Salaam, Tanzania Publishing House, 1972, p. 114; see also pp. 104–23

10   W. E. Burghardt Du Bois, *The World and Africa: an inquiry into the part which Africa has played in world history*, New York: International Publishers, 1969, pp. 44–68

11   Robin Hallett, *Africa to 1875*, The University of Michigan Press, 1970, p. 13

Questions for discussion

1   How have Africans viewed their history?

2   What problems does the historian face in trying to write African history?

3   What role does physical environment play in the evolution of culture?

4   Has the impact of environment on man in Africa diminished or increased in the twentieth century?

Suggestions for further reading

Fage, J. D. *A history of Africa*, London, Hutchinson, 1978

Gabel, Creighton and Bennett, Norman (eds.). *Reconstructing African cultural history*, Boston University Press, 1967

Gibbs, James L., Jr. (ed.), *Peoples of Africa*, Holt, Rinehart & Winston, 1965

Henige, David P. *The chronology of oral tradition: quest for a chimera*, Oxford University Press, 1974

McCall, Daniel F. *Africa in time perspective: a discussion of historical reconstruction from unwritten source*, New York, Oxford University Press, 1969

Rodney, Walter. *How Europe underdeveloped Africa*, Dar es Salaam, Tanzania Publishing House, 1972

Turnbull, Colin M. *Man in Africa*, Garden City, New York, Anchor Press, 1976

Vansina, Jan. *Oral tradition: a study of historical methodology,* Chicago, Aldine Publishing Co., 1965

2 Internal African migrations and the growth of cultures

Jolayemi Solanke

Migration

It is appropriate to begin an account of African cultures with a study of the related theme of migration. This makes it possible for us to address the vital questions of how different African societies came to be where they are; how cultures, civilisations and states evolved; and to what extent external influences or internal forces can be used to explain the growth of African cultures. This chapter will be devoted to the elucidation of these questions.

However, there are problems. Trying to recapture a very distant past without written sources is difficult if not impossible, for the 'long ago' of oral tradition is hard to date even approximately. There is hope, however, for some advance in knowledge with the co-operation of archaeologists, linguists, anthropologists and other specialists. Our knowledge of Africa's prehistoric origins must be wrung from oral tradition (to a very limited extent), from such ancillary subjects as anthropology, archaeology and linguistics, and from a few written records – in Arabic, for example. By the very diverse nature of our subject, all we can hope to present here is a survey to show the historical links between migrations and the growth of cultures.

The two major developments which both led to and resulted from internal migrations and the growth of cultures were the evolution of food-producing societies and the introduction of metallurgy, especially iron technology. Both these developments gave man a greater degree of control over his environment and offered him opportunities for cultural growth heretofore unknown or inconceivable.

Prehistoric man in Africa was nomadic, a hunter–gatherer who, uninhibited by pressure of population, was free to move where game and wild foods were plentiful. The material culture of these early societies was of necessity simple as was their social organisation; they existed in an intimate, precarious balance with nature and their environment.

The next phase in the growth of prehistoric societies centred on the domestication of animals. The herding societies whose livelihood depended on their stocks of cattle, camels or goats were also nomadic, but their migratory movements were directed more to the search for grazing lands and water than for food and game. Social and political institutions were somewhat more complex but still lacked the centralised structure which was to appear later in the settled agricultural societies.

The domestication of plants, a momentous if long-term achievement, had vast repercussions for man in Africa. The impulse for man to turn from hunting and gathering to raising crops was somewhat retarded in sub-Saharan Africa by the sheer abundance of edible wild foods and plentiful game. The shift from nomadism to cultivation, when it did come, was the key factor underlying the growth of civilisations and the rise of city-states. With the more sedentary forms of existence which farming required, larger communities and cities could grow and flourish. Production of agricultural surpluses led not only to a rapid growth of population, but also to labour specialisation within society. Not everyone needed to engage in farming, and consequently classes of administrators, craftsmen, priests and soldiers arose in response to an increasingly more sophisticated and more populous society.

This evolutionary process of cultural development which we have just outlined did not, of course, occur everywhere at the same time. Even today in Africa all three 'stages' of the evolution – the remnants of hunting–gathering societies, numerous herding groups, and large agricultural societies – are encountered. The dating of these evolutionary steps and even the reasons and impulses for them remain obscure. Stone Age Africa, excluding Egypt, is now thought to have lasted until some time towards the end of the first millennium B.C. when metallurgy was introduced.

The transition from a nomadic way of life to a sedentary agricultural one first appeared in Africa in the fertile Nile Valley during the fourth millennium B.C. with the civilisation of Egypt. Irrigation from the waters of the Nile and the exceptionally fertile flood plain made possible agricultural surpluses which, in turn, stimulated the growth of political and social institutions. Here a highly centralised political authority emerged, sanctioned by religious belief and supported by the accumulated wealth of the kingdom. Here artistic skills and monuments surpassed any then known to the world. Dynastic Egypt flourished for about two millennia, after which (c. 1000 B.C.) decadence set in and Egypt began to be overrun firstly by people who were militarily more powerful and who came from the Upper Nile regions and later by the Romans.

For all its achievement, Egyptian civilisation lacked the art and science of iron working (although other forms of metallurgy were known and practised), and its direct cultural influence did not extend much further than the Nile Valley. The successor kingdom of Kush with its capital at Meroe (not far from Khartoum) flourished for about one thousand years and was conquered by Axum around A.D. 300. Much of the archaeological record of the vanished civilisation of Meroe is yet to be explored, but it is well established that iron working had reached here, most probably from the Arabian peninsula.

The introduction and spread of iron technology throughout Africa was of crucial importance in the development of cultures. The availability of iron tools and iron weapons transformed societies and opened up new possibilities for mastering the environment and for military conquest.

Other metals, particularly gold and copper, had been known and used in the Nile Valley and in West Africa for hundreds of years before iron appeared. But it was iron that had by far the greatest impact on the growth of cultures. The knowledge of iron smelting became a highly valued skill, and an aura of mystery and a cult of secrecy enshrouded the craftsmen who were its masters. Iron working was known in Meroe some

Fig. 2.1   *Ruins of the Kushite civilisation at Meroe*

six centuries before Christ, and is thought by some scholars to have spread from there across the Sudanic trading routes to West Africa. The secrecy surrounding iron technology no doubt prolonged the time that it took for the knowledge to spread, but its diffusion could not be arrested indefinitely, and by the beginning of the Christian era, iron working was established in the regions of West and Central Africa. There is some archaeological evidence, such as Saharan rock paintings depicting chariots, which suggests that iron technology reached West Africa across the Sahara from the region of Phoenician settlement in North Africa at a slightly earlier period. But both theories are in agreement in supporting diffusion rather than independent invention in explaining the origin of iron working among the peoples of West Africa.

During the first millennium, iron working continued to spread through Central and Southern Africa reaching as far south as present-day Angola. Indeed, the first twelve or thirteen centuries A.D. witnessed the true beginnings and growth of African civilisations, and it is no exaggeration to state that the primary stimulus for these developments was attributable to iron. This seems also to have been the era of the great migrations which are the foundations of African society and ethnic dispersal as we know them today.

As long as population densities remained low and people were wholly nomadic, a relative ecological stability prevailed over much of prehistoric Africa. The shift to agriculture necessitated, among other things, establishing more clearly territorial claims and rights. As noted before, population grew rapidly in farming societies, and pressures on land and other resouces intensified faster. These pressures, in turn, provided strong motivations for peoples to migrate to new lands, to spread out, to search for more fertile fields for cultivation. Herding peoples, too, spread out in short migratory waves when fresh grazing or new watering holes were needed. Migrations also resulted from situations of conflict and warfare with families, clans or other small groups striking out in search of new farming areas untroubled by neighbouring communities. These migrations were seldom long moves made in single brief spans of time, but rather short, periodic ebbs and flows of people taking place over hundreds of years.

Migrations of this sort have been occurring on the African continent for hundreds of years. They were the means by which empty or sparsely populated land came under cultivation or became the hereditary grazing lands for pastoral people. More important, they were the conduit through which new ideas and beliefs, new techniques and skills, new food crops and products were channelled into ever more far-flung regions. When people moved into lands already occupied by an indigenous population their response was usually to adapt themselves to unfamiliar ways rather than to adopt those ways wholesale. Local environmental conditions and pre-existing cultural and political forms would determine the degree of acceptance and assimilation. Certain unfamiliar food crops, for example, would be found more suitable to some areas than to others; the horse could survive and breed in the Sudan but not in the forest to the south. The concept of divine kingship would mean little in a stateless society where there were no other centralising forces. Migrations of peoples certainly facilitated and encouraged the cultural diffusion of iron technology, and this metallurgical knowledge, in turn, had a crucial impact on the growth of cultures.

While it is valid to regard migration as one mode of cultural growth and diffusion, there have been over the years a number of dubious interpretations attached to this process of migration. In particular, it was postulated that an ancient people of white racial stock migrated onto the African continent at some very early unknown period, intermingling with the indigenous black populations. It was supposedly these 'Hamites' who brought 'civilisation' to the less civilised primitive societies with whom they came into contact. A consequence of this 'Hamitic hypothesis' was to reinforce those theories which persisted in ascribing Africa's achievements to outsiders. The stone edifices of Zimbabwe, the bronze sculptures of Ife and Benin, and, indeed, any manifestations of cultural or artistic accomplishment, were attributed to outside influence. Although the Hamitic hypothesis has fallen into desuetude as an explanation of cultural development, its demise has, nonetheless, been slow and uncomfortably recent.

West African states

More than any other factor, the desiccation and steady expansion of the Sahara were responsible for the migration of food producers and pastoralists southward into the western Sudan from about the end of the second millennium B.C. This is confirmed by archaeological evidence and also to some extent by the recurring theme in oral tradition prevalent in West Africa of ancestors migrating to present locations from somewhere in the north or north-east. The migrants coming in these southward waves settled across West Africa, and were very much part of the trans-Saharan trade which contributed to the emergence of trading centres in the region. These communities were by now familiar with the techniques of iron smelting, which made it possible for them not only to improve their agricultural implements but also to develop better weapons of war. These, together, allowed them to build and sustain more complex societies, which arose from about the fifth century A.D. Ghana, Mali and Songhai in turn dominated large parts of the western Sudan from around A.D. 500 to A.D. 1600. All three shared a common economic base: control over the lucrative caravan trade routes between North Africa and West Africa.

The earliest of these states (for which the term 'empire' seems appropriate) was Ghana – from which contemporary Ghana derives its name, even though it does not occupy any of the territory of the original Ghana. Old Ghana grew in the region which is now part of the modern state of Mali. Its early history is obscure, but it has been speculated that its first rulers were migrants from the north who settled among the Soninke people living in the area. The potentialities for a powerful trading empire were soon realised, and a strong, centralised government emerged. A later dynasty of Soninke kings ruled over a relatively stable and prosperous state whose strength lay not only in military might but also in economic power. Gold, ivory and slaves from the southern forest areas were exchanged for salt, copper and other trade goods from across the Sahara, and the kings of Ghana maintained absolute control over this trade, exacting sizeable profits as overlord middlemen. Their rule was further buttressed by the divine status accorded them; this was one of the most pervasive characteristics of these west Sudanic states of the first millennium A.D.

According to the fourteenth-century Muslim historian, Ibn Khaldun, Ghana was subjected to incursions around the mid-eleventh century by the Almoravids, a movement of Muslim reformers among the desert Sanhaja. This seems to have resulted in, or been accompanied by,

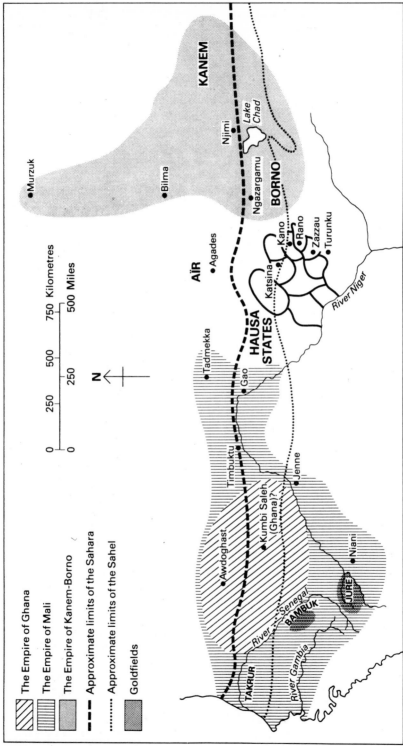

Map 2.1 *The empires of Ghana, Mali, and Kanem-Borno*

the conversion of many of the people of this Sudanese empire. Eventually, the power of its rulers declined, and the capital was captured by the neighbouring Soso. A number of small successor states appeared, one of which was the nucleus of the next empire of the western Sudan, Mali.

The Mandinka people of Mali had a long tradition as traders and middlemen, and they utilised this accumulated experience and knowledge to full advantage. They were also agriculturalists, cultivating rice and other crops. This enabled them to generate surpluses which in turn gave them a basis for trading. A third source of cohesion and strength of the kingdom of Mali was Islam, to which its rulers had converted; some of its kings even made the pilgrimage to Mecca. During the thirteenth and fourteenth centuries Mali dominated the western Sudan, achieving political stability and territorial expansion. At the height of its power, the boundaries of Mali reached to the Atlantic in the west and beyond the big bend in the Niger to the east.

The most celebrated of the kings of Mali was Mansa Musa, who ruled during the first half of the fourteenth century. Under his reign Mali not only experienced an expansion of trade and acquisition of new land but also enjoyed a cultural flowering and a burgeoning scholarly tradition. The ever-wandering fourteenth-century chronicler Ibn Battuta describes in vivid passages the might and greatness of Mali at its zenith to which he was eye-witness.

The overlordship of Mali was subsequently challenged by one of the city-states within its wide realm of influence. Gao, a prosperous trading centre of the Songhai people situated on the Niger, had paid tribute to Mali during its era of domination, but, following the death of Mansa Musa after a quarter of a century on the throne in 1337, Gao became independent. Finally, by the beginning of the fifteenth century, the Songhai armies had openly threatened Mali and were launched on full-fledged wars of conquest. The imperial reign of Sonni Ali, one of Songhai's greatest rulers, witnessed not only ruthless territorial expansion but also a higher level of administrative control than that attained in either Mali or Ghana. Traditional political hierarchies in the cities were eclipsed by royal appointees, and a governmental bureaucracy loyal to the king was created. Sonni Ali, though nominally a Muslim, drew his support from the people in the rural areas who had retained their traditional religious beliefs, while maintaining political balance with the Muslim factions in the urban areas.

His successor, Askia Muhammed, who came to power after defeating the son of Sonni Ali, instituted a number of reforms yet gradually lost the support of the traditionalists in the countryside who continued to resist conversion to Islam. This inherent source of instability came to the surface on the passing of Askia Muhammed. However, a more important source of instability was the lack of any clear rules for succession to the throne, so that subsequent Songhai rulers experienced growing insecurity and became ever more vulnerable to external encroachments. In 1591 Songhai was defeated by an invading Moroccan army with its superior weaponry. The defeat was decisive and political disintegration quickly followed. Nevertheless the collapse of Songhai seems to have had little impact on the economic life of the region, and caravan traffic remained active between the Maghrib and the western Sudan.

Contemporaneous with Ghana, another empire less spectacular but more enduring was arising far to the east in the region of Lake Chad. The old Kanem empire grew and developed out of the intermingling of peoples across the heartland of Africa between the Nile and the Niger. Like Ghana, Mali and Songhai, Kanem enjoyed the economic benefits of her situation at a crossroads of the Saharan trade, except that gold was not a mainstay of this more easterly trade. The people of Kanem had also mastered the techniques of iron smelting. Under the dynasty of Kanem, known as the Sefuwa, a feudal form of rule was established, reinforced by military conquest and held together by skilful administrative overlordship. Islam, which was introduced in the eleventh century, was another unifying factor in Kanem. From its emergence around the ninth century until its decline in the eighteenth century, Kanem and its successor kingdom of Borno to the west (in present-day Nigeria) remained an important power, achieving greater sophistication of government and a higher degree of stability than had been evident in West Africa up to this time. Borno reached its political apogee under the reign of Mai (king) Idris Alooma in the late sixteenth century. Kanem–Borno withstood outside pressures for a thousand years, resisting even the Fulani invasions of the nineteenth century under the leadership of al-Kanami (founder of the present dynasty).

Little is known of the small Hausa states of the Katsina, Kano, Zaria and Gobir before the mid-fifteenth century, but they seem to have arisen as extensions of the typical walled town (*birni*) and came to share in the trade arising at the southern ends of the Saharan caravan routes. Islam too became a potent force, being probably first introduced from the west Sudan rather than directly from North Africa. By the sixteenth century Kano and Katsina, with their Mediterranean and North African links, were important commercial and intellectual centres. However, they remained essentially Muslim city-states until the nineteenth century jihads of Uthman dan Fodio gathered them into the vast Fulani–Hausa empire.

The non-Islamic states of the southern forests – Oyo, Benin, Dahomey, Asante – were the products of similar historical factors. The forest had effectively halted the southward spread of the savannah empires, but cultural influences and ideas continued to filter down. Instead of acting as political overlords, the Sudanic states became trading partners with these forest states. The Guinea forest states were agriculturally based, although trade and commerce played an important role in their economies. Artists and skilled craftsmen thrived, creating a superb, largely courtly art, examples of which survive to our day. The Benin kingdom, for example, produced the famous bronze sculptures, so refined and exquisitely crafted that European visitors found it difficult to believe that this art had truly African origins, while skilled gold metallurgists from Asante designed and fashioned the famous miniature gold weights. Divine kingship was a prominent feature of these forest states, but the kings and courts required metal not only for religious and social artefacts, but also for weapons, since warfare, too, was a common theme running through the history of their states.

Fig. 2.2   *A Benin bronze head*

The Oyo kingdom of the Yoruba on the northern fringes of the forest zone seems to have been at the height of its power in the late sixteenth and early eighteenth centuries. Oyo kings (*Alafin*), commanding large armies and a cavalry force, established their hegemony over peoples from Dahomey to the Niger. Trade with the savannah peoples across the Niger to the north was a likely stimulus to the growth of Oyo and to enable its rulers to support their military forces and pursue ambitions of conquest. An elaborate governmental hierarchy, with built-in constitutional sanctions and safeguards, made for effective and vigorous rule in Oyo, but it was not immune to internal dissension and rivalries. Although the position of Oyo in the eighteenth century was threatened by the encroachment of slave trading from the south and the influence of Islam penetrating from the north, it seems in reality to have been internal political difficulties which mainly brought about the devastating civil wars of the nineteenth century.

The Oyo kingship traditionally derived from Ife, the spiritual home of the Yoruba, which possibly flourished at an earlier period, around the eleventh to fourteenth centuries. That Ife supported a divine kingship and royal court is attested by the splendid bronze and terracotta sculptures which have been found there. Ife, however, probably did not have an extensive military and political domain as did Oyo at its height, but it never lost its spiritual primacy among the Yoruba kings, even after its decline.

Benin similarly claims religious and political descent from Ife, and oral traditions even indicate a direct dynastic link between the two. The people of Benin were not Yoruba, they were Edo-speaking, but proximity and cultural closeness meant that the Benin kingdom resembled the Yoruba states in many ways. Benin had early contacts with European coastal explorers – from the last half of the fifteenth century – but neither these contacts nor the slave trade had the impact one might expect. Benin's ultimate decline, like that of Oyo, resulted more from internal troubles than from external interference.

The fate and fortunes of the state of Dahomey, on the other hand, were inextricably bound up with the slave trade. Competition with other neighbouring coastal city-states for control over the trade led to the rise of Dahomey in the late seventeenth century. The military supremacy which Dahomey attained over her neighbours posed a threat to Oyo on whose western borders Dahomey held sway, and in 1730 Oyo, after a series of invasions, succeeded in imposing a tributary relationship on Dahomey. But even so, Dahomey retained a certain degree of autonomy and continued to deal heavily in slaves.

Although the view that the kings exercised a monopoly over the slave trade has recently been convincingly challenged, the kingship was nevertheless very powerful, officials being royal appointees rather than hereditary holders of office. With the decline of Oyo in the late eighteenth and early nineteenth centuries, Dahomey regained complete independence under its strong monarchy, until the ending of the transatlantic slave trade brought about the deterioration of her position.

The people of the Akan states in the Volta River region of West Africa also trace their origins to migrants from the savannah regions who intermingled with indigenous inhabitants. Here, as in the Yoruba states, demand for forest products and growth of the Saharan trade gave rise to prosperous trading centres. Trade in gold was the most lucrative of all, and proved to be the economic mainstay of the powerful Asante state which dominated the hinterland of the Gold Coast from the seventeenth until the late nineteenth centuries. From the unifying reign of King Osei Tutu (d. 1712) until the defeat of the kingdom by a British colonial army toward the end of the nineteenth century, Asante evolved a relatively stable, centralised governmental bureaucracy with several layers of civil servants who were appointed on merit. Trading was rigidly controlled by the state from the capital at Kumasi. The divine kingship with its symbolic Golden Stool further served to weld and unify the Akan peoples into a cohesive empire.

Bantu migrations and Bantu civilisations

The Bantu, as a linguistically related group of peoples, are believed to have originated on the eastern fringes of the West African forest zone, possibly in the Benue River valley near Nigeria and the Cameroons. The basis for this hypothesis (admittedly very controversial) rests largely on linguistic evidence which further suggests a migration south and eastwards from that location into the Congo forests at some time perhaps around the first century A.D. It was from the Katanga region that the Bantu pushed outward over many centuries in different directions, expanding eastward into East Africa beyond the Rift Valley toward the coast and south into south-central Africa, where the civilisation of Great Zimbabwe grew and flourished. Bantu migrations in north-easterly directions into the region of the Great Lakes and further on into East Africa encountered an opposing southward migration of pastoral Nilotic peoples from north-east Africa and the Horn.

The migrating Bantu were mainly cereal or grain agriculturalists who had acquired the knowledge of iron working. Both these factors gave them certain advantages over the indigenous people who had neither the metallurgical skills nor the settled character of Bantu culture. However, the Bantu migrations seem not generally to have been ones of military intrusion and conquest, but rather, they were culturally integrative, being characterised by the assimilation and infusion of divergent economic, social and linguistic patterns. The nature of these initial contacts between the Bantu and the indigenous Neolithic groups of hunters and gatherers was not wholly one-sided. Indeed, the Bantu expansion throughout the vast regions of Southern, Central and Eastern Africa is in itself testimony to their adaptability to a great variety of environmental and economic conditions. The great differences in physical types of present-day Bantu also reflect the differences in the peoples they assimilated.

The Bantu culture, spanning out across sub-equatorial Africa during the period from the first century A.D. to about 1700, produced several large politically centralised kingdoms. The best known was Zimbabwe whose massive stone ruins stand as evidence of a cultural complex which thrived in the area between the Zambezi and the Limpopo rivers. These stone structures are believed to have witnessed several successive occupations from the fifth to the fifteenth centuries A.D. Trading in gold and ivory was established with coastal Arab traders near Sofala as early as the thirteenth century. The successor states of Monomotapa and Changamire came increasingly under the disruptive influence of the Portuguese who, by the sixteenth century, had established themselves on the East African coast.

The Arab presence on the coast, which antedates the European arrival by many centuries, led to a particularly interesting example of cultural synthesis – the Swahili language and culture. There are conflicting views about the origin of this on the East African coast. The earliest Arab migrants, who travelled down the coast during the first millennium B.C., came for trade, not conquest. They settled, intermarried, learned local languages and established trading centres. Fresh influxes of Arabs over the years assured the preservation of an Arab identity in spite of constant interaction with the Africans. The Swahili culture, though basically Bantu – that is, truly African – has nevertheless been much modified by Arabic influences. From the seventh century onwards, the Arabs settling on the coast brought with them their Islamic religion; by the middle of the fourteenth century, population centres like Kilwa, Mombasa, Mogadishu and Zanzibar had become largely Muslim in character. This, of course, affected the character and flavour of the Swahili culture, but it never lost its essentially African base. The Swahili culture created not only its own language, but a body of

Fig. 2.3 *The outer wall of Zimbabwe, evidence of a cultural complex which thrived in the area between the Zambezi and Limpopo rivers*

poetic literature. It also produced some distinguished buildings, many of whose ruins still survive, although much archaeological investigation remains to be carried out.

Further to the north, in and around the Great Lakes region, other Bantu-speaking peoples founded small kingdoms which at a later period were partially absorbed and enlarged by the Luo, herding peoples moving southward into the Lakes region from the Upper Nile, The Bunyoro and Buganda kingdoms were two such states whose kings ruled through many generations – in fact, until the coming of the white man disrupted the existing political stability and order. Similarly, the kingdoms of Rwanda and Burundi were the cultural and historical products of an intermingling of iron-working Bantu farmers and cattle-raising Nilotic groups with all the elements of true statehood: political hierarchies, social stratification and labour specialisation. The Kongo kingdom situated near the mouth of the Congo River had also achieved political and cultural autonomy by the time the Portuguese reached that part of the west coast in the fifteenth century.

Conclusion

The main intention of this chapter has been to emphasise the two-way interplay throughout much of the early history of Africa between migrations and the growth of cultures. At the simplest level, migrations contributed to the growth of cultures by bringing in new ideas, skills and products; this in turn resulted in further migrations and movements of peoples as populations expanded and new horizons opened up. The major factors which gave rise to this historical interplay were two: (1) the food-producing revolution or the domestication of plants, and (2) the acquisition of iron technology.

The growth of cultures in Africa may be viewed as an evolutionary process from simple, relatively unstructured societies to highly organised, complex political states. In such a schema, state formation can be seen as an advanced stage of cultural and political development. Yet this is not meant to impute any value judgement as to the superiority of state societies organised into large or relatively large political and economic units as compared to 'stateless' ones; it is merely a measure of increasing complexity and more varied cultural patterns. Indeed, the African states were a great deal less stable and more transitory over long historical time than the older, simpler ways of life. Moreover, stability is not to be confused with stagnation. Ancient prehistoric African societies were dynamic and changing; it is only that in the last hundred years or so, the pace of change in Africa has quickened beyond all previous experience – as, indeed, it has in the rest of the world.

Questions for discussion

1   The most significant age of metals in prehistoric Africa was clearly that of the Iron Age. Why was iron so crucial to the growth of culture?

2   Discuss the concept of cultural diffusion as a factor in the growth of cultures.

3   Discuss the 'Hamitic hypothesis'. Why has it fallen into disrepute? Based on present knowledge, what would be a more realistic hypothesis to explain the growth and spread of culture in Africa?

4   On a map of Africa, trace the Bantu migrations from their postulated origins to their ultimate expansion. Why were the Bantu able to spread so rapidly and to adapt so thoroughly?

5   State formation in the western Sudan and the Guinea forest was possible for several reasons. Discuss these underlying factors.

Suggestions for further reading

Ajayi, J. F. A., and Crowder, M. *History of West Africa*, I, Longman, 1971, 1976

Bovill, E. W. *The golden trade of the Moors,* 2nd rev. ed., Oxford University Press, 1970

Clark, J. Desmond. *The prehistory of Africa,* Praeger, 1970

Crowder, M. *West Africa: an introduction to its history,* Longman, 1977

Davidson, Basil. *East and Central Africa to the late nineteenth century,* Longman, 1968

Davidson, Basil. *Old Africa rediscovered,* Longman, 1970

Davidson, Basil, and Buah, F. K. *A history of West Agrica, 1000–1800,* 2nd ed., Longman, 1968

Fage, J. D. *A history of Africa,* London, Hutchinson, 1978

Fisher, H. J. 'Leo Africanus and the Songhay conquest of Hausaland', *International Journal of African Historical Studies,* XI, 2, 1978

July, Robert W. *A history of the African people,* New York, Charles Scribner, 1970

Oliver, Roland. 'The problem of Bantu expansion', *Papers in African Prehistory.* J. D. Fage and R. A. Oliver (eds.), Cambridge University Press, 1970, pp. 141–56

Oliver, Roland and Fagan, Brian M. *Africa in the Iron Age,* Cambridge University Press, 1975

Turnbull, Colin M. *Man in Africa,* Garden City, New York, Anchor Press, 1976

Vansina, Jan. *Kingdoms of the Savanna* University of Wisconsin Press, 1966

3 Traditional social and political institutions

Jolayemi Solanke

Traditional African social and political institutions, like those of pre-industrial societies all over the world, embody patterns of culture which have evolved over hundreds of years and which represent man's success, or degree of success, in integrating himself into his environment. Given the limitations imposed by the physical environment, the availability of natural resources, and the level of technology achieved, African societies developed remarkably viable and enduring social and political institutions, many of which are surviving the relentless onslaught of the twentieth century. The changes in the traditional ways of life wrought by the incursions of Western technology, modernisation and political independence are themselves legitimate subject for study, but they are not the focus of the present chapter. In this brief survey we examine some of the salient and characteristic features of traditional African society in its multiplicity of patterns and forms. The important point to bear in mind is that, when speaking of 'traditional African society', one is really referring to many different societies each of which is in some respects unique. Yet the sheer number and diversity of African societies force one to attempt some degree of generalisation and categorisation in order to superimpose a framework for the study of African culture. Otherwise, we would be confronted with a mere miscellany of cultures.

We will consider first the predominant types of social groupings centring on but not restricted to the family unit. Secondly, we will discuss the political systems which fuse local social groups into broader or wholly self-contained entities, ranging from simple stateless societies to centralised bureaucratic states. Thirdly, we will examine some of the social mechanisms which provide stability and control to the society, enforce its social and moral codes, and legitimise its political authority.

Social institutions

The key concept in understanding African social organisation is that of the corporate group. Every individual belongs to several overlapping groups which provide the frames of reference for his daily life. Social groupings are of three kinds: those based on kinship (family, lineage, clan); those based on association, or non-kin groups (age grades, secret societies, craft guilds); and those based on residence or locality.

Kinship ties

Kinship ties are those which bind an individual to a family group either through birth or marriage. There are basically two kinds of kinship: (1) consanguinity, or the blood relationships of *descent* and *filiation*; and (2) affinity, or marriage bonds. Filiation refers to the relationship between parent and child, whereas descent denotes the extension of one's filial ties back through several generations.

Consanguinity

Descent is reckoned in several ways in African societies, the most widespread being *unilineal descent*. This means essentially that a man traces his descent through only one side of his family, either the father's line (patrilineal) or the mother's line (matrilineal). 'Patrilineal descent' means that a person's line of descent is through the males on his father's side, while 'matrilineal descent' is traced through females on the mother's side. Of these two forms, patrilineal descent is the more common in Africa. In a few societies *double descent* is the rule, whereby a person traces descent patrilineally and matrilineally with a sort of social balance struck between the two lines. A fourth descent system, quite rare in Africa, is the *bilateral* one in which a person traces his descent through both sides of both the mother and the father.

These lines of descent are known as *lineages,* and it is not uncommon for people to trace their lineage back to some remote and revered ancestor, even if not all the intervening generations are recalled with accuracy. Separate lineages which claim a common ancestor are said to belong to the same *clan.* Lineages and clans thus comprise not only living persons but also dead ancestors and unborn children. In a real sense a lineage is thought of as a continuum of one's line of descent. Throughout Africa the ancestors are highly respected and they wield authority over the living members.

Through natural social pressures over time, lineages tend to divide into distinct lines, thus preventing their growing too large. This division might be brought about by a relocation of one portion of the lineage with a resultant break-up of the lineage group. Lineages also segment, or form new subdivisions within the main descent group, as when the sons of the same lineage head found their own descent lines.

Not all societies have clans, nor is clan structure and organisation equally powerful in different societies. Clans may own farming or grazing lands in common as well as other property, as is the case among the pastoral Somali where clans are quite important and powerful. Or they may be geographically dispersed and function as a corporate group only for certain social or religious purposes.

The lineage, as a corporate group, has a recognised head, who is usually the oldest living male member. This is true also of lineage segments whose male heads in turn defer to the overall lineage head. The lineage head has authority over members of the lineage and represents them to outsiders on matters of importance. In addition to overseeing communally owned property, especially land or cattle, the lineage head also has ultimate responsibility for arranging the marriages of the young men and women from the lineage. Since marriage is almost always *exogamous*, in the sense of being outside the descent group, this particular duty of the head may be seen as another kind of control of resources of the lineage – that is the reproductive capacities of the woman whose marriage settlements will bring in a bride price. Even in rare instances of *endogamous* marriages, or marrying within the descent group, it is the lineage head who supervises the marital negotiations.

The lineage has as its basic component the family: the nuclear family, consisting of parents and children, and, equally important in African society, the extended family. The extended family is a grouping of related nuclear families which quite often live together in the same compound or homestead and constitute the group most readily identifiable and most important for the individual in his or her daily life.

Affinity

Marriage, or a relationship of affinity, is the second type of kinship bond. It takes many forms in African society, but there is usually some material exchange or settlement between the two families before the marriage can take place. This transaction serves to legitimise the marriage and to give stability to the arrangement since marriage is viewed as more than the linking of two individuals: it is a means of bringing about social cohesion between families and lineages. The marriage settlement compensates the bride's family and at the same time ensures that the new husband will meet his obligations. Marriage payments, known as *bride price*, are most commonly made in goods, such as livestock or currency, but they may also be made in service or kind. *Bride service* exists sometimes as a supplement to bride price, but it is also found as the chief marriage payment among peoples who are poor in material wealth. In San (Bushman) society a young husband is required to live with the bride's parents and render bride service which is usually hunting. He is expected to stay with them until three children are born, which may be several years.

A third form of matrimonial transaction is known as *exchange marriage*, whereby two women from different kin groups are exchanged, each marrying a man from the other's group. Although relatively rare in Africa, exchange marriage was practised among the Tiv in Nigeria until it was proscribed by the colonial government in 1927 and a form of bride price substituted.

Monogamous marriage, or that which considers the sole husband and the sole wife as the only permissible form of marriage, is rare in African society. Most African cultures permit *polygyny*, or the marriage of one man to two or more women. This does not mean, however, that all marriages in such situations will be polygynous, since the normal sex ratio would result in some degree of monogamy. Economic factors also restrict the number of wives taken by a man, many wives being a sign of wealth. The other kind of polygamous marriage – *polyandry*, or one woman with two or more husbands – is extremely rare in Africa.

Polygyny is of two types: *sororal* and *nonsororal*. Sororal, or sister marriage, occurs where two sisters marry the same man and become co-wives; nonsororal marriage involves co-wives who are not related by consanguinity. Another kind of preferred marriage is between cousins. The pastoral Fulani of the western Sudan practise this form of endogamous marriage, whereby marital partners are found primarily within the descent group according to carefully prescribed principles. Certain rules exist in some polygynous societies making provision for the remarriage of widows by another member of the deceased husband's kin group. If the deceased husband's brother 'inherits' the widow, that is known as the *levirate*.

Women tend to marry at a younger age than do men; consequently they are more likely to be widowed and remarry, thus maximising their fertility potential which after all serves the ultimate aim of marriage – procreation. Polygyny is found in both patrilineal and matrilineal descent systems; whether patrilocal (living with the husband's family), or matrilocal (living with the wife's family), the usual pattern is for each co-wife to be given her own separate room or hut where she lives with her children. Although jealousy and hostility among co-wives are not infrequent, the polygynous arrangement does offer security and convenience. The monogamy first insisted upon by the Christian missionaries has probably been far more socially disruptive than otherwise.

The legal termination of marriage through divorce is discouraged by the investment of the kin groups in the continuation of the bond. Divorce may mean the return of all or part of the bride wealth. It is possible, therefore, for a couple to live apart without officially severing the marriage contract. Patrilineal societies tend to be somewhat more stable than matrilineal ones, since here the husband retains his children in the event of a dissolution of the marriage. In a matrilineal society, the children would remain with the mother's kin group. Barrenness or sterility is often sufficient grounds for declaring a marriage null and void, except in a few societies where surrogate husbands or wives are allowed in such cases.

Non-kin groups

Non-kin groupings comprise the second major type of social organisation. These associational groups, whether voluntary or prescribed, play a remarkably important role in society even where kinship groups are considered fundamental to the structure of the society. The most prevalent kinds of associations are the age-grades, the so-called 'secret societies', co-operatives, craft guilds and specialists' organisations.

Age-grades, found most commonly among the pastoral societies of Eastern and Southern Africa but also quite widespread in West Africa, are usually men's associations based on contemporaneity: a man belongs to that set of men who are his age mates, and their set moves through the several age-grades as the men go through life, beginning with their initiation into manhood as adolescents. Membership in an age set is not voluntary, and it carries with it both obligations and privileges. Typically, age sets pass through some four grades comprising (1) newly initiated men in a training period; (2) the warrior grade responsible for defence;

(3) adult men responsible for governing; and (4) the society's elders.

As can be readily imagined, age-grades have undergone vast changes in modern Africa, but traditionally they have formed a vital part of the social structure. The Swazi of Southern Africa, for example, had age-grades which were formed about every six years, each with its own distinguishing totem, songs and insignia. No man could marry until his age set had received permission from the king to do so. Each group had an officially designated leader, and as young men they were in the service of the king. Membership in an age set was prescribed, and young men were drawn from all villages and homesteads so that the age set cut across kinship boundaries. Passing from one grade into the next was ritually celebrated, and a set survived as long as its members lived. Unlike lineages, the age set did not own property nor have a continuing corporate being. Today, with warfare prohibited and adult men engaged in migrant labour, the Swazi age-grades no longer play a significant role, although they do survive in radically modified form. This is true of all societies which traditionally had age-grade systems. Before the colonial period, the Ekiti Yoruba of Nigeria had a thriving system of age-grades in which there were five clearly established grades each with distinct duties and responsibilities, the last two of which were warrior grades. Today these have been rendered obsolete and replaced among the Ekiti, as well as in other parts of Yorubaland, with the *egbe* or men's informal society based on voluntary, mutual-interest association. These are usually formed in adolescence and endure for many years, perhaps throughout a lifetime.

Another type of association which plays a vital role in the social structure of societies in certain areas of West Africa and the Congo basin is the secret society. Most frequently a men's fraternity, the secret society serves to exert forms of social control and to condition and train young initiates for adulthood. Elaborate and protracted initiation rites are characteristic of secret societies, and they may last for several years. Their power and influence are backed up by strong religious sanctions. Such societies frequently own a sacred grove where many of their activities are conducted, and they always have identifying symbols and ritual artefacts. One of the best known and widespread of secret societies is the Poro, found among several culturally related peoples in Sierra Leone and Liberia. In fact, the Poro cuts across ethnic boundaries to link separate ethnic groups. The Ogboni society among the Yoruba is another example of a strong and active secret society.

Other associations found in some African societies are labour co-operatives which perform communal farm and village work for individual members. Among the Kpelle of Liberia, where co-operative work groups are very important, a group is voluntarily established by people living in the same area, and it may contain from six to forty persons who go in turn to every member's farm to work. A day of labour always includes much conviviality and a feast provided by the host.

Residential groupings

Residential groupings and geographical proximity, the third major type of social organisation, are determined in significant part by kinship patterns. Although quite naturally family and lineage groups tend to live in close proximity, there are other factors at work apart from kinship which influence residential groupings. These factors relate to the environment and to the level of technology found in the society.

Where natural resources are scarce and the environment can support only a limited number of people scattered over a wide area, residential groups are relatively small and are most likely to be migratory or nomadic, moving from place to place in response to their needs for water, grazing lands, firewood and game. The low level of technology in such societies contributes to this mobility, since these societies lack the means, for example, to drill a deep well for water instead of continually searching for surface deposits. Migratory patterns vary from society to society and are certainly far from being random wanderings. Transhumance movements, such as those practised by the Fulani, are long-established seasonal movements between (usually) north and south in the dry and wet periods of the year which reflect the intimate ecological balance between man and environment. Other pastoral peoples, living in the environmentally different areas of East Africa, reside more or less permanently in the few well-watered areas and migrate outward during the rainy season.

Where technological advancement is greater and the environment is less harsh, larger populations can be supported, as is the case in the larger states. The economic basis of life, whether agriculture, pastoralism or hunting, likewise plays a decisive role in determining residential patterns. Farming requires considerably less land than does either grazing or hunting – although this land is utilised more intensively – so that people in agricultural societies live in much closer proximity and greater density. Residential patterns in sedentary farming groups differ according to the types of cultivation practised. People may live in scattered villages, as do the Igbo of eastern Nigeria, or they may dwell in more highly concentrated population centres, such as are found among the Yoruba of western Nigeria or the Asante (Ashanti) of Ghana. Some societies, such as the Nuer of the Sudan, subsist in a dual farming and cattle-raising economy which combines semi-permanent village dwelling with short seasonal migrations.

One of the more unusual residential groupings is found among the Nyakyusa of Central Africa where rudimentary age-grades are the basis of residence. The young men of a given age set leave their natal villages and establish a new village to which they will bring their wives when they marry and where they will raise their children. Military and administrative leadership then passes with each generation from the older villages to the younger ones, rather than through the normal channels of inheritance. Kinship ties are nevertheless important, even though the social principles of association and residence appear to predominate.

Political organisations

Traditional African political systems are built around kinship structures within the societies, and indeed the close interrelationship between social and political organisation is a predominant feature in Africa. The range and variety of political systems found in Africa defy attempts at definitive classification into types of political organisation. What can, however, be used to illustrate the diversity are three broad, general characterisations of the ways which different peoples organise themselves politically.

'Stateless' societies

At the simplest level one finds 'stateless' societies in which the political system is coterminous with the kinship group, either the lineage or the clan. These societies are culturally homogeneous and notable for their small size, possibly with people living in bands of no more than one hundred. They are nomadic, hunting and gathering over a large area with a relatively low density of population. They have a low level of technology and a simple material culture. There is virtually no political differentiation, although lineage heads function as 'political' leaders for the purpose of making decisions relating to the life of the community. Such small-scale societies are increasingly rare in Africa today. The San of the Kalahari Desert and the Pygmies of north-eastern Zaire are two prominent surviving examples of this type of political organisation. Yet they exist in quite different ecological settings and social circumstances vis à vis their neighbours The San family group or band roams that area of the desert over which it has rights, each group existing quite independently of other groups both economically and socially. Among bands of San people the family head functions as political, social and religious leader over his own small group. The Pygmies, in the tropical rain forest, live in proximity to their Negroid neighbours, trading their trapped game and gathered forest products for food grown by their farming neighbours in what has been described as a symbiotic relationship. Leadership within the Pygmy bands is diffuse and co-operative with no single person being responsible for all decision making for the group.

Middle-sized societies

The next and most widespread political pattern found in Africa is that of the middle-sized societies which do indeed seem to fall between the smallest groups, just described, and the highly centralised states which comprise the third pattern of political organisation; this second type is often described, like the first, as 'stateless'. Within these middle-sized societies are found groups ranging from several hundred to several thousand; the politically independent groups may constitute a larger unit culturally and linguistically, but this has little meaning in daily life and constitutes little more than a convenient classification for the anthropologist. The Nuer in the Sudan and the Masai in East Africa are examples of societies in which political groupings share cultural similarities with surrounding groups but are really quite independent; no group dominates the others. Middle-sized societies may be based on agriculture or herding; they may be sedentary, like the Tiv of the Plateau region of Nigeria, or nomadic, like the Somali of the Horn of Africa; they have higher population densities and higher levels of technology; some degree of specialisation of labour is observable; and social differentiation, usually based on wealth, is not uncommon.

Most autonomous political units tend to break up or segment when they grow too large; both ecological and social pressures may be responsible for this self-restraining tendency. New groups form which are based also on kinship or lineage ties or on residential patterns. Although political centralisation is rare among these societies, one may find internal subdivisions along kinship lines or villages groupings. Leadership is vested in an acknowledged head who is often assisted by a council of advisers. Religious and judicial authority is likely to reside in different persons – that is, there is some specialisation of leadership. The role of political leadership is more clearly defined here than it is with the smaller societies because of the greater complexity of relationships both internally and externally. Ownership of property, especially land and cattle, and the numerous dealings with outside groups for purposes of marriage settlements, trade or disputes require a more highly developed and well-established political leadership. Warfare and raiding were traditionally part of life especially among the East African herding societies with their warrior age-grades, but these forays were carried out to seize property or exact revenge rather than for territorial expansion.

Centralised states

The third tier, the centralised states, are politically the most complex and sophisticated. Although less numerous than the middle-sized societies, the large African states are among the best-known societies in Africa – for example, the Ashanti and the Yoruba, the Swazi, the Zulu and the Ganda. These large centralised states share certain characteristics and patterns of life. They have a relatively high population density and are usually sedentary, being engaged in farming and herding. Indeed it has been argued that complexity of political organisation is an accompaniment of population density, that is, the denser the population, the more highly centralised and internally hierarchical the political system. States of this kind have a higher level of technology; there is some accumulation of wealth, deriving from the generation of surpluses; trading plays an important part in the economy. Labour specialisation is more sharply delineated; society can support full-time specialists such as craftsmen, administrators, priests or cult leaders and so forth. Social stratification is also evident, usually with an upper ruling class, the mass of commoners, and possibly a slave class on the lowest rung. In some societies craftsmen are accorded a special status, placing them above the commoners.

Within the ruling class authority is centralised with a pattern of hereditary leadership. There is usually an established administrative centre associated with the chieftainship. At the pinnacle of this political hierarchy is the head chief, or king, who is advised by an inner council. Often an outer layer of councillors is comprised of representatives of various wards or sectors in the villages in the kingdom. Although the ruling class is clearly recognised, a certain amount of instability and political intrigue is generated within the ruling groups arising from factionalism and rivalries. Internal segmentation does exist, often quite pronounced, and it is likely to be based on geographically distinct districts each with its own local rulers. The sub-units usually pay some form of tribute to the central authority, while at the same time enjoying some local political autonomy.

The caste system as the basis for political authority is perhaps most clearly seen in the kingdom of Rwanda where three sharply different castes – the Tutsi, the Hutu and the Twa – live within one political entity. Here clientship, or the system of allegiance whereby members of the socially inferior caste could become clients of the king, served to protect and maintain the domination of the ruling Tutsi over the conquered Hutu. Among the Hausa of northern Nigeria, clientship together with kingship and titled offices are part of the social fabric reinforcing the political order. Clientship provides benefits to both lord and client, linking as it does persons of unequal wealth and status. It is also possible for a person to be a client to a nobleman, while at the same time he maintains clients of his own.

The centralised states have established judicial systems for settling disputes in a peaceful manner, rather than resorting to feuds and warfare as may happen in the middle-range societies. Disputes are adjudicated at all levels of the society, depending upon who is involved and the nature of the offence.

The histories of the African states invariably include episodes of warfare, conquest and territorial expansion. Indeed armies (and very occasionally even standing armies) and military support units were integral parts of the political order, and some differentiation of military function had been developed in pre-colonial armies. The superior force of the imperialists' firearms heralded the demise of traditional African warfare, and, once colonial rule was firmly implanted, these large military units were disbanded.

Social control and law

Social control within African society rests on the seminal concept of the individual as part of a corporate group. The perception of belonging to a group – whether family, age-grade, village, clan or nation – is almost always paramount over a sense of individuality. One acts as a member of a group and is responsible to that group. An offence against another member of one's group, say theft or adultery, is dealt with by the group through its elders as its representatives rather than between the two people involved. Serious crimes against a group member may result in a fine or even banishment for the criminal. Religious beliefs are intricately bound up with attitudes and behaviour toward social transgressions. It is believed that the miscreant will fall victim to illness, bad luck or some other misfortune as a result of his bad behaviour. Having offended not only the group, but also its ancestral spirits, the guilty persons will be punished by them. These beliefs act as a strong deterrent to crime and immorality. Witchcraft is another expression of the supernatural form of social control, whereby those persons possessing malevolent powers of witchcraft invoke them against the criminal.

Retribution in criminal cases involving persons of two different groups is also dealt with at the group level, since an offence against an outsider is seen as an offence against that outsider's group. Defending a member's property or seeking justice and compensation for him becomes the responsibility of his group. This may be handled by discussion and negotiation (and 'palaver'), adjudication or, in extreme cases, violent means.

Formal legal systems with courts and judges are found most often in the centralised states and less frequently in the middle-sized societies. Land and other property cases seem to constitute the most common type of litigation. Court proceedings, while not written, have many features of modern legal systems: judges, witnesses, presentation of evidence and testimony, argument and counter-argument, and sentencing. The overriding objective in these traditional trials appears to be to arrive at an acceptable and conciliatory settlement rather than to dispense an impersonal 'justice'.

Cases do arise where the most earnest and judicious efforts to achieve a satisfactory resolution fail, and appeal must be made to some spiritual arbiter, most commonly an oracle. One of the most famous oracles was the Aro Chukwu oracle which was a powerful spiritual force over much of southern Igboland. Diviners may also be consulted in particularly difficult cases; their role is to act as intermediaries to interpret the wishes of the ancestral spirits. The message transmitted from the oracle or through the diviners is considered final in determining guilt or innocence.

Finally, among the larger states, and even in smaller and 'stateless' societies, a form of 'international law', based on widely accepted principles of customary law, has been identified. This may be seen in such matters as declarations of war, the negotiation of peace treaties and the treatment of ambassadors – for diplomacy too flourished in much of pre-colonial Africa.

These highlights of traditional African social and political institutions offer some insight into the richness and complexity of African cultures, but, we must caution, they should not be considered as in any way comprehensive. Rather, the survey is intended to encourage an appreciation and understanding of traditional African society which may stimulate our interest in continued and more thoroughgoing study.

Questions for discussion

1 Distinguish among the three basic types of descent: *unilineal, double* and *bilateral.*

2 For what reasons do you suppose the institution of age-grades evolved? That is, what function and purpose do they serve within the social order?

3 Given that marriage is virtually universal in African society and that there are more or less equal numbers of men and women, how do you explain the existence of polygyny?

4   What is the social role of bride price?

5   Consider the position of males in a matrilineal society. How does it compare with that of males in a patrilineal setting?

6   The large, centralised African states are always politically and socially more complex than the stateless societies. What factors account for this consistently observable pattern?

7   The individual in African society is subordinate to the group. Discuss.

Suggestions for further reading

Bohannan, Paul, and Curtin, Philip. *Africa and Africans*, rev. ed., Garden City, New York, Natural History Press, 1971

Cohen, Ronald, and Middleton, John (eds). *From tribe to nation in Africa*, San Francisco, Chandler, 1970

Davidson, Basil. *The African genius: An introduction to African social and cultural history*, Boston: Little, Brown, 1969

Fortes, Meyer, and Evans-Pritchard, E. E. (eds). *African political systems*, Oxford University Press, 1961

Gibbs, James L., Jr. (ed), *Peoples of Africa*. Holt, Rinehart & Winston, 1965

Mair, Lucy. *Primitive government*, Indiana University Press, 1962, 1977

Maquet, Jacques. *Power and society in Africa*, Weidenfeld and Nicolson, 1971

Ottenberg, Simon, and Ottenberg, Phoebe (eds). *Cultures and societies of Africa*, Random House, 1960

Radcliffe-Brown, A. R. and Forde, Daryll (eds). *African systems of kinship and marriage*, Oxford University Press, 1950

Schapera, Isaac. *Government and politics in tribal societies*, New York, Schocken Books, 1967

Smith, R. S. *Warfare and diplomacy in pre-colonial West Africa*, Metheun, 1976

Stevenson, Robert F. *Population and political systems in tropical Africa*, Columbia University Press, 1968

Truden, Arthur, and Plotnicov, Leonard (eds). *Social stratification in Africa*, New York, Free Press, 1970

4 Islamic penetration of Africa

Richard Olaniyan

Islam, like other great world religions such as Christianity, Buddhism or Confucianism, is doctrinally concerned with ultimate causation, truth and morality, and with man's relation to his Creator. With its own code of ethics and set of beliefs, Islam enables people from different parts of the world to share in what its adherents consider to be universal truths and the culture associated with that dispensation. In other words, Islam is both a religion and a culture, a way of life. Like Christianity, the duty of extending the frontiers of the faith falls on the believers, who are charged along with their religious leaders to win new converts.

Thus, the agents of Islam would include virtually all segments of the believing community – soldiers, traders, immigrants, teachers and preachers, belonging to many nationalities. Historically the Arabs were the first agents. Between the death of Islam's founder in A.D. 632 and the middle of the eighth century, the Arabs carried the new faith to all parts of the Middle East, the Mediterranean, central and western Asia, and North Africa in a very short space of time. In their wake, they left a new civilisation proposing a new universalism and based on their own language and means of writing. In time, much of the rest of Africa was opened to Islamic religious and economic penetration. How did it all begin? How did Islam enter the African continent? What impact did it have on African societies? In this chapter, we will take a continental view as we examine these questions. First, let us examine the origin and tenets of Islam.

Muhammad

Muhammad, the founder of the Islamic faith and recognised by the Muslims as the last of the prophets of God after such other acknowledged prophets as Moses and Jesus, was born in Mecca in about A.D. 570. Having lost his parents at an early age, he was brought up by his grandfather and an uncle. When he was about twenty-five, he took for a wife a forty-year-old wealthy widow named Khadija.

Being disposed to a life of solitude and meditation, Muhammad sought peace and quiet annually in the month of Ramadan in the hills near Mecca. It was after one of these retreats in A.D. 610 when he was about forty that he claimed to have received divine messages. Preaching a new faith based on these messages, he and his followers met with hostility from the people of Mecca. In order to escape from their persecution

Muhammad in 622 fled to the town of Medina, about 120 kilometres away. This flight from Mecca to Medina is often referred to as the *hijra* or holy flight. At Medina Muhammad was well received and not only gained a position of great influence but was also soon able to wage a successful war against the people of Mecca, leading to his triumphal return to the town of his birth in 630. From this time on Islam started to gain influence and followers far beyond the immediate vicinity of Islam's twin strongholds of Mecca and Medina.

Extremely important to the new religion was the Koran, the collection of divine messages which God commanded Muhammad to preach. Though the Prophet continued to receive divine revelations until his death in 632, these were not collected together to form the Muslims' holy book, the Koran, until some fifteen years after his death. Liberally, 'Islam' means 'submission' – submission to the will of God. It is the belief of the Muslims, the followers of Prophet Muhammad, that Allah's will is enshrined in the Koran. It contains virtually all that a Muslim ought to know and do in order to be accepted as a true believer. In addition to the relationship of man with his Creator, which is the essence of all religions, the Koran also lays down Muslim law and precept, and a morality which ranges from matrimonial laws and obligations, inheritance laws and laws governing drinking and eating habits, to laws regulating inter-personal relations. It goes even further, for it also contains political ideas which were used to establish relationships in a political system based on Islamic beliefs. Those receiving a Muslim education are required not only to memorise the Koran but also to study the *hadiths*, a collection of the sayings and actions of Muhammad, as a basis of the Muslim way of life.

The adherents of the Islamic faith are required to fulfil certain obligations. First, they must affirm the oneness of God, Allah, as expressed in the declaration that 'There is no God but Allah and Muhammad is his Prophet'. This is the basic, fundamental confession of faith, and the distinction should be noted: Muhammad is not God but his Prophet. Secondly, all believers are obliged to pray, facing towards Mecca, at five specified times daily. The third duty is to participate in the thirty-day fast in the month of Ramadan. As their fourth duty, Muslims are encouraged to give alms to the needy. Finally, all believers are enjoined to go on pilgrimage to Islam's holy cities of Mecca and Medina at least once in their lifetime, provided they can afford to do so. These form the five pillars upon which the Islamic faith is based.

Regional distribution and spread

The Muslim population of Africa today is estimated to number about 102 million – 4 million more than the Christian population – in a total continental population of about 436 million. As to specific countries and regions, Muslims are heavily concentrated in Nigeria, Senegal, Guinea, Niger and Mali, more so than in Liberia, Ghana and Togo where they form small minorities. They make up almost the entire populations of Zanzibar, the Somali Republic, several of the other West African countries and, to be sure, all the North African countries, and form a clear majority in the Sudan. In Ethiopia and mainland Tanzania, they remain a substantial element, and form small groups within the populations of Uganda, Malawi, Zimbabwe and Zaire. In South Africa a few thousands, made up principally of the descendants of the Indonesians brought there by the Dutch in the seventeenth century and the nineteenth century Indian immigrants, adhere to the Islamic faith. How did Islam spread to all these parts of Africa?

In order to answer this question effectively, it is expedient to divide the continent into four, namely: Egypt and North Africa, West Africa, eastern Sudan and the Horn, and East and Central Africa. This is necessary partly for convenience based on geographical propinquity and partly because this 'regionalisation' is based on shared experiences in the patterns and thrusts of Islamic penetration and development in Africa. [1]

Egypt and North Africa

Following its conquest by the Arabs about 639, Egypt became the first stronghold of Islam on the African continent, remaining thereafter the most important and enduring source of Islamic proselytisation in and even beyond North Africa. It was from Egypt that the Arab immigrants began in the seventh century to fan out in large numbers in different directions, conquering and converting as they went. Through military conquest, followed by religious and cultural domination, they extended their sway to the Maghrib – Libya, Tunisia, Algeria and Morocco. The Berbers, who were the major indigenous ethnic group in this vast area, revolted against Arab domination but eventually accepted Islam, though in a characteristically Berber form. The northern stretches of Mauritania also came into the expanding Muslim orbit. The initial effort to establish a military presence in North Africa was modest, and hence Islam was limited at the beginning to the coast. But by the beginning of the ninth century, the Berbers had become active agents of Islam, first into the immediate interior and then over the trans-Saharan trade routes.

The city of Kairouan, built by the Arabs in Ilfriqiya (the eastern half of the Maghrib, or Tunisia) in 670, became the base of military operations into the Berber territories. The invasion of Ilfriqiya by the Hilali Arabs in the eleventh century led to a more permanent and significant peopling of North Africa by Arab immigrants more numerous than the original attempt in the seventh century to establish a foothold. This was the prelude to the thirteenth- and fourteenth-century Arab migrations into the Maghribi hinterland, thereby overwhelming much of the area with Arabic as well as purely Islamic culture.

It was among the militant Berber Muslims in the interior that the Almoravid and Almohad revivalist movements emerged during the eleventh and twelfth centuries respectively. Their religious ideology (if one may call it that) – the former preaching a strict adherence to the traditional interpretation of the Koran, and the latter stressing the direct contact of the individual soul with God – dominated the thinking and the politics of the Maghrib until the mid-thirteenth century. Each in turn ruled an empire which comprised southern Spain as well as the western (and in the case of the Almohads also the eastern) Maghrib. The period from the thirteenth to the sixteenth centuries witnessed the emergence of Sufism – a Muslim mysticism – which soon became an active agent of Islamisation; the period also witnessed the full Islamic flowering in the Maghrib.

Thus it was the Berbers who now dominated the Saharan trade routes, and they accompanied their religious proselytisation with intense commercial activity. From the south of the Sahara came slaves (who were used to provide cheap labour and as domestics), gold, and to a lesser extent, ivory, to the northern commercial and religious towns of Kairouan and Tunis in Tunisia, Tahert in Algeria, Sijilmasa, Fez and Marrakech in Morocco. In return, camel caravans carried manufactured goods such as textiles, steel weapons and metal bars from North Africa, or at times imports from Europe, across the Sahara. Salt, produced in Saharan mines at Taghaza and Bila, was an important part of the thriving trans-Saharan commercial activity linking the Maghrib with the western Sudan. The market towns and the major oases in the desert region became vital to the Muslim commercial and religious enterprise.

These commercial links were maintained for centuries, bringing considerable prosperity to the North African states. By the turn of the sixteenth century, almost every corner of North Africa had been Islamised and Arabised. Although during the nineteenth century and early part of the twentieth the region was subjected to European colonial rule, Islamic faith and culture have in no way been diminished by this: Egypt and the Maghrib countries, now all independent, remain the most strongly Islamic and Arabised region of Africa.

West Africa

Islam in West Africa is closely linked with the Maghrib, for it owes its origin in many areas (though probably not in Hausaland) to the converted Berbers who had for many years been involved in the trans-Saharan trade.[2] They and the nomadic Tuaregs began making converts in the western Sudan from about the ninth century. The introduction of this new and widely-based religion was of great importance in that it provided a common bond and a sense of community among various ethnic groups and commercial interests.

Traders were then the most effective agents in the penetration of the western Sudan by Islam, although there are also instances of the imposition of the faith by military means. The Berbers and their neighbours the Tuaregs controlled the caravan routes across the Sahara and monopolised the lucrative gold trade from the ancient kingdom of Ghana. From its situation north of the mountain sources of the rivers Senegal and Niger, this ancient Soninke kingdom became, according to al-Idrisi, the Arab geographer, the most powerful and largest commercial centre of the western Sudan. Arab writers report the conversion of Ghana to Islam, an event which probably occurred in the late eleventh century at a time when the empire was apparently subject to incursions by the Almoravids, a reformist movement of Berber Muslims. This conversion may have entailed a change of dynasty, but in any case the administration was subject to Islamic influence; Muslim clerics, for example, were employed as envoys and interpreters in domestic matters and external contacts. A century or so later, however, Ghana was in decline, and was then overwhelmed by its non-Muslim neighbours, the Soso.

But the political tide changed. The Malinke kingdom of Mali on the upper Niger emerged about the middle of the thirteenth century as the leading power in the western Sudan under its Muslim rulers and remained so during the following century. No doubt the development of new trade routes and trading centres to the south, among other factors, contributed to Mali's emergence as the new power. Black African Muslim traders now became more prominent and influential than their co-religionist Berbers who had carried their religion and trade to the gates of the tropical forest zone. These Sudanese traders became part of a wider economic system and made contact with North African Muslim merchants, thus acquiring an outlook broader than their own cultural backgrounds.

The western Sudanese traders were not, to be sure, the only ones exposed to the influence of Islam. The rulers reaped huge benefits from trade; they employed Muslim scholars as advisers, ambassadors and administrators. Yet few rulers in the eleventh century became Muslims: the kings of Gao and of Kanem-Borno, with the probable addition of the kings of Ghana, are important exceptions. Even where the king converted to Islam, the common people did not rush to renounce their traditional faith. Nor did the king himself abandon the old verities which bound traditional society together; it was often a pragmatic choice, a matter of accepting the best of the two worlds. Thus, a religious dualism, an accommodation of the traditional and Islamic faiths in peaceful coexistence, assured social harmony.[3]

In the thirteenth century the expansion of the Mali empire led to the overthrow of the Soso successors to the power of Ghana and the extension of the Islamic frontiers in the western Sudan. During the reign of Mansa Musa (c. 1312–37), an administration based on a literate bureaucracy was establishing contact with distant lands, especially Morocco and Egypt, and centres of Islamic learning in Timbuktu, Jenne and other places. The Mali rulers went on pilgrimages to Mecca; Mansa Musa's pilgrimage in 1324–25, during which he spent some time in Cairo, revealed to the Mediterranean world the wealth of this Sudanese empire.

The enterprising Malinke-speaking Dyula merchants, protagonists of Islam, carried not only their wares but also Islam to most parts of West Africa. These traders, according to the Arab historian Ibn Battuta who visited Mali in 1352–53, were famed for their entrepreneurial skills and wide commercial network and enjoyed an enviable economic power in the market communities in western Sudan. Their contribution to the diffusion of Islam in the savannah belt across West Africa from Guinea to northern Nigeria, in the period from the mid-fourteenth to the nineteenth century, is generally acknowledged.[4]

However, the empire had grown so large that effective control became difficult: the Mossi, the Tukulor and the Tuaregs raided Mali from different directions with virtual impunity. By the middle of the fifteenth century another state, Songhai, had arisen on the Upper Niger. By the early sixteenth century it had greatly expanded its already large

Fig. 4.1 *The Sankoré mosque in Timbuktu, which was one of the great centres of Islamic learning.*

domain. But Songhai suffered from political instability caused by rivalry for leadership and the conflicting claims of the various army generals contending for supremacy. Moreover, Morocco coveted the Songhai salt mines and, even more, the gold of the Sudan. Internal rebellion weakened and fragmented the empire, but it was the Moroccan invasion of 1591 that dealt the fatal blow.

We noted earlier the establishment of centres of Islamic learning in Timbuktu and Jenne. By their strategic locations at the crossroads of commercial activities, they were able to disseminate Islamic culture to different parts of the region. Like Harar in the Horn of Africa, the mosques of Timbuktu and Jenne could be considered universities in their own right, centres of intellectual ferment and academic disputation where students and scholars from far and wide occupied themselves with theological and canonical questions. Their activities fostered the spread of Islam as the disciples of each scholar in turn trained another generation of Muslim teachers. Many became itinerant scholars. These two centres continued to contribute to the spread of Islam until well into the seventeenth century.

Much earlier, a thriving Islamic culture had been established in Kanem-Borno in the Chad Basin. For centuries, until about the middle of the fifteenth century, Kanem was the dominant of the two regions. It maintained a strong military force and by its control of the Fezzan was able to safeguard its commercial and diplomatic relations with the Hafsid rulers of Tunis. By the last quarter of the fifteenth century, Borno had become the dominant area in the state, and under a succession of able rulers in the sixteenth century, including Idris Alooma (1570–1602), greatly extended the territory. In spite of later decline, it continued as an independent power until British colonialism put an end to its autonomy at the end of the nineteenth century.

To the west of Borno the Hausa city-states of Kano, Katsina, Gobir, Zaria and others emerged, probably at some time during the fourteenth century (but see Chapter 2), and thrived on long-distance trade selling textiles, leather and metal goods. By the late fifteenth century these city-states were becoming important centres of Islamic learning and could boast the presence there of accomplished scholars from other lands. Two centuries later Islam reached the Yoruba kingdoms in south-western Nigeria.

Nevertheless, perhaps the most dramatic and revolutionary period in the penetration of Islam in West Africa was the eighteenth and nineteenth centuries, a period that could be called the Age of Islamic Revolutions since it witnessed a series of jihads or holy wars, led mainly by Fulani zealots, preachers and warriors. The Fulani, a pastoral people, had moved eastwards from their original home in the Senegal valley in search of better grazing. In the process, they left in their wake large Fulani settlements in Futa Toro, Futa Jallon, Macina, Sokoto and elsewhere. The Fulani jihads began from these settlements towards the close of the eighteenth century. Why was this? In looking for explanations for the revolutionary movement, some historians have argued that in addition to the need for grazing land for their cattle, there were dominant religious and political motives: the Fulani wanted to conquer new lands for Islam; then, ambitious for the interests of their own nation, they sought political and economic control of the area in which each jihad was waged. They made claims too (of a kind familiar in our own days) that they were fighting to reform alleged political and social abuses in the lands they conquered.[5]

The Fulani 'holy war' in West Africa can be divided into some five main phases or separate wars.[6] The first broke out in Futa Jallon in 1725 and led to the fall of the pagan rulers there and the creation of a Muslim state. Then followed in 1775 a second jihad in Futa Toro; the third, the most famous, led by Usman dan Fodio, began in 1804, so that by 1808 the major Hausa states in northern Nigeria – Gobir, Kano, Katsina and Zaria – had been overwhelmed. The Sokoto caliphate which emerged from these military successes represented the most extensive and impressive political achievement by Islam in the western Sudan. There were at least two other jihads – of Shehu Ahmadu in Macina in 1818 and of al-Hajj Umar in the Bambara states of Segu and Kaarta in the middle of the nineteenth century. Much as we may concede differences in leadership, circumstances and strategies between all of these jihads, there is no doubt that the Sokoto experiment inspired the two succeeding nineteenth-century jihads. Nor could the leaders have been unfamiliar with the earlier successes in Futa Jallon and Toro. All told, the jihads created a number of new polities which brought new lands and peoples into the Islamic fold.

In summary, we can see that the introduction of Islam into West Africa benefited from long-distance trade and trade routes linking many important parts of the region with North Africa and the eastern Sudan. The *tariqas*, or Muslim brotherhoods, most popular in western Sudan – the Qadiriyya and the Tijaniyya introduced to the region in the sixteenth and eighteenth centuries respectively – contributed in their own way to the spread of the faith, while the Ahmadiyya, a much more recent phenomenon, is gaining adherents especially in Nigeria. We have also seen how Islam provided a cultural focus which in turn enhanced political integration in many of the ancient polities of the area. At Sarakole in Timbuktu and in other centres of Islamic learning across the western Sudan, Islamic traditions of scholarship have flourished in the African environment. Finally, during almost a century of colonial rule which was Christian in religious orientation but essentially tolerant of other faiths, Islam continued to gain more converts in West Africa, albeit with varying degrees of success and constraints from one colony to the other, while the post-colonial era has created a climate still more favourable to the spread of Islam.

The eastern Sudan and the Horn of Africa

As in North Africa, although much later, the eastern Sudan encountered the Islamic faith through direct influence from Egypt, in this case along the Nile; but unlike North Africa, the eastern Sudan also experienced direct contact with Arabian Islam from across the Red Sea. Thus, the eastern Sudan was subject to Islamic influence from two directions, Egypt and Arabia, each leaving its mark on the socio-cultural development of the area.

Egyptian efforts in the seventh century to conquer the area were repulsed by the Christian kingdoms of Nubia. What was beyond the capacity of force, however, was then accomplished through a slow process of interaction and mixing of Arab nomads and immigrants from Egypt with the indigenous Hamitic peoples of the northern Sudan. Islamic culture became so well entrenched in the area that the demographic composition was permanently altered. By the second decade of the fourteenth century, Islam and Arab culture had been firmly planted among the former Christians of Nubia.

About the beginning of the sixteenth century, Arab teachers from different parts of Arabia took up the task of proselytisation. Most of them were *sufis* or mystics and belonged to the *tariqas* or such Islamic fraternities as the Shadhiliyya and Mirghaniyya. These Islamic orders, often built around individual holy men and their families, dominated the religious scene and confirmed the basic Islamic patterns of Sudanese society.

This direct encounter with Arabian Islam and culture largely explains the sense of belonging to an Arab, rather than an African, nation which is prevalent among the Muslim majority in the Sudan Republic. As a historian puts it, 'more than for most other Muslim peoples of Africa, for the Sudanese to be a Muslim is to be an Arab'.[7] The predominantly Nilotic and negroid ethnic groups in southern Sudan, however, remained until recently unaffected by these religious and cultural influences. Nevertheless developments in the nineteenth century provided other integrative factors which ultimately brought the two sections together to form the modern Sudan Republic. In 1820 the Turco-Egyptian forces under the instigation of Muhammad Ali Pasha, the Ottoman Turkish governor of Egypt, invaded the Sudan and occupied the northern and

Fig. 4.2 *The Mahdi, Muhammad Ahmed ibn Abdallah (1846–1885)*

central regions. After a period of 'pacification' which included the south and with the conquest of Darfur in 1874, Islam began to spread westwards along with the Turco-Egyptian administration.

In the nineteenth century the spread of Islam and the establishment of the new administration went hand-in-hand with the expansion of the slave trade. By 1880, social discontent, political turmoil and interference by the colonial administration with slave trading had made the Egyptian regime unpopular. The different sectors of society which opposed the Egyptian regime, including both religious leaders and slave traders, looked for a Sudanese liberator – a *Mahdi*, or a second coming of the Prophet – and found one in Muhammad Ahmad ibn Abdallah. With popular support and messianic fervour the Mahdist movement soon overwhelmed the regime. During the Mahdist period, from 1881 to 1898, there was some modicum of stability. Then, with the dislodgement of the Mahdists in 1898, there began the Anglo-Egyptian colonial period (or 'condominium') which ended with the proclamation of independence in January 1956.

In at least one significant respect, Islam in the Horn of Africa (Ethiopia, Eritrea and Somalia) was similar to its position in the Sudan: the existence of the *tariqas* or Muslim brotherhoods. Here, as in the Sudan, membership in the Muslim fraternities and veneration of saints and holy men were highly regarded; *tariqas* like the Qadiriyya, Ahmadiyya and Salihiyya, had and still have large followings. However, Muslim influence came to this region not from Arab immigrants from Egypt but rather from Muslim Arab and Persian merchants and teachers who had established trading posts on the Red Sea and Indian Ocean coasts in the early days of the Islamic expansion.

Islam failed in its attempt to gain converts in Ethiopia because of the vigorous resistance to it by the Christian Amhara. However, other Semitic-speaking peoples in the Horn, such as the Bait Asgade, the Mensa and the Marya in Eritrea, the Beja of eastern Sudan and Eritrea, have embraced Islam. Furthermore, Islam has also made progress among the Hamitic language and cultural groups like the Afar (Danakil), the Somali and the Saho.

Between the beginning of the eighth and the end of the tenth centuries, several Muslim settlements were established on the coast. In Zeila, Mogadishu and other Muslim settlements, there was much intermingling of cultures among the Muslim Arab and Persian merchants on the one hand and the local populations on the other. From about the tenth century, Arab proselytisers and traders and converted Somali pastoral nomads began carrying the new faith into the hinterland from the port of Zeila. Several important Muslim settlements developed in the process of expanding commerce and Islam in the interior. However, the Islamisers soon came into conflict with the Christian kingdom of Abyssinia. The long struggle for supremacy between the Muslims and the Christians ended in the defeat of the former in 1542. This failure in Ethiopia ended Muslim hopes of penetrating the highlands, and left a legacy of conflict and distrust between the Christian and Muslim communities of the region.

East and Central Africa

The coastal area of East Africa from the Horn down to Mozambique has a long history of commercial contact in the pre-Islamic era with Egypt, Arabia, India, Assyria, Greece, Rome, Phoenicia and even China.[8] By the eighth century A.D. Muslim settlements had been established on the Sudanese and Somali coasts where slave trading was the chief commercial occupation. There is, however, disagreement among historians about when Islam first came to East Africa. The Kilwa Chronicle states that the town of Kilwa on the coast south of Dar es Salaam was established in A.D. 957 with the arrival of the Bantu, Arab and Persian immigrants. This seems to be a safe date for the earliest Islamic presence in the region. Between the end of the tenth century and the beginning of the sixteenth, over three dozen Muslim coastal settlements had developed with Mogadishu on the Somali coast and Kilwa in the south being the most prominent. These settlements attracted Arab merchants dealing in gold, which was brought to the coast from the mines in the Zambezi–Limpopo region; they also traded in ivory, iron, timber, copper, hides and skins, and slaves. They carried these products together with slaves in their dhows to the emporia of Arabia, Persia and India.

Unlike the experience of eastern Sudan, the Horn, and elsewhere, Muslim trading activities in East Africa were for long restricted to the coast. What could be responsible for this? In the first place the hinterland peoples were not Muslims. Secondly, it may well be that the under-populated hinterland failed to attract the Arab merchants other than those trading in slaves, ivory and gold coming from the interior, an exploitative commerce which failed to develop into a two-way exchange between the hinterland and the coastal settlements. This was the situation until the end of the eighteenth century.

However, although Islam failed to make headway in the interior, the picture was markedly different on the off-shore islands of Zanzibar, Pemba, Mombasa, Comoros and Mafia. These, along with the coastal settlements, were monopolised by Muslim culture until the nineteenth century. Here, between the beginning of the fourteenth and the end of the fifteenth centuries East Africa witnessed an Afro-Arab cultural efflorescence which culminated in the emergence of a new language and culture, Swahili, a Bantu–Arab admixture rooted in Islamic culture.[9] Perhaps originally evolved on the Kenyan coast, it soon spread to the coastal settlements and islands. Swahili is now widely spoken in East Africa and in parts of the central African countries including the eastern parts of Zaire; Tanzania has in fact made Swahili its official language.

In the opening years of the sixteenth century a Portuguese presence began to be felt in the political and trading circles of East Africa. A Portuguese maritime expedition led by Pedro Alvares Cabral reached Kilwa in 1500, and two years later Vasco da Gama on his second journey to India forced that settlement to pay tribute to Portugal. In 1509 Portugal occupied Zanzibar, Pemba and Mafia. This and such subsequent actions as the occupation of Mozambique, facilitated by superior naval technology, made it possible for Portugal to extend its political sway and commercial interest to much of the Indian Ocean region. One significant effect of this was the almost total ruin of Muslim commercial concerns in the area for almost two centuries. In the process, however, the Portuguese alienated Africans, Arabs, Indians and other Europeans by their high-handed policies, and they were subsequently forced to withdraw to their stronghold in Mozambique.

The restoration of Arab influences and Islamic culture followed the invasion, beginning in 1652, of Zanzibar, Pate and the coastal settlements by the state of Oman in southern Arabia. By the beginning of the eighteenth century, the Omani hegemony had been established in the coastal towns and on the islands with governors loyal to Oman appointed to administer and collect taxes. In the seventeenth and eighteenth centuries most of the inhabitants, Arab as well as Bantu, in the coastal settlements were converted to Islam.

The reign of Sultan Said, the Omani ruler (1804–56), witnessed important developments: the Arab and Swahili merchants began penetrating the interior in the 1820s; Said moved his capital from Muscat in Oman to Zanzibar in 1840 where slave markets had been established; he allowed the Indians to settle in Zanzibar, while European and American merchants were also active there. The upshot of all this was an expanding commerce and an intensification of Arab participation in the slave and ivory trade in the established markets of the coast and the newer ones of the hinterland. Islam also gained converts through proselytisers and mystics who fanned out to various parts of East Africa. European colonialism (British and German), established at the turn of the century, did not curtail its growth.

In Central Africa the only Islamic contacts were provided by the incursions into the Congo region of Zanzibar and Swahili merchants seeking slaves and ivory in the first half of the nineteenth century. Later attempts to spread the faith by Egyptian preachers and Sudanese Mahdists were rendered ineffective by the opposition of the colonial powers, especially Britain, to the disruptive potential of their aggressive messianism.

Colonial rule and Islamic penetration

It would at first sight seem that colonialism in Africa – a Euro–Christian socio-political phenomenon – would be antithetical to the cause of Islam, but on the contrary it created in many places conditions in which Islamisation and even Arabisation found encouragement. This came about in three main ways: through the social disruptions caused by the advent of colonial rule; through policies which enhanced the status of Islam and its agents; and finally, through the consolidation of Islamic gains, a consequence of socio-political stability and increased social mobility. These were interdependent, interrelated processes which all facilitated the spread of Islam.[10] With colonial administration came educational and economic opportunities which freed many people from traditional authorities and obligations. This was apparent in the attitude of the youth to religious beliefs and rituals. New educational values replaced old traditional values contributing to the growth of secularism and materialism. While Christianity claimed the loyalty of most of those who attended mission schools, others became disposed to Islamic conversion. In the circumstances, Islam, as an integrative social force with a universal outlook, provided a ready and acceptable alternative to the old verities that were now on the decline. Reaction against Christianity as the religion of the white man and colonial authority accounted for some conversions, while the weakening of traditional social and religious values provided a fertile field for Islamic penetration.[11]

Furthermore, certain colonial policies fostered the spread of Islam. In particular, those policies relating to the expansion of commercial opportunities and contacts, the development of roads and other means of communication, the growth of urban areas with their characteristic secular and detribalised cultures and social and political harmony, provided Moslem preachers, traders and other proselytisers with the opportunity to reach larger audiences and distant communities.

Although the European administrators did not set out to promote the Islamic cause, they nevertheless, especially in the early stages of European rule, recognised that Muslims constituted the literate elements of the newly-subjected population. Many were employed in the lower rungs of colonial administration; with an enhanced position in the colonial organisation, they persuaded many adherents of traditional religion to convert to Islam. Chiefs who were Muslims received greater support and authority in their domains from the colonial powers. Islamic law and institutions were allowed to thrive because the colonial governments appreciated the peace, order and stability that they provided. This favoured position given Muslim chiefs was the basis of the British policy of 'indirect rule' in Northern Nigeria where vast numbers of adherents to traditional religions became subjects of Muslim rulers. The system deliberately discouraged Christian proselytisation in many cases, whereas Western-type education was introduced in a way which made it possible for Islam to make widespread gains in the region. Basic to this development in the colonial and post-colonial periods was the improvement in communications, railways and roads opening up vast areas to the spread of the faith. By the middle of this century the Muslim population of Northern Nigeria had risen to more than 75 per cent.[12] By the close of the last century and the beginning of the twentieth, Islam had penetrated as far as south-western Nigeria winning Yoruba souls for Islam; progress was also impressive during the same period all across West Africa, in British as well as French territories.

There were other factors which contributed to the expansion of Islam during the colonial period. Even though Islam was originally alien, it had become part of the way of life in most of the areas where it had taken root by the last decade of the nineteenth century. In such areas it only needed further expansion and was no longer looked upon as 'foreign'. The inadequacy of the chiefs in their resistance to colonial conquest led Africans – in Senegal, for example – to look for leadership to the Muslims. In some areas it received support because it was considered a religion opposed to the political and cultural imperialism of the West, while in others its success was an unintended consequence of colonial policies.

These trends in combination with a third – a process of Wolofisation of Islam – were clearly at work among the Wolof of Senegal. Briefly, until the later half of the last century only a small proportion of commoners among the Wolof had become Muslims in spite of a history of early contact with Islam. The process began under the leadership of Amadou Bamba (d. 1927), who received a 'call' in 1886. After evolving a strategy for Islamic propagation, he embraced the peaceful method and emphasised the dignity of labour in agriculture. A deeply religious and fiercely nationalistic leader, he founded a *tariqa* (the Muridiyya) and soon became a saint-hero with divine pretensions. Other Muslim 'saints' among the Wolof similarly built up their movements, all with the support of the French colonial power. Thus the Wolof adopted Islam not as individuals or as a class but as a people and thus were able, as Trimingham says, 'to preserve their social life and all essential institutions intact and resist the disruptive effects of the legal code of Islam'.[13] Using the Murid movement as an agent of Islamisation, they then embarked upon a successful colonisation and absorption of neighbouring lands and peoples. Islam has thus enabled a relatively benign government in post-colonial Senegal to maintain stability, although somewhat to the disadvantage of the rural population.[14]

In East Africa, the Islamisation of the Yao who inhabit eastern Malawi, southern Tanzania and northern Mozambique provides an example of a people embracing Islam *en masse*. Although their participation in trade had brought them into contact with Islam much earlier, it was not until late in the nineteenth century that the Yao began to fan out along the trade routes and adopted Islam. This followed the disruptions brought about by the slave trade and the establishment of colonialism. Like the Wolof, they were able to maintain their ethnic identity.[15]

Islam faced its stiffest opposition during the colonial era in the Belgian Congo where Islamic schools were disallowed and proselytisation was frowned upon. But considering everything, we can confidently say that Islam made tremendous progress during the European occupation of Africa as a result of the perceived coincidence of interests and exploitation of opportunities provided by the interaction of the two cultures, African and Arabic.

Conclusion

Our concern has been the history of the Islamic penetration of Africa. Islam has influenced Africa in many ways and in like manner Islam in Africa has acquired cultural traits from the host populations in the various communities where it has taken root. Trimingham has identified three aspects in the process of the Islamic penetration of Africa, namely: cultural reciprocity leading to the evolution of a new religio-social order; assimilation; and 'dualism', which, with time, changed to 'parallelism'.[16] Since, as has been said elsewhere, religion permeated every aspect of African life, any form of religious assimilation found the African cultural element to be vital and dynamic. For example, the institution of marriage retained many of its indigenous features with the tradition of bride price remaining essentially unmodified. In the rural areas Islam was more apt than in the towns to be affected by indigenous elements. Examples of cultural dualism and parallelism were not uncommon in West as well as in East Africa, especially at the early stages of conversion. Even where Islam was widely accepted, prayers in countless communities were still directed to spirits as well as to Allah because it was believed that spirits, being always near and capable of being induced to give favours, needed constant propitiation.

In general, African societies retained those traditional practices which were considered essential to their cultural identity and social harmony while at the same time professing the Islamic faith. We need to remember that we are not here dealing only with a religion, a set of doctrines, but a culture as well, with its own *mores* and laws, its language, its system of justice and concepts of government. It is only with these in mind that we can account for the relative speed with which Islam reached all regions of Africa. [17]

At first the early leaders of Islam accepted the concept of the holy war as the prime weapon for the growth of the new religion. Islam made its earliest serious effort to penetrate the African continent through Egypt and thence to the Maghrib. Here military conquest as a strategy for spreading Islam was used by the invading Arabs across the northern littoral converting the Berbers and imposing their culture on them. Again, in the various jihads which swept West Africa in the eighteenth and nineteenth centuries, it was the sword that broke the resistance to Islamisation and established Muslim polities. Yet, as we have seen, other means of proselytisation were available, and in many places and situations these may be seen to have been more effective than the sword.

In general, Islamisation owed more to traders and the trade routes than to military conquest not only in western Sudan but also in East Africa. In many respects, as was certainly the case in West Africa, Islam followed the trade routes utilising the network of market towns and the oases across the Sahara which linked West Africa with North Africa and the eastern Sudan; these in turn linked up with the Muslim world of the Middle East through the Red Sea ports. Every major commercial centre became Islamised. This was clearly the case in East Africa on the off-shore islands and along the coast, whereas it was only in the nineteenth century that the search for slaves and gold forced the Muslim Arab and Swahili traders into the interior and southward also to Central Africa. Furthermore, among the adherents of the traditional religions, conversion to Islam became one way of escaping the bondage of slavery.

In this respect, special mention must be made of the contribution of the Dyula, the Hausa and the Karimiya of Kanem – all intrepid traders who traversed vast areas of West Africa and beyond, selling their wares and proselytising as well. We must also stress the significant role of other groups as agents of Islamisation: the Lebanese, the Syrians and the Indians in West Africa; the Arabs, Persians and Indians in North and East Africa; and the Berbers and the nomadic Tuaregs in western Sudan.

Another factor which fostered the spread of Islam in Africa was population movement and migration. In the various regions of Africa, with the probable exception only of the East, population movements proved advantageous to Islamisation. This was of particular significance in North Africa, the eastern Sudan and West Africa.

The traders themselves played an important part in winning converts to Islam, for many were also teachers and holy men whose business successes, proselytising oratory and exhortations, and religious devotions won them admiration and followers. But there were teachers and holy men who did not engage in commercial activities. Such clerics (*alfa*) ran schools, leading their Muslim communities in religious activities and dispensing charms, treating illnesses attributed to supernatural causes, soothsaying and preventing bad omens or interceding with forces that the traditional methods had found intractable. These clerics were considered not only learned but were believed to possess supernatural power or *baraka*. They were seen as practitioners of a mysterious art to which they alone, by virtue of their familiarity with the secrets of the Koran, were privy.

Traditional rulers were captivated by what Islam and the Muslim scholars could offer. They employed Muslim scholars as secretaries, envoys, advisers and negotiators. Crucial as the Muslim influence could be in such circumstances, the rulers were often cautious in undertaking conversion to Islam themselves, taking this step only if it seemed politically expedient. Again, it sometimes happened that a king and his immediate chiefs adopted the new faith while the majority of the people retained their traditional beliefs. Islam was not wholly inimical to local traditions. It was possible to be a religious leader and still to accommodate many local customs. Askia Muhammed of Songhai (1493–1528), for example, did not find it amiss as a Muslim leader to allow traditional obeisance to him as a divine ruler. This pragmatism, still very much part of the contemporary scene, proved especially advantageous for the spread of Islam in societies where traditional leaders maintained a halfway position.

To what extent were the centralised states instrumental in the diffusion of Islam, especially in the western Sudan? There can be no doubt that in Mali, Songhai and Kanem–Borno, to mention three cases, the imperial impulses and needs and the religious commitment of these states facilitated the expansion of Islam. But let us put the question the other way around: to what extent was Islam a crucial factor in the evolution of the Sudanese empires? Here it is possible to overstate the facts by offering the generalisation that without Islam these states could not have come into being. The significance of Islam in this question is, of course, not in doubt; however, it is also indisputable that the so-called 'pagan' states – Ghana, for example – had advanced far along the road to state formation before the coming of Islam. In other words, Ghana's evolution was indigenous. But where Islam became the state religion, as in Mali and Songhai, it did accelerate the development, introducing social, political and administrative innovations, and it was instrumental in refashioning the traditional strategies for political integration. There were, of course, other forces at work – economic, demographic, political and others – some of which were stimulated by Islam. A last category comprises those states – for example, the Hausa–Fulani emirates – which were entirely the creation of the jihad, and in which Islam, not surprisingly, occupies a special position.

At the level of the individual, Islam derived its appeal from the power and prestige which accompanied membership in a new religion and culture, the acquisition of a new and widely-spoken language with a rich literature, and the adoption of a new mode of dress. Generally, membership did not entail any difficult initiation beyond mastery of the fundamentals of worship. Moreover, the local *alfa*, familiar with the spiritual concerns of his community, used local language and drew analogies and created imageries from familiar circumstances to illustrate lessons from the Koran and the *hadiths*. We may also add here that the belief of an individual that he belonged to a larger community of believers, the *umma* of Islam, might consolidate his faith and be a source of inspiration to his neighbours. A final point is the social significance which is attached to the holy pilgrimage to Mecca, a religious duty which confers on the individual a title (*Al-hajj*) and an instant social status. All this helps to make Islam more attractive to the status seekers, the rising middle class, in an increasingly urbanised Africa.

Notes

1   J. S. Trimingham identifies seven culture zones based on geographical, ethnological and cultural factors. See his *The influence of Islam upon Africa*, Longman, pp. 5–33. See also I. M. Lewis (ed), *Islam in tropical Africa*, Oxford University Press, 1964

2   For this section, J. Spencer Trimingham, *A history of Islam in West Africa*, Oxford University Press, 1970, is indispensable

3   Lewis, p. 311; Nehemia Levtzion, *Muslims and chiefs in West Africa*, Oxford University Press, 1968, p. 55, 172

4   Trimingham, *A history of Islam in West Africa*, p. 143; Lewis, pp. 24–6

5   Mohammad Al-Hajj, 'The Fulani concept of Jihad – Shehu Uthman dan Fodio', *ODU, University of Ife Journal of African Studies*, I(1), July 1964, 45–58; see also H. F. C. Smith, 'The Islamic Revolutions of the nineteenth century', *Journal of the Historical Society of Nigeria*, II (2), 1961

6   N. S. Booth (ed), *African religions: a symposium*, New York, NOK Publishers, 1977, pp. 312–15

7   Lewis, p.5

8   J. Spencer Trimingham, *Islam in East Africa*, Oxford, Clarendon Press, 1964, is especially good for this area.

9   Gervase Mathew and Roland Oliver (eds), *History of East Africa*, Oxford University Press, 1963, p. 113

10   See Trimingham, *A history of Islam in West Africa*, pp. 224–31

11   W. Montgomery Watt, *Islam and the integration of Society*, Routledge and Kegan Paul, 1961, p. 137

12   Joseph Greenberg, *The influence of Islam on Sudanese religion*, Seattle, University of Washington Press, 1946, p. 359

13   Trimingham, *A history of Islam in West Africa*, p. 227

14   D. B. Cruise O'Brien, *Saints and politicians, essays in the organisation of a Senegalese peasant society*, Cambridge University Press, 1975, *passim*

15   Booth, *African religions,* p. 324

16   Trimingham, *The influence of Islam upon Africa,* pp. 44 ff.

17   *Ibid.,* pp. 38–42

Questions for discussion

1   Trace the history of the Islamic penetration of your country.

2   Assess the significance of the trans-Saharan trade routes in the diffusion of Islam in the western Sudan.

3   Discuss the influence of the traditional religion and culture on the development of Islam in your area.

4   The role of Islam in the evolution of the Sudanese empires remains a controversial issue. Discuss.

5   'The age of Islamising revolutions': do you agree with this view of political and religious developments in the eighteenth and nineteenth century in West Africa?

6   Examine how Islam profited from colonialism.

Suggestions for further reading

Ajayi, J. F. A., and Crowder, M. *History of West Africa,* I, 2nd ed., Longman, 1976

Booth, Newell S. (ed.) *African religions: a symposium.* New York: Nok Publishers, 1977

Cruise O'Brien, D. B. *Saints and politicians: essays in the organisation of a Senegalese peasant society,* Cambridge University Press, 1975

Holt, P. M., Lambton, K. S., and Lewis, Bernard (eds.) *Cambridge history of Islam,* 2 vols, Cambridge University Press, 1971

Josephy, Alvin M., Jr. (ed.) *The horizon history of Africa,* American Heritage, 1971

Kritzeck, J., and Lewis, W. H. (eds.) *Islam in Africa,* Van Nostran Reinhold, 1969

Lewis, I. M. (ed.) *Islam in tropical Africa,* Oxford University Press, 1964

Lombard, Maurice *The golden age of Islam,* Amsterdam, Holland, 1975

Trimingham, John Spencer. *A history of Islam in West Africa,* Oxford University Press, 1970

—— . *The influence of Islam upon Africa,* Longman, 1968

—— . *Islam in East Africa,* Oxford, Clarendon Press, 1964

—— . *Islam in the Sudan,* London, Frank Cass, 1965

5 Africa and external contacts

Richard Olaniyan

Discussion of Africa's relations and interaction with other parts of the world and people involves the following interrelated themes: early contacts between Africa and other continents; European intruders in Africa; the cultural, political, economic and psychological impact of the Euro-African interaction; the era of the slave trade; missionary activities; the explorers; the partition of Africa; and the installation of colonial administrations.

Early contacts between Africa and other continents

Africa has never been completely isolated from or unknown to other parts of the world. She has influenced and has been influenced by forces which have shaped the history of the world. A century and a half before the beginning of the Christian era, North Africa was drawn into the Roman empire as a result of the struggle for supremacy in the Mediterranean between the Roman republic and the empire of Carthage, whose capital was located near the modern city of Tunis. The Carthaginians had established a far-flung commercial empire which, in addition to the coastal lands of North Africa, included Sicily and settlements in Spain, Sardinia and mainland Italy. The bitter rivalry led to the three Punic wars of 264–241 B.C., 218–201 B.C., and 149–146 B.C. As a result of their successive defeats (in spite of the heroic leadership of Hannibal, in the second war), Carthage was reduced to ruins by the invading Romans. With the initial aim of preventing a resurgence of Carthaginian power, Rome gradually extended its rule over all the agricultural coastlands from Egypt to Morocco, turning the region into the bread-basket of the empire.

Through liberal laws which extended citizenship rights and privileges to all free men, many indigenes of North Africa were able to participate in the administration of the empire. Indeed, the emperor from A.D. 193 to 211, Septimius Severus, was an African, born in Leptis Magna in Tripolitania. Aurelius Augustinus, better known as Saint Augustine, the leading Christian philosopher of his day and bishop of Hippo (modern Bône on the Algerian coast) from 396 to 430, also hailed from Roman Africa.

But even earlier than the Roman intrusion into North Africa, the Greeks had been interested in and had had contact with Africa. The Greek historian Herodotus describes Carthaginians trading down the west coast of Africa and also refers to the 'silent trade' or 'dumb barter' by which goods were exchanged between the Africans beyond the Straits and the Carthaginians. He himself is said to have travelled in Egypt and Libya in the fifth century before the Christian era. He writes about the Nile with some familiarity and gives intimations of the kingdom of Kush further up.[1] Subsequently Greek mariners reached the Red Sea ports and parts of the East African coast. Quite early in the Christian era and before the advent of Islam, the Arabs had established trading links with the East African coastal towns.[2] A new religious movement would benefit from these early links.

As stated in the last chapter, the Arab Muslims invaded Egypt in the seventh century, and by the beginning of the eighth century had spread over the former Roman provinces in North Africa. Early in the same century, African Muslims (or Moors) participated in the Muslim invasion of the Iberian peninsula; Gibraltar, derived its name from the Berber general who commanded the invasion. The influence of North African Muslim leaders was to remain significant there until the fifteenth century. African contact with Europe was not all peaceful or wholly commercial although trade continued even in times of belligerency. In the tumultuous era of the crusades in the thirteenth century, the saintly king of France, Louis IX, attempted unsuccessfully to recapture Egypt and Tunisia from the Muslims. Peaceful propagation of the Christian faith was also initiated in North Africa by Dominican and Franciscan missionaries.

The spread of Islam by external agents and their interaction with Africans in the various regions of Africa was considered in the last chapter, and we need do no more than stress that in terms of its impact on African history and culture, Islam is equal only to Christianity. Islamisation and Arabisation brought Africa into contact with an extra continental culture which, over the centuries and in many parts of Africa, has become a significant force affecting both individual lives and the destinies of nations.

As we have also noted, the Africans had been involved in extensive internal commercial activities using long-distance trade routes which connected the different regions and linked the continent with Europe, Arabia and the Indian Ocean emporia. They traded in gold, slaves, ivory, copper, cloth, leather products, salt, other minerals and a variety of foodstuffs. The market and exchange system was well developed; Dyula and Hausa trading captains were, for example, the ubiquitous practitioners of the commercial art in most parts of western Sudan. The wealth of Africa, especially its gold, remained a great lure to the Europeans and attempts to reach its source in the fourteenth century by daring European seamen proved unavailing. The Portuguese were to succeed in the following century.

The intruders: the Portuguese

The Portuguese were the first Europeans to make concerted efforts to explore the coast of Africa. For this purpose Prince Henry, known as the Navigator (1394–1460), established a school of navigation where he assembled the leading cartographers, astronomers, shipbuilders and sailors. Political stability at home, advanced maritime technology, royal support, and Prince Henry's leadership and enthusiasm combined in making the Portuguese explorations successful. But how can we account for this surge of interest in Africa?

· Reports of the wealth of western Sudan, especially its gold, had long been well-known in most West European courts. But apart from his ambition that his countrymen should capture and control this flourishing trade, Prince Henry hoped to find a southerly route to the sources of the Asian spice trade, avoiding the Mediterranean, the eastern ports of which were by the fifteenth century already controlled by the Muslim Turks. In · other words, the commercial prospect of circumventing the trade restrictions and heavy duties imposed on imports from the Orient passing through the Middle East and the Mediterranean by the Ottoman Turks became a compelling reason for backing overseas voyages. In addition to this economic motivation, it was also hoped that the venture would facilitate the spread of Christianity and bring enlightenment to the peoples of these unknown lands. Finally, such exploratory voyages might make it possible for Portugal to establish contact with Prester John – the legendary, powerful Christian potentate in the interior who might prove co-operative in the crusade against Islam.

The first of several expeditions during the fifteenth century set sail in 1417. In 1418 the Portuguese mariners reached Madeira; sixteen years later Gil Eanes arrived at Cape Bojador; in 1441 Nuño Tristao and Antao Gonzalves rounded Cape Blanco; in 1444 Dinis Dias reached the mouth of the Senegal River and Cape Verde. In 1460 and 1471, the coasts of Sierra Leone and Ghana respectively were explored; the mouth of the Congo River was reached in 1482; and in 1487, Bartholomew Dias rounded the Cape of Good Hope. Finally in 1497–99, Vasco da Gama with his party following Dias' course, went past the Cape of Good Hope and touched at Mozambique, Mombasa and Malindi; he arrived in Calicut, India, in 1497, thus achieving Prince Henry's ultimate objective.

In all these places, the Portuguese took some account of the indigenous political institutions and were especially impressed by the mineral wealth, especially in gold, in both West and East Africa. They built forts on the coast of modern Ghana at Elmina, Axim and Accra. They also established sugar plantations on the Canaries, Madeira, the Cape Verde, São Tomé and Fernando Po islands on which African slave labour was used. Two interests were paramount in this contact between the Portuguese and Africa: commerce and conversion. On the islands where they established plantations, in the areas around their forts on the coast, in the kingdom of Benin (in modern Nigeria) and the Kongo (in modern Angola), they made some effort to introduce Christianity to the local inhabitants. Their evangelisation met with some success in the Kongo although elsewhere in West Africa it rapidly came to an end.

Commerce was also vigorously pursued. The cane plantations on the off-shore islands of Cape Verde, São Tomé and Fernando Po yielded sugar for export. The Portuguese traders obtained ivory from the coast of modern Ghana and Ivory Coast. They also participated in and benefited from the gold trade on the coast of (modern) Ghana to the extent that they named it the Gold Coast. In exchange they sold to the Africans spirits, iron, copper, cloth, horses, hardware and guns. To the African

Fig. 5.1   *A view of Elmina Castle, Ghana,
constructed by the Portuguese*

the Portuguese commercial link was, except for the guns, not crucial since many of these items, or their substitutes, were produced locally. Nevertheless, import of these goods increased to satisfy the consumption demands of an emerging African elite. By the end of the fifteenth century, gold and slaves had become the major imports of the Portuguese from Africa. Between 1441, when the Portuguese sent the first group of slaves (a dozen of them) to Portugal, and the end of the fifteenth century, the annual number of slaves exported from the Senegambia area and the Kongo to Portugal and their plantations on the off-shore islands rose by about 168 per cent. Eighteen years later the first direct export of slaves to the New World was inaugurated.

But the insatiable lust of the Portuguese for more and more slaves to be used on the sugar plantations in São Tomé disrupted relations between the Portuguese and the people of the Kongo. This led ultimately to the collapse of the Kongo state and the end of the first major Afro-European experiment in economic and cultural relations.

The Portuguese record in Angola was even more discreditable. With the help of some Portuguese slave traders, the Ndongo state declared itself independent in 1556 after a successful military confrontation with its former suzerain, the Kongo. The charter to establish a Portuguese colony was granted to Paulo Dias de Novaes in 1571. With the founding of Luanda in 1575, the four centuries of Portuguese colonial rule in Angola was begun. It was from here that the Portuguese supplied their plantations in the New World with cheap African slave labour. In spite of the fact that missionaries were usually part of the Portuguese colonising processes, we find the Portuguese administration characterised by brutality and complete lack of sensitivity to the African way of life.

In East Africa, the Portuguese defeated the Afro-Arab Muslims in 1509 and proceeded to control the commerce of the coastal city-states and the off-shore islands. They remained unchallenged there for almost a century. Here as in West Africa, their preoccupation was to capture the lucrative gold trade from the hinterland. They decided therefore to tap it at its source in the interior by building a fort at Sofala very early in the sixteenth century. Furthermore, a Jesuit missionary was sent to the interior where he succeeded in converting to Christianity the king of the Monomotapa empire and his leading chiefs. Father Gonzalo de Silveira's murder by the Arabs in 1571 was used as a pretext by the Portuguese to invade the region in 1571 and again three years later. When these invasions failed because of distance and disease, the Portuguese caused the deposition in 1629 of the Monomotapa ruler and the enthronement of a puppet ruler. But the deposed king, Nyambo Kapararidze, soon recaptured his throne after a humiliating defeat of the Portuguese.

The picture that emerges in the history of the Portuguese in East Africa is that they were never without vigorous opposition or challenge. When the challenge to their dominant position in the Indian Ocean region came in 1698, the Portuguese could not resist the joint assault on Fort Jesus in Mombasa by the combined forces of the Omani Arabs from south-eastern Arabia and the Afro-Arabs in the coastal settlements. This decisive defeat entailed the restriction of the Portuguese to their Mozambique stronghold.

Ethiopia, a Christian state since the fourth century, was during the fourteenth and fifteenth centuries facing a challenge from the Muslim Somali and Danakil people in the lowlands. In the 1520s the Ethiopians were overwhelmed by the invading Muslims. The Ethiopian ruler in the early decades of the sixteenth century, Lebna Dengel (1508–40), sought the help of the Portuguese in regaining his kingdom. In the military confrontation with the Muslims during the reign of Galandewod (1540–59), the Ethiopians and their Portuguese allies defeated the Muslims in 1543 and drove them back to their coastal lands, leaving the Ethiopians on the highlands. For a while, Portuguese and Spanish Catholic priests were welcomed in Ethiopia, but in the 1630s the Amhara Coptic Christians expelled them; for over two centuries Ethiopia cut almost all contacts with Europe.

The Portuguese impact on Africa before the nineteenth century scramble is a little difficult to assess. To some extent, it is a record of lost opportunities, especially in the Kongo where a more rational approach to cross-cultural development would have yielded greater dividends. On the positive side, Africa's contact with the Portuguese led to the introduction of numerous food items from the New World such as maize, groundnuts, cassava, rice, and pineapples, tomatoes, sugar cane and tobacco also came from the same source. It must, however, be pointed out that the Portuguese record of oppression was in direct contrast to the hospitality which the Africans showed in their dealings with them. Their mission to evangelise the Africans was a dismal failure because of the misrepresentation of the Christian message of brotherhood and a cultural arrogance that created the master–servant superiority complex in the intruders. Finally, the Portuguese lacked the resources to overcome the traditional African beliefs or to suppress the tenacious religious practices.

The intruders: other Europeans

During the seventeenth century the race for Africa began in earnest among other European powers, outstripping the Portuguese pioneers. The French established settlements in Senegal; the Dutch gained a foothold on the Gold Coast in 1612 and within thirty years the Dutch West Indies Company had taken over all the Portuguese forts on the Guinea coast; the English entered the scene on the Gold Coast officially in 1660 with the granting of a royal charter to a company of adventurers doing business with Africa. In the same century other Europeans established forts on the Gold Coast: the Danes in 1642, the Swedes in 1647, and the Brandenburgers in 1682. In all, the Europeans had built about twenty-eight forts or trading posts on the coast by the close of the seventeenth century.

The establishment of forts in West Africa provided the Europeans with the security they needed against other European rivals and served as trading bases with their African hosts. At this stage of the contact between the Africans and the Europeans, it was clear that the latter were tenants who had to pay rent on the land they occupied and observe a code of conduct in order to maximise their commercial interests. The Africans controlled the trade along the coast and in the interior, and had enough military power to humble any recalcitrant European settlement as was the case in 1693 when the Akwamu occupied the Danish fort of Christiansborg in Accra and only returned it a year later following payment by the Danes. In other words, the Africans were by no means the underdogs in their relations with the Europeans in this area.

The era of the slave trade

There was, however, a consensus of interest among the Europeans on the Guinea coast: their major objective was to assure their countries a steady supply of slaves for their colonies in the New World. Systematically, they shipped off men and women in their prime to plantations in distant North and South America to satisfy the mercantilist proclivities of the rising nation states. Why was there this great demand for African labour?

It is important to emphasise that the transatlantic slave trade was not the first or the only time when Africans were sold into slavery. It is believed that Nubians were sold by the Egyptians to Europe and the

Middle East. The Carthaginians employed large numbers of slaves from the Sudan on their estates and in their armies. Rome and Greece also bought slaves from the North African markets. There was in East Africa a thriving business in slaves in which Arabs, Persians and Indians participated, and their human exports to India were to be found in Bengal, Gujarat and Deccan. As early as the tenth century, African slaves were being sent to China and other countries of the Far East. The western Sudanese empires of Ghana and Mali, the Hausa states and others received substantial revenues from the slave trade.

It is also appropriate here to point out that there were different categories of slaves in different African societies as there were in other countries of the world, ranging from people in voluntary servitude to domestic servants and those used as pawns for debts. This aspect of slavery cannot be compared with the Atlantic slave trade in its brutality and callous inhumanity, for in African societies slaves enjoyed rights and privileges and were considered not mere property but as members of the families they served. In some African societies slaves could and did hold certain political offices.

The transatlantic slave trade

It was the active participation by the Europeans in West Africa in the seventeenth century that introduced a new chapter in the history of the African slave trade across the Atlantic. The slave trade across the Sahara and from East Africa was also intensified at about the same time because of increasing demands in the Mediterranean and the Middle Eastern markets, but this cannot be compared (or, at any rate, has not been conclusively compared), in volume with the transatlantic slave trade.

The development of a plantation system in the New World (North, Central and South America and the Caribbean islands) by the Europeans for the production of cotton, sugar, tobacco and indigo created a large demand for cheap labour. The Amerindians (native Americans) were ill-suited for the hard work needed on the plantations and their mortality rate was alarmingly high, whereas black labour was both cheap and superior. Consequently, the Europeans – Spaniards, Portuguese, British, French, Dutch and others – turned to Africa for slaves to work on their plantations and mines. And as Eric Williams maintains, it was a purely economic decision, not racial.[3] The first batch of black slaves to the Americas in 1501 came from Spain; the first direct shipment from West Africa to the Americas was in a Spanish ship in 1518; the Portuguese followed fourteen years later; the English joined in 1562 when John Hawkins took his cargo of slaves to the West Indies; and in 1619 the Dutch deposited the first twenty African slaves in Jamestown in Virginia on the North American mainland. But why was it easy for them to obtain slaves?

The Europeans themselves did not go into the interior to capture slaves but maintained forts and trading stations along the coast of West Africa where African kings and chiefs came to sell or barter their own slaves or servants and certain categories of criminals and war captives. The growing demand for slaves in the Americas encouraged the African rulers and local merchants to look for a supply of slaves outside their own sources by conducting raids and wars; slaves were now more in demand than either gold or ivory. Furthermore, Africans had begun to demand, more and more, certain European goods, especially spirits, tobacco, gunpowder and firearms, which Europeans would in most cases make available only in exchange for slaves. A tragic cycle was thus created: if the African chiefs and merchants wanted more luxury goods and fire-arms, they had to produce more slaves; the availability of arms increased the chance of waging successful wars on neighbours and capturing more prisoners to become slaves. With the introduction of firearms, the seven-teenth century began a time of trouble in West Africa; the Portuguese turned life in the Kongo and Angola, especially the latter, into a long nightmare as devastation spread and all kinds of methods were employed to meet the ever-increasing demands for slaves in Brazil. From the seventeenth century to about a decade before the mid-nineteenth century, the slave trade was a major preoccupation on the West African coast and in the Kongo–Angola region.

There has been some controversy about the number of slaves taken from these areas of Africa to the New World. In a recent study of the statistics of the trade an American historian, Philip D. Curtin, came to the conclusion that some eleven million people were forcibly removed from Africa and shipped to the Americas between the sixteenth and the nineteenth centuries, when the slave trade was finally abolished. He does not include in this figure the slaves involved in the trans-Saharan traffic or those who perished in the slave-raiding wars which often preceded the sea-voyage.[4] Other historians have put the figure at about fifteen million.[5] The exact count will never be known. All told, taking into account the

Fig. 5.2 *Conditions on board a slave trade ship*

mortality rate during the notoriously dehumanising 'Middle Passage', which must have been high, and the casualties of the brutal slave-raiding wars, it would probably be close to the truth to say that as many as twenty million Africans in the prime of their lives either perished or were taken from their homes to work in the mines or on plantations in the Americas. Thus as many as the present populations (1978 estimates) of Ghana, Ivory Coast and Liberia put together – or, one person out of every twenty-four Europeans or, approximately one out of every eleven citizens of the United States, perished or were enslaved in the Americas.

Perhaps the following figures will give an idea of the staggering scale of the slave traffic:

> In 1760, 146 ships sailed from British ports to Africa with a capacity of 36,000 slaves. In 1771 there were 190 ships and 47,000 slaves. The British colonies between 1680 and 1786 imported over two million slaves. By the middle of the eighteenth century Bristol owned 237 slave trade vessels, London, 147, and Liverpool, 89.

In terms of active participation and volume, Liverpool and Bristol were in the lead among British ports in what Du Bois calls the 'rape of Africa'.[6]

As we have pointed out, the responsibility was not wholly that of the Europeans since they could not engage in the trade without the co-operation of the African leadership – kings, chiefs and merchant princes – who suplied the slaves in the various areas. An English visitor to many West African slave-trading areas in the 1780s reported to the Privy Council Committee in 1789 that the African rulers were often 'incited by the merchandise shown them, which consists principally of strong liquors', and would 'give orders to their military to attack their own villages in the night. . . .'[7] They needed to do this in order to obtain the gunpowder and the firearms, spirits and luxury goods offered by the European slavers. The competition among the Europeans not to be outdone or displaced by their rivals ensured lively trading conditions, while the African suppliers too competed among themselves to provide the slaves in their struggle for economic and political advantage. '"The European traders taught the African to sell other Africans as they had taught them to sell gold-dust and ivory . . . for third rate articles" – and for cheap brandy and costly (as they would prove in the end) guns.'[8]

Even though attempts to oppose the slave trade by some African rulers proved ineffective, they are significant if only to recognise that there were men of principle and courage who stood out against the forced exportation of fellow-Africans to a life of bondage in the Americas. The earliest known example was in 1526 when King Nzinga Mbemba of the Bakongo state of the Kongo (also known by his Christian name of Affonso) wrote to the king of Portugal complaining about the bad effect the slave trade was having in his kingdom. He complained about de-population, and insisted that the Portuguese traders be recalled because 'it is our will that in these kingdoms of Kongo there should not be any trade of slaves nor any market for slaves'. Instead, Affonso wanted from his Portuguese counterpart 'priests and people to teach in our schools, and no other goods but wine and flour for the holy sacrament'.[9] Not only did the appeal fall on deaf ears but even the Kongolese chiefs and merchants themselves could not easily abandon the lucrative trade.

A second example which has been suggested (on the basis of a contemporary opinion) is the action of King Agaja of Dahomey in attacking his neighbours in Ardrah and Ouidah in 1724, interpreted as being intended to suppress the slave trade there. Most historians now agree, however, in preferring the explanation for the attack (also based on a contemporary source) that the king's aim was to gain unrestricted access to trade with the Europeans on the coast.[10] A more convincing case is that of the Almamy of Futa Toro who in 1789 forbade passage through his domain to slaves who were being exported. The local chiefs, who had much at stake if the law was effectively carried out, and the French captains waiting for their human cargoes on the coast both appealed to the Almamy to rescind his order, but instead he returned the French company's gifts and refused to change his stand. In the end the traders stayed away from the Almamy's vicinity on the Senegal River and looked for another route to the coast. Finally, the kings of Benin refused for a long time to co-operate with the European slavers and only yielded to pressure towards the close of the seventeenth century to allow the capture of males for the purpose of the Atlantic slave trade. These four instances all ended in failure because the principals in these episodes were dealing with what had become a complex commercial and political network affecting four continents. For it to come to an end, it was necessary to halt the demand for slaves in the Americas.

Assessing the impact of the slave trade on African societies at this stage of our discussion may appear premature, but to attempt such an assessment may elucidate further developments elsewhere on the continent and in Europe. The social and racial troubles of the present day have their roots in the invaders' irruption into Africa, disrupting and destroying traditional African social order, political development and economic life.

The history of the slave trade in Africa is a history of violence and destruction, kidnapping and the degradation of human dignity. The magnitude of the rape of Africa during the four centuries preceding 1870 was unprecedented in the history of the human race. In order to capture slaves wars were fought and raids carried out. There were, of course, wars that were occasioned by other reasons – economic and imperial, for example – but which nevertheless produced slaves. The need to acquire more firearms led to the need to produce more slaves, and the supply of more firearms further increased tension and the incidence of warfare.

The Europeans were eager to supply firearms because they needed the slaves. The internecine wars of the nineteenth century produced millions of slaves. However, it is also true that the slave trade aided the expansion of empires like Oyo, Dahomey and Asante. These powerful empires, which flourished in the eighteenth and nineteenth centuries, turned their attention towards the coast in order to establish direct dealing with the European traders, and in the process had to fight wars to eliminate the middlemen. The effect in Angola and on the East African coast was different. Decline and disintegration were the lot of the states that were in existence when the Portuguese began their drive for slaves in these areas – the Manikongo in the Kongo, the Mbundu in Angola, the city-states on the East African coast and the great empire of Monomotapa. Smaller states – in the Niger delta, for example – which grew and prospered as slave posts never grew to be as powerful as the empires whose beginnings antedated the slave trade.

In political terms, therefore, the slave trade produced inter-state conflicts which were directly or indirectly connected with the capture of slaves. This situation weakened political stability and institutional development both in the communities from which slaves were captured and in those who supplied the slaves and adversely affected all other trade.

Another effect was that the slave trade contributed to the depopulation of Africa. It was not just the question of the millions taken into slavery but also that it was people in their prime between early youth and middle age who suffered most. This meant that the affected societies were deprived of a vital productive age group which would normally have contributed in diverse ways to their development. This constituted a serious demographic impoverishment, so that the prevalent agricultural economy could not expand, remaining instead in many places at the subsistence level. Africans were so preoccupied with the lucrative slave trade that they neglected to learn the relevant technology from Europe which might have helped to transform their economy. Furthermore, the nature of the slave trade and its high profit margin prevented the Africans from developing their own technology to cope with the needs of their societies. Finally, in such an atmosphere the traditional arts and crafts of Africa were unable to flourish, and a long period of decay set in.

All told, therefore, the slave trade can be said to have initiated the underdevelopment of Africa. Finally, one major legacy of this era that seems to be still much with us is the racial attitude that ineluctably developed from the relationships of the white slave owners to the black slaves. The feeling of superiority which originated with the white owners of estates and mines replaced the initial respect and equality that characterised the first contacts between Africans and Europeans and still to some extent poisons relations between black and white peoples in the world.

South Africa

The Dutch took over Portuguese interests in the East Indies as well as on the Gold Coast, and made the Cape of Good Hope their midway station between Europe and East Indies. In 1652 in order to avert the danger of other European powers establishing themselves there, the Dutch East India Company commissioned Jan van Riebeeck and about ninety men to set up a victualling station. Less than a decade later the post had a fort, a hospital, houses, a mill, workshops, fruit and vegetable gardens and herds of sheep from which India-bound Dutch ships could draw their supplies. Orders were given that the area should not be colonised or the local Africans molested. However, what was originally intended to be a small station began to expand when fresh immigrants arrived from Holland (free farmers or burghers), followed after 1688 by some two hundred Huguenots from France. By the close of the century the settlement had expanded as far into the interior as Stellenbosch with the result that the Cape had indeed become a veritable European-run settlement which comprised some 17 000 slaves, the Dutch company's European employees, the 1 600 Dutch burghers (or Boers), a group of French Huguenot refugees, and finally a 'coloured' population – the products of white–black unions.

The local population whom the Dutch met in South Africa included the Khoisan-speaking peoples – the San (Bushmen) and the Khoikhoi (Hottentots);[11] the former were hunters and gatherers and the latter cattle herders living in the coastal area of the Cape and along the eastern littoral of the Transkei. There were also the Bantu-speaking peoples – the Zulu, Xhosa, Pondo, Tembu, the Sotho-Tswana, the Herero and the Ambo – living in the different regions of southern Africa. (The argument that there were no Africans living in the area when the Europeans came is an invention by apologists for the policy of apartheid.)

The early history of contact between Africans and Europeans in South Africa was replete with confrontations: the Khoikhoi and the San had encountered invaders as early as the closing decades of the fifteenth century; with the Bantu-speaking people the confrontation came in 1702. (If there were no indigenous peoples, how can we account for the Khoikhois' affray with Bartholomew Dias and Vasco da Gama's followers or the open hostilities with the Portuguese in 1503 at Table Bay or in 1510 at Gao during which sixty Portuguese lost their lives?) Land was a crucial commodity for both the Africans and the land-grabbing Boers; hence the clashes of 1658–70 and 1673–77 over grazing. But the Africans were ultimately defeated: liquor and tobacco and the white man's diseases such as smallpox broke the resistance of the Khoikhoi. They finally joined the devil they could not defeat by becoming laboureres and domestic servants. But the San were only finally subdued through a systematic policy of extermination and the mass expulsion of the survivors into the arid regions of northwest Cape and the Orange River. Resistance had fizzled out by the middle of the eighteenth century through the application of superior technology and the use of firearms. The suppression of the last group of resisters, the Bantu-speaking people, started in the eighteenth century and has continued to this day with varying degrees of intensity.

Looking over the contact between the Africans and the Europeans, we can now identify three main areas of semi-permanence, namely Angola, Mozambique and South Africa. In the case of the last, between 1835 and 1843 more than 12 000 Afrikaners, descendants of the Dutch, moved away from the Cape region in the Great Trek in search of new land and to free themselves from the English who in their turn had displaced Boer rule. With the defeat of the Ndebele in 1836 and of the great Zulu army in 1838, the Trekkers appropriated regions of the Transvaal and the Orange River. In the meantime, English settlers had occupied the Cape and Natal provinces. The clash between the two groups, the Boers and the English, consequent upon the discovery of diamond and gold towards the end of the nineteenth century, was to determine the nature of the South Africa that would emerge and the racial policy that would be enunciated and entrenched by the Afrikaner political majority in 1948, and which has been guiding South Africa to this day.[12]

The new orientations

Even before the close of the eighteenth century, new forces began to impinge upon relations between Africa and Europe. In the first place, influential consciences had been roused to the point that a move to suppress the slave trade started to gather momentum; this was later accompanied by the advocacy of 'legitimate' trade. Secondly, there was the unfinished work of unravelling the mystery of the so-called 'Dark Continent' and opening it up to the outside world. The participants would include two classes: the intrepid explorers and scientists, and the exploiters whose ambition was the acquisition of territory for the various European nations. In the last quarter of the nineteenth century, this sequence would change to scramble, partition and consolidation, the last being the installation of colonial administration. Finally, the century also witnessed a revived interest in Christian evangelisation, a pattern that seemed to be inseparable from colonial advances. These new orientations, or in some instances reactivations of former impulses, were to dominate the nineteenth century.

The abolition of slavery

The serious effort to come to grips with the evils of slavery and the slave trade in the Atlantic and Indian oceans began in Britain, and she was to bear the brunt of the anti-slavery measures until well past the mid-nineteenth century. How can we account for this anti-slavery movement in Britain at a time when other nations were willing to continue the exploitation of Africa for the easy profit it assured them?

In both Britain and America, almost three hundred years of iniquity towards a segment of the human race had left scars on the consciences of both the slavers and their clients. There were those who felt strongly enough to appeal to the British Parliament to stop the human traffic, and who formed pressure groups made up of individuals who became famous in their commitment to save civilisation from this blot, like Granville Sharp, John Wesley, Thomas Clarkson and William Wilberforce. Sharp's persistence in his desire to see the trade outlawed led to the famous ruling of Chief Justice Lord Mansfield in 1772 that slavery had no legal basis in British law. What the learned jurist did was to create a population of abandoned free slaves without any legal responsibility by their ex-owners; slavery was still legal in the colonies. Undaunted, Sharp devised a scheme with official support to send the freed slaves to Africa. The 1787 attempt to settle about four hundred blacks and whites in the colony of Sierra Leone among the unsympathetic indigenous Temne was doomed to fail. Another attempt under the auspices of the Sierra Leone Company in 1791 led to the foundation of Freetown with some 1 200 ex-slaves who had been loyal to the British in the American War of Independence; others joined them from the Caribbean. With official support and a royal charter for the Sierra Leone Company in 1800, the settlement attained the status of a crown colony, a haven for freed slaves and a base for naval action against slavers in West Africa. Whatever initial birth pangs the settlement experienced arising from the difficulty of integrating the expatriate Africans into the indigenous population, the experiment worked.

A similar experiment was undertaken by the American Colonisation Society. In 1822 groups of black Americans and recently freed slaves under the aegis of the A.C.S. and with support from the administration of President James Monroe and others arrived in West Africa to establish Liberia where they hoped to be free from the racism in the United States. Liberia too went through the clash of interests between the indigenous Africans and the invading returnees from America, disease and other problems of such resettlement experiments; the new American offspring came of age in 1847 when it declared its independence. This American element in the history of Liberia has contributed to the problems of national integration, but there is increasingly hopeful evidence that antagonism between coast and interior may be a thing of the past.

The abolitionists, however, would probably have been unable to achieve what they did without a fortunate sense of timing and an auspicious co-operation of forces. In the first place, there was a rising and influential climate of opinion informed by the liberal ideas of the eighteenth-century Enlightenment. These ideas in part contributed to the revolutionary thinking and mentality that culminated in the American and French revolutions in the last quarter of the eighteenth century. The revolutionary movement attacked all forms of oppression and increased pressure for an end to slavery and the slave trade.

A leading scholar on the subject argues that it was the rise of industrial capitalism which led to the abolition of the slave trade and slavery. His contention is that with the legitimisation of the independence of the American colonies in 1783 an economic change of fortune had taken place. In addition to the economic loss this meant that the British sugar planters in the West Indies now had to compete with their French counterparts who, for a combination of reasons which included efficiency and good soil, proved to be more than a match for them. For example, in 1789, French planters in Saint Domingue alone exported over a third more sugar than all the British West Indies put together. This new colonial economic climate forced Britain to shift her centre of imperial economic operation to India. The loss of the American colonies shattered the advantageous British colonial monopoly which had hitherto formed the bedrock of the imperial arrangement. What was astonishing was that the volume of free trade between the United States and Britain after 1783 actually increased, disproving the theories of colonial monopoly and mercantilism. Consequently, the case for the abolition of the slave trade was made less difficult and the attack on the West Indian mercantilist monopoly more effective.

This thesis has, however, recently been disputed by Drescher and Anstey who have shown that the British parliamentary decision to abolish the slave trade cannot be satisfactorily explained on economic grounds. In fact, far from declining, the West Indies were increasing their production and share of British overseas trade in the twenty years before the abolition Act of 1807.[13]

Among the long-term factors that led to the abolition of the slave trade and slavery was the growth of the Industrial Revolution in the late eighteenth and nineteenth centuries in Britain, which turned the leading slave-trading nation into the workshop of the world and made the world her market. British capital, manufactures and skills were exported to many parts of the world; and by 1830, the West Indies had become insignificant to British capitalism and the new industrial order – an order in which an economy based on slavery and the slave trade – had become simply anachronistic.[14]

In any event, a strong attack was mounted in Britain on slavery and on the slave trade. This anti-slavery movement of the late eighteenth and nineteenth centuries included Christians, humanitarians and philanthropists as well as those capitalists who found a common enemy in the 'peculiar institution' whose profitability was now questionable. The Industrial Revolution generated a similar antipathy towards the slave trade and slavery in other countries. Thus the interlocking impact of political and economic motives made it possible for the reformers to bring about the passage in the British Parliament of the law of 1807 which made the slave trade illegal and that of 1833 which abolished slavery in British possessions.

For the following two decades the Royal Navy performed its task with earnestness, exacting penalties for every slave found on a ship and confiscating the erring vessel itself. This approach succeeded in virtually extirpating the trade among British merchants.

The United States abolished the slave trade in 1808, Sweden in 1813 and the Netherlands the following year. France, after experiencing what we may call 'Hamlet's complex' from the revolutionary days of 1794 to the triumph and tragedy of the Napoleonic era, made the civilised genuflection in 1818. Denmark had earliest of all abolished her slave trade in 1804. Yet, for the anti-slavery policy to be really effective Britain had to enlist the support of other countries in combating illegal shipments. This met with stiff opposition, especially from the Americans and the French. Finally Britain concluded agreements with arrangements for compensation with a number of countries: Portugal in 1815 and 1817 and Spain in 1817, while Brazil, following upon her independence, accepted the British anti-slavery policy in 1831. But even with these legal and treaty arrangements, trading persisted. The Atlantic trade was finally ended only in the early 1860s, due perhaps more to action on land against the traders and their accomplices than to the admittedly exacting efforts at sea of the British and other navies, while the East coast and Indian Ocean trade lasted even longer.

By the 1840s, however, the success of the abolition laws and the British naval patrols had begun to have a serious economic impact and to render increasingly less lucrative the slave trade among the African slave barons, especially on the Niger coast – Bonny, Brass, Calabar and the Cross River. The upshot of this was a search for alternative economic pursuits – the change to legitimate trade. Soon the groundnut in the Senegal area and palm oil in the Niger delta region came to be developed as viable exports to replace the old traffic in human beings. These products were needed in the expanding soap industry in England. By the third decade of the nineteenth century, West African entrepreneurship in palm oil production had begun to meet the demands of the English soap factories. A new development in the commercial relationship between the old slave coast and Europe was taking shape, and the Africans all along the west coast either as farmers or as oil-palm plantation owners became active trading partners with Europe; this created a new race of merchant-princes on the west coast, especially in the oil rivers. Moreover, there were other exciting prospects which fed the imagination of the Europeans. Africa contained, Europeans earnestly believed, immense deposits of minerals that could turn a lucky pauper into an instant millionaire. Cotton was also more and more in demand as the American Civil War of the 1860s interrupted the supply of raw material to the Lancashire mills.

Exploration

The economic motive was, therefore, significant in the exploration of Africa, but there was another dimension to the new interest. The scientific advances of the late eighteenth and early nineteenth centuries had expanded the frontiers of man's knowledge of his planet and of the universe. The combined harvest of research in the various scientific disciplines – geography, astronomy, archaeology, ethnology and others – in America and Europe had produced an adventurous outlook which amounted to a revolution. In Africa the way forward was pioneered by young scientists looking for professional laurels. In 1788, the African Association was formed with the expressed purpose of sending scholars to gather scientific information on the continent. Many of their collaborators included businessmen, missionaries and others interested in Africa. Soon, this British experiment was emulated by other nationalities: the Geographical Society of France was formed in 1821, for example, and that of Prussia in 1828. In Egypt, Napoleon set on hand the study of Egyptology; and in Zimbabwe (Rhodesia), the British imperial enthusiast, Cecil Rhodes, put his money where an abundant return seemed assured: the collection of information on the gold deposits of the region. In short, the new outburst of scientific pursuits was to prove beneficial and at the same time serve as a prelude to the other new orientations.

The other development in the relations between Africa and Europe, as we noted at the beginning of this discussion of the new orientations of the nineteenth century, was the 'discovering' of Africa. Except for the coastal enclaves and trading stations, much of Africa and almost all the interior, remained unknown to the Europeans, so that the eighteenth-century English satirist, Jonathan Swift, could make the point in rhyming couplets:

> So geographers in Africa maps
> With savage pictures fill the gaps
> And o'r unhabitable downs
> Placed elephants for want of towns.

The nineteenth-century explorations aimed to discover the waterways, open up Africa for 'legitimate commerce', and initiate a new missionary effort to bring Christianity to the 'dark continent'. These motives were compatible, and together they provided the impetus for the exploration of Africa and furthered Africa's contact with the outside world.

We must here sound a note of caution, otherwise we may be carried too far by admiration for the admittedly lofty ideals of this group of Europeans who boldly ventured to advance man's knowledge of the

African continent. The use of the word 'discovery' is tendentious. Of course the regions and physical features concerned had been known to the Africans for generations. The pioneering explorers drew on the Africans' knowledge and rarely did an explorer embark upon any scientific excursion without using groups of local people as pathfinders. Nevertheless, to the European explorers belongs the credit of making information about the interior of Africa available to the wider world outside, thus contributing to the growing pool of human knowledge.

The explorers of Africa of the late eighteenth and nineteenth centuries shared certain characteristics: they were daring, idealistic, curious, inventive and persevering. They faced the dangers of climate and diseases. The problem of the source and course of the River Niger provided an early challenge in West Africa. A young Scottish doctor, Mungo Park (1771–1806), under the auspices of the African Association, reached Segu on the Niger in 1796 and realised that the river flowed northeastward. In 1805, he returned to trace the course of the lower river but met sudden death at Bussa. The greatest mystery of the Niger was unravelled in 1830 by Richard and John Lander, who travelled downstream from Bussa to the Bight of Benin. The intention of the British government was to use the Niger as an access to the commercial possibilities of the interior. Disease was the scourge that prevented subsequent attempts to make a success of the venture, which had to be abandoned in 1842. It was the use of quinine which changed the situation by giving protection against malaria, so that the Niger expedition led by Blaikie in 1854 suffered no fatality. Other British or British-sponsored travellers were meanwhile exploring the Muslim regions of modern Nigeria – travellers like Oudney, Clapperton and Denham.

West African exploration received great encouragement from the successful exploits of the German explorer Heinrich Barth (1821–65), sent out by the British government, who travelled from Lake Chad across to Say on the Niger, thence to Timbuktu, Sokoto and Borno, and discovered in the process the upper parts of the Benue River. He returned to England in 1855 loaded with invaluable information on the history, geography and culture of the entire region. His book, *Travels and Discoveries in North and Central Africa,* remains a mine of information.

The exploration of West Africa, with its greater commercial interest, went ahead faster than that of East Africa. The Arabs and the Portuguese had, however, earlier extended the frontiers of contact with the Africans there. Then, under the aegis of the Anglican Church Missionary Society two Germans, Johann Krapf and Johann Rebmann, scored early success: the former was the first European to see Mount Kilimanjaro in 1848; the latter sighted Mount Kenya the following year. Their glowing reports on the region and the snow-capped mountains encouraged others to follow them. Then two Englishmen, Burton, a talented linguist and prolific writer, and Speke, both Indian army veterans, discovered Lake Tanganyika in 1858, while Speke was the first white explorer to identify in 1862 Lake Victoria Nyanza as the source of the River Nile.

The French and Italians were also involved in the East African exploration. The French scholar Antoine d'Abbadie (1810–97) immersed himself in the history and culture of Ethiopia, acquiring and cataloguing valuable documents.

However, by far the most celebrated explorer was the Scot, David Livingstone, who arrived in Cape Town in 1841; exploring the interior of Africa, he reached the Zambezi in 1850 and Luanda in 1854, and then trekked across the continent reaching Mozambique two years later. His contribution went beyond his role as a missionary doctor; he compiled valuable information on geography, botany, ethnography, anthropology, tropical medicine and other areas of knowledge. Above all, though, Livingstone is remembered as one who combined in a single life the main currents of the era: humanitarianism, missionary zeal, scientific curiosity and commercial pursuits.

Fig. 5.3 *Dr David Livingstone, one of the best-known European explorers of Africa*

Evangelisation

Missionaries of various kinds descended on Africa in great numbers in the nineteenth century – all committed to bringing Christianity to the pagan populations; they were involved also in the suppression of slavery and the slave trade, introducing the alternative legitimate commerce and in general forwarding the modernisation of African society through European technology and education.

We should perhaps stress that the missionary zeal of the nineteenth century was a reflection of the same intellectual and ethical climates in Europe which sent out traders, scientists and soldiers to distant corners of the globe. However, unlike earlier attempts to Christianise Africa, the new impetus depended much less on the political apparatus of the state than on individual contributions and the support of the laity. The Protestants in northern Europe and North America dominated missionary enterprise in Africa and formed powerful organisations devoted to the cause of overseas evangelisation.

By the closing decades of the eighteenth century, numerous missionary groups had been formed: the British Methodists led the way in 1787; then the Baptists; the London Missionary Society was formed in 1795 by the Congregationalists in London; the Church Missionary Society, which was to play a prominent role in the missionary endeavours in Africa, was established in 1799 by a small group of Anglicans. Other nationals followed the growing phenomenon: the Basel Missionary Society was inaugurated in 1815; the Paris Evangelical Missionary Society in 1828. In the United States, missionary enthusiasm was closely linked with the anti-slavery movement and the resettlement of blacks in Africa. An interdenominational institution, the American Board of Commissioners for Foreign Missions, was set up with the chief objective of training Africans to carry out missionary work among their own people; their first destination in 1834 was Liberia. The Roman Catholics set up their Institute for the Propagation of the Faith at Lyons in 1822; the Church itself supported the founding of religious orders dedicated to missionary enterprise abroad.

Propitiously for the new missionary efforts, there was a consensus of opinion in Europe at the time about the need to carry the Gospel and civilisation to the backward parts of the globe. In West Africa, Sierra Leone and Fernando Po became the early entry points; in East Africa, Zanzibar was used by missionaries intended for service in the mainland missions; Cape Town played a similar role in South Africa. From these overseas outposts came reports which filled the ecclesiastical journals at home. Their main concern, however, was to stamp out all manifestations of the Devil. Unhappily, many overzealous evangelicals tended to decry all indigenous practices and institutions out of a feeling of superiority. Yet in spite of their cultural arrogance and other faults, the missionaries made a great contribution to African culture, especially in the committing of African languages to writing and in translating the Bible, which was of great value in the development of a written African literature.

How did the Africans view this missionary endeavour? And how can we account for the fact that while there were no European colonies at the beginning of the nineteenth century other than small outposts, by the close of the century almost the whole continent had been occupied by alien forces?

Reaction to the missionaries varied from one area to another, from open and enthusiastic welcome among the Yoruba to one of cool toleration further in the interior. A diplomacy of give-and-take developed between the chiefs and the missionaries. The friendship of the latter was much valued, for example, during the internecine, fratricidal wars in the Yoruba country in the nineteenth century when access to firearms was a decisive diplomatic leverage which the missionaries often had at their disposal. The missionaries' involvement in local politics exposed them to the charge that they were agents of imperialism.

This connection between the missionaries and the eventual annexation of the relevant territories during the scramble was well illustrated by the role of the British missionaries in the annexation of Kenya and Uganda, as parts of the British empire. However, it must also be pointed out in fairness to the missionaries that on numerous occasions they protested to the colonial authorities against any alienation of the rights of the Africans.

It must not be forgotten also that the missionaries provided institutions that accelerated the process of change, change that ultimately would spell the demise of the colonial structure. The provision of schools, the inclusion of Africans in church committees, the tradition of allowing Africans free access to the Bible – all these contributed to sharpening political awareness and raising hopes for future political autonomy. Perhaps this was an unintended advantage of the 'civilising mission'. During the closing decades of the last century, especially in the Niger Mission, the earlier policy of encouraging Africans to take over leadership in the missions was given less rather than greater prominence. The emergence of African separatist churches can be traced to this era, especially in Nigeria.

In spite of the racial overtone in the missionary administration of religion in South Africa, and even in Central Africa and the Belgian Congo where a paternalistic approach was practised, the Africans found opportunities, religious and political, for expression in their separatist churches. In South Africa especially, racial oppression forced the Africans to give racial interpretations to the Bible, and it was even preached that Christ was black and would return to save his African brethren. In the 'Ethiopian' movement, politics and religion became bedfellows, at times advocating violence to underscore opposition to the racial injustices of South Africa. It is clear from even a cusory look at the missionary factor in Central and East Africa that the opportunity for European settlement and economic possibilities greatly affected the original missionary objectives. West Africa, however, was saved from European settlement and large-scale alientation of land, by, among other factors, the bad climate and the prevalence of malaria which turned the region into the 'white man's grave'.

It has been necessary for us to consider at length the impact of the Christian missions because they profoundly affected the social and political development of the continent. They were a vital force, and, indeed, their impact is still with us to this day.[15]

The scramble for and partition of Africa

How was it that within a hundred years nearly the whole of Africa and its people had been subjected to external domination? It must be emphasised first that this change was neither sudden nor wholly explicable in terms of developments taking place on the African continent alone; we have to look at developments taking place in Europe as well.

The abolition of the slave trade and the encouragement of 'legitimate' commerce started a pattern of change in the relationships between Europe and Africa. In the meantime, Britain had become the leading industrial state and, with the other European nations, looked to other lands to meet the expanding needs for raw material of the Industrial Revolution. Thus, while the motive for African colonisation was essentially economic and political, the weapons were Europe's technological superiority and military strength (opposed to African technological inferiority and lack of political unity). Historians are still debating the causes and the motives behind European imperialism: some emphasise the economic, others stress the political and strategic factors. The truth seems to lie in a combination of the two.

Competing and clashing nationalisms among the European countries, the need for a balance of power whereby no one country or a combination of countries would be in a position to threaten the peace of Europe or its political equilibrium, and the urge for national glory exacerbated the quest for colonies during the years between the mid-nineteenth century and 1900. There was also keen competition among the European countries to find new markets for their manufactured goods and new sources of raw materials. We must also consider the strategic factor. Because Britain had interests in the Middle East, India and Asia, the control of the Suez Canal was of strategic importance to her. This was the major reason for the occupation of Egypt in 1882.

We have already noted that many Europeans felt that they had a duty to extend the benefits of their civilisation and religion to what they saw as the backward parts of the world. This last motive for conquest and colonialism grew out of the ethnocentric ideas of the time in Europe, based on evolutionary theories. It was the belief of such men as Charles Darwin, Herbert Spencer and even Karl Marx that it was the responsibility of the 'higher' forms of civilisation (the European in this case) to conquer the 'lower' or backward civilisations in order to effect 'progress' in the world. The racial purists were also at this time strongly asserting the racial superiority of the white race.

Against this intellectual background, the leading West European countries – Britain, France, Germany, Italy and Belgium – laid claims to different parts of Africa without any consideration for the rights and wishes of the inhabitants. In order to avoid military confrontations over the partition of Africa, the Berlin West Africa conference was held in 1884–85. It was there agreed that any European country claiming an African territory must have 'effectively occupied' it before its claim could be recognised and respected. It was at the Berlin conference that the Congo Free State was recognised as a personal possession of Leopold II of Belgium.[16]

Whichever way one looks at it, colonialism was really the political, economic and cultural domination of weaker peoples by stronger and technologically more advanced peoples. Several African leaders resisted this foreign domination: the story of Samori Touré who fought valiantly against the French in West Africa, though defeated, remains one of the most memorable examples of resistance against colonial conquest.[17]

Africans in diaspora

To conclude our survey of Africa's external contacts, some consideration must be given to the Africans in diaspora – Africans beyond the seas. The slave trade has been the major exporter of African culture to North America, the Caribbean and South America in the New World and to Europe and Asia. The pattern and variety of African cultural survivals vary from place to place. The most obvious reminder of the African influence in many lands is the existence of black populations whose historical roots go back to Africa. For example, by the beginning of the nineteenth century, half the populations of Brazil and Venezuela were of African ancestry. African cultural characteristics can also be found in the Caribbean republics and Surinam; but even in the other countries in the Americas, from Canada in the north to Argentina in the south, no country has been without African cultural contact; the difference was one of degree. It is probably not widely known in Africa that the black population of the United States (25·2 millions in mid-1977) makes her the fourth largest 'black power' in the world after Nigeria, Ethiopia and Zaire. These are a key people in a key country.

The contribution of the blacks to the growth and development of the various communities in which they have found themselves can fill volumes of national histories. However, briefly, for our purpose here, it is significant to mention that the founding of the Republic of Haiti (formerly the French sugar-producing colony of Saint Domingue) following the French Revolution of 1789 was the crowning achievement of the courage, determination and leadership of the African slaves, led by nationalists like Toussaint L'Ouverture (1744–1803), a man of Napoleonic qualities. Even though L'Ouverture died in gaol in France ignored and unsung, Haiti declared its independence in 1804. In the United States recent historical writing is giving due recognition to the role of the black Americans from the inception of the republic. A great military tactician of African descent who led the struggle for Cuban freedom from Spain in 1868, Antonio Maceo, is regarded as one of the founding fathers of that island republic. These are only a few examples; there are many other instances of black revolts against the life of bondage. Elsewhere the story of genius, heroism and creativity was recorded by many former African slaves who regained their freedom to contribute their quota to man's march of civilisation.

A significant African cultural survival in Brazil and Cuba that continues to fascinate contemporary African visitors to the New World is found in religious rituals. The Yoruba traditional religion seems, for various reasons, to have retained many adherents in Brazil and Cuba in spite of years of separation from the ancestral home; but what is even more striking is the current phenomenon in the southern United States, in Harlem, in Washington, D.C., and in several other black communities, of people embracing Yoruba religion and culture with a purity of purpose and sincerity of devotion rarely observable among the urban elite in Lagos or Ibadan.

Even in areas, North America in particular, where African religions and cultural observances were unable to develop fully among the slaves, the African soul expressed itself. Those who had become Christians still worshipped their adopted deity with typical African exuberance, dancing and singing and rejoicing as the Psalmist commanded. It was a quiet but enduring victory for the slave to be able in this way to reclaim part of his African heritage without the threat of reprisals from the slave masters. Moreover, contributions by the African slaves in material culture, music, art and dance to the cultures of the Americas are no longer in dispute, and, like their agents, they have become part and parcel of the continent's cultural heritage. Brazilian music, for example, is heavily indebted both in composition and variety to its all-pervading African heritage; American jazz, in inspiration and vitality owes much to its African roots. All this arose inevitably from years of cultural contact and interaction of which the former masters and their erstwhile slaves have become beneficiaries in a cultural dynamism that every day enriches the world.[18]

This brief consideration of the Africans in diaspora is only an indication and certainly not the whole picture. It can even be misleading by its brevity for, as we have noted earlier, African contacts in classical antiquity enriched Rome and Greece, and the black man was neither a passive agent of Islamisation in his own continent nor in the Mediterranean world; he has contributed to the civilisations of the Orient. The sad situation is that his place in mankind's universal history has been for long neglected or misrepresented. Africans are only just beginning to insist that Africa's history is longer than the two major documented phases of external contact in our Odyssey, the periods of the slave trade and of colonial rule. We may conclude with the words of Winwood Reade (1838–75), an Englishman who travelled extensively in and wrote profusely on Africa, who writes:

> He who writes the history of the world must not neglect to observe and describe the black stream of humanity which had poured into America from the Soudan. It has fertilised half a continent with its labour, and set a world on fire with its wrongs; it has influenced the progress of commerce, culture and morality in Europe. . . .[19]

Notes

1   Elspeth Huxley, *The challenge of Africa*, London, Aldus Books, 1971, p. 21. No student should fail to read E. W. Bovill's *The golden trade of the Moors*, 2nd rev. ed. and with admirable additional material by Robin Hallett, Oxford University Press, 1970. Also Robin Hallett, *Africa to 1875: a modern history*, Ann Arbor, University of Michigan Press, 1970, pp. 3, 123–4; and an important article by Robin Law, 'The Garamantes and trans-Saharan

enterprise in classical times', *Journal of African History*, VII, 2 (1967)

2   This point is well underscored in Colin M. Turnbull, *Man in Africa*, Garden City, New York, Anchor Press, 1976, pp. 235–42

3   Eric Williams, *Capitalism and slavery,* New York, Capricorn Books, 1966, pp. 9, 19–20

4   Philip D. Curtin, *The Atlantic slave trade: a census*, Madison, University of Wisconsin Press, 1969; see also J. D. Fage, 'The effect of the export slave trade on African populations', in *The population factor in African studies,* R. P. Moss and R. J. A. R. Rathbone (eds), University of London Press, 1975, pp. 15–23

5   Hallett, *Africa to 1875*, p. 167

6   W. E. B. Du Bois, *The world and Africa,* New York, International Publishers, 1969, p. 54; see figures indicating the Portuguese rapacity in Freda Troup, *South Africa*, Penguin Books, 1975, p. 33.

7   Quoted in *The Horizon history of Africa*, A M Josephy, Jr. (ed.), American Heritage, 1971, p. 318

8   Troup, *South Africa,* p. 33

9   Quoted in Basil Davidson, *A history of West Africa to the nineteenth century,* Garden City, New York, Anchor Books, 1966, pp. 296–7

10   See Robin Law, 'Royal monopoly and private enterprise in the Atlantic trade: the case of Dahomey',*JAH*., XVIII, 4(1977), expecially p. 559, n. 24, for a summary of views on Agaja's motives in attacking Allada (Andra) and Hueda (Ouidah) in 1724.

11   The Africans prefer their own name 'Khoikhoi' to 'Hottentot' which the whites use rather abusively. For the same reason 'S'n' is preferred to 'Bushman'.

12   Troup, *South Africa, passim*

13   Williams, *Capitalism and slavery,* should be read in the light of Anstey, *The Atlantic slave trade and British abolition* and Drescher, *Econocide,* which both provide an authoritative corrective.

14   Williams, *Capitalism and slavery,* pp. 126–34

15   Recent assessments of their impact in Nigeria, for example, include: J. F. A. Ajayi, *Christian missions in Nigeria 1841–1891: the making of a New Elite,* Longman, 1965; and E. A. Ayandele, *The missionary impact on modern Nigeria 1842–1914: a political and social analysis,* Longman, 1966.

16   See S. E. Crowe, *The Berlin West African Conference 1884–1885,* Westport, Connecticut, Negro University Press, 1970

17   Michael Crowder (ed.), *West African resistance: the military response to colonial occupation,* New York, Africana Publishing Co., 1971, for this and other examples

18   The six articles in *Tarikh*, (4), 1978, form an excellent introduction to this fascinating theme.

19   W. Winwood Reade, *The African sketch-book*, London, Smith, Elder, 1873, 2, pp. 511–12

Questions for discussion

1 Account for the beginning of the Atlantic slave trade and show why it lasted so long.

2 What were the consequences of the slave trade on African societies?

3 Assess the nature of the Portuguese contact with Africa and account for its failure.

4 Account for the scramble for Africa.

5 Discuss the motives which led to the political control of your country or a former African colonial country of your choice by an alien power.

6 Discuss any case of African colonial resistance of your choice and assess its significance.

7 Compare the impact of European involvement in West and in East Africa in the nineteenth century.

8 Briefly discuss what policy recommendations you would make to your government to foster co-operation with the Africans in diaspora.

Suggestions for further reading

Ajayi, J. F. Ade, and Espie, Ian (eds). *A thousand years of West African history,* Ibadan University Press, 1965

Anene, Joseph C., and Brown, Godfrey (eds). *Africa in the nineteenth and twentieth centuries,* New York, Humanities Press, 1972

Anstey, R. *The Atlantic slave trade and British abolition, 1760–1810,* London, Macmillan, 1975

Beachey, R. W. *The slave trade of Eastern Africa,* New York, Barnes & Noble, 1976

Bennett, Norman Robert. *Africa and Europe: from Roman times to the present,* New York, Africana Publishing Co., 1975

Curtin, Philip D. *The Atlantic slave trade: a census,* University of Wisconsin Press, 1969

Davidson, Basil. *Africa: history of a continent,* London, Hamlyn, 1972

Drescher, S. *Econocide: British slavery in the era of abolition,* Pittsburgh University Press, 1977

Du Bois, W. E. Burghardt. *The world and Africa,* New York, International Publishers, 1969

Josephy, Alvin M., Jr. (ed.) *The Horizon history of Africa,* New York, American Heritage, 1971

Rodney, Walter. *How Europe underdeveloped Africa,* Dar es Salaam, Tanzania Publishing House, 1972

Williams, Eric. *Capitalism and slavery,* New York, Capricorn Books, 1966

6 Colonial policies and independence movements

Oluwole Omoni

Despite the differences in the policies pursued by the European colonial governments in Africa, their basic goal appeared to be essentially the same: the political domination and economic exploitation of the Africans. This implies that the colonial system in Africa was one of dependence of the exploited African majority on the dominant but few European imperialists, who treated the colonial peoples as social inferiors incapable of governing themselves. However, it was only after the drawing of political boundaries in Africa in the 1880s that colonial policies started to take shape.

British policy

In many of her African colonial territories Britain (at different periods) adopted a system of indirect rule. In their efforts to maintain law and order for effective free trade, the British depended on the traditional institutions, especially the traditional government of the colonised peoples.[1] The officials believed that African traditional systems of government were the most suitable for the Africans, provided that these were rid of features which did not conform with the British sense of justice. This belief formed the core of the respect which the British officers accorded the African chiefs, who were treated as separate yet equal colleagues. It must be noted, however, that this British dependence on traditional political institutions arose less from a theory of the government of dependent territories and people than as a pragmatic and economical solution to the financial, personnel, defence and communication problems which confronted them. Bearing this in mind, the British may, to a small extent only, be regarded as more 'liberal' than the French or any other colonial power in the style of their colonial policy.

It would appear also that the British had the intention of preparing their colonies, especially the large ones (Nigeria and the Gold Coast, for example), for independence at a future date, though this future remained remote. They hoped to do this by imposing their particular brand of parliamentary government on the African peoples. This is why the colonies inherited Houses of Assemblies and Chiefs along the patterns of their British overlords. Although the British may have accepted the self-imposed burden of bearing responsibility for the advancement of their colonies in Africa, they did not assume that Africa would one day become an extension of Britain, or that Africans would one day become 'Britons'.

The relationship between the British officers and the African elite forms another basic feature of British colonial policy. The British officer usually felt uneasy before the educated African, and sometimes expressed contempt for the few educated elements in the colonies. The irony of this situation was that it was Britons who trained these Africans, mostly in their mission schools, and Britons who now disowned them, regarding the supporters of the 'radical' nationalists especially as mere 'verandah boys'.[2]

French policy

The administration of French African colonies was highly centralised. France treated her colonies as a political and economic unit, and simply regarded them as 'Overseas France'. This meant that the territories under the French empire were legally part of France proper even though they were culturally different, and physically separated by water and distance. The French officially had the basic aim of assimilating the inhabitants of their colonies into French culture and civilisation – a civilisation which they assumed to be the best in the world. This policy, in which, however, they in large measure failed, was informed by egalitarian ideas which had been gaining ground ever since the French Revolution. As a result, the French started out with the intention of creating a system that would transform Africans into French citizens in order to enjoy the same rights and privileges as those actually born in France proper.

The French assimilation policy never took account of the diversities of the African peoples. This is not surprising because the colonial administration was intended to make French citizens of Africans. Compared, therefore, with the British policy, it is clear that France had no aim of granting independence to her colonies. She believed in retaining the colonies as an annexe to the homeland or metropolis, allowing them to send their political representatives to the French National Assembly in Paris.

To pursue the policy of assimilation, educational opportunities in the colonies were designed for advancement within the French system. These opportunities, however, remained limited. This implies that the French failed to provide adequately for the means through which the African was supposed to be assimilated into French society and culture. Only those colonial subjects who fulfilled all the requirements stipulated by the French authorities would be accepted as French citizens. Such requirements included: the passing of a test in the French language; becoming a Christian; and assimilating French customs and traditions. This dual policy divided the colonial peoples into two categories: the assimilated French citizens who enjoyed all the rights and privileges of French citizenship, and the colonial subjects to whom the 'Indigénat' applied. The 'Indigénat'[3] was a system introduced in the 1880s, whereby any commandant in the colonies could summarily punish the Africans for certain specific offences without trial. No appeal was allowed under this sytem.

In the event, while many Africans appeared, in spite of their French citizenship, to prefer their traditional customs, the French themselves soon realised the folly in following assimilation policy rigidly. They saw that the French empire in Africa was expanding rapidly, and that soon the colonial population would be greater than that of France herself, thus creating a situation whereby the colonial peoples could become masters over their French overlords. Moreover the practical difficulties of assimilation on a large scale were such that in most places (Senegal being the most prominent exception), the policy had to be abandoned in favour of one of 'association', or paternalism, whereby local chiefs were used as agents of the colonial administration.

Belgian policy

The Belgian colonial administration was direct and absolute. Leopold II, King of the Belgians, administered most regions of the Congo Free State as his private property from 1885 onwards. Because he believed that colonies should directly benefit the metropolis, he tried to extract maximum profit from the Congo (now Zaire) through his officials. There was compulsory cultivation by the Africans, and public work became common. Flogging, mutilation and even killing of Africans were common occurrences under this administration. Indeed, the desire for profits and positions by colonial officials themselves led to the dehumanising and exploitation of the Africans.[4]

The brutal means by which exploitation was pursued aroused international sympathy for the Congolese. Leopold II was therefore forced in 1908 to transfer his personal rule over the Congo to the Belgian Government. The transfer brought about some reforms which only tempered the sufferings of the Congolese.

The Belgian policy after 1908 was often described as 'sternly paternalistic' with control over the colony the paramount objective. The Africans were to be treated as children who required the fatherly direction of the imperial country. The primary objective of the Belgians was economic development, hence the colony was controlled by a coalition of the state, church and business cartels. Direct control over the colony was exercised by the Belgian administrators, who were responsible to the Belgian Government in Brussels. The Governor-General represented the King in the colonies. The Congolese had no say in the administration of their territory, for all edicts and laws were made from the Belgian capital. Roman Catholics occupied most of the senior government posts, through which they exercised great influence. The Catholic church was given control of education, thereby establishing an alliance between church and state. By 1952, it was reported that five holding companies controlled nearly 70 per cent of all business in the Congo. The state held a strong interest in these five and other companies in the Congo. The result then was of double advantage to the Belgian administration at the expense of the Congolese: the state collected taxes as well as dividends from the companies.

Amenities, though below those of the Europeans, were provided for

African families. The aim was to justify separate facilities for blacks and whites on cultural rather than racial grounds. Food, medical care and clothing were provided in order to maintain satisfied and healthy labourers. The small amount of education provided for the Congolese was geared only towards the training of senior administrative and management personnel. Indeed, the Belgians recognised the labour-supply problems that confronted them, and they were ready to solve these through any means. For instance, the Congolese in the countryside were often forced to marry very young, in order to expand the population and thereby solve the labour-supply problem. There is no doubt, then, that the Africans were given some opportunities, although not on an equal basis with the whites. There was physical segregation in the cities, with the white sections heavily favoured in all respects; the Congolese had to carry a permit while travelling; he could not possess firearms and was allowed to drink nothing stronger than beer. The Congolese was given a limited education; he could become a technician but not an engineer, a medical assistant but not a medical officer. He could not become a lawyer since the Belgians regarded law as politics, and politics as an exclusive area for the whites. Furthermore, it was very difficult for a Congolese to secure admission to a Belgian university.[5]

From the above, it is clear that the Belgians pursued a policy of isolationism in the Congo. White settlement was discouraged in order to prevent land alienation by the whites, though this policy became a means through which contacts between Africans and other nationals were minimised. The Belgians did not want the Congolese to see how other nationals, especially the Europeans, lived. The major intention of the policy, then, was to breed contented Africans, and thereby avoid the rise of political activists who would agitate against black inequality.

German policy

The Germans established a highly centralised administration in their colonies. The colonial officials who supervised this administration were responsible through the chancellor to the emperor. In the areas most suited to agriculture, the African indigenes were excluded in order to make room for the European settlers to acquire more fertile land. This created problems and hardship for the colonial peoples, who were deprived of pasture for their cattle and land for their own existence. In this situation, the Africans had no choice but to submit as labourers on European farms and establishments until such time as they could organise themselves to challenge the European encroachment.

All along, the Africans, especially those in German East Africa, Togoland and the Cameroons, were subjected to forced labour for road construction and other public works; traditional laws were subordinated to the German codes; and the African women were often indecently treated or assaulted by the German officials without any check.[6] Like the other colonial policies, it can be observed that the German colonial policy, as drafted in Berlin, sometimes went through several changes before being applied in the territories for which they were intended.

There was always a major personality involved in their implementation, and he might decide to make such amendements as he considered necessary for practical application, although within the general spirit of the German colonial policies.

Portuguese policy

The Portuguese colonial policy, like the Belgian, can be regarded as paternalistic. The declared objectives had always been to 'christianise, colonise and civilise'.[7] though the means through which the Portuguese intended to pursue these were arbitrary. Their rule was strict and harsh. The Africans in Angola, Mozambique and Portuguese Guinea (now Guinea-Bissau) were deprived of political rights; many were forced to work on sugar and cocoa plantations without pay; and the economic resources of the colonies were tapped to replenish the impoverished treasury of Portugal.

Like the French, the Portuguese came to regard their colonies as 'Overseas Portugal' and followed an assimilationist policy. They had no plan to grant self-government to their colonies since there was 'only one state, one territory, one population, one citizenship, and one government'.[8] The colonies were overseas provinces, merely separated geographically from Portugal itself. The Portuguese accepted two categories of Africans: the assimilated and the unassimilated. The former could hope to enjoy all the rights and privileges of Portuguese citizenship if they could speak Portuguese fluently, were Christians, had good character, paid taxes, remained loyal to the Portuguese-controlled administration, and had sufficient resources to support a family. But only few Africans could aspire to this standard. Consquently, the majority of the Africans remained unassimilated and were treated as children, frequently disciplined even with the whip.

Because Portugal herself lacked many necessities of a modern diversified economy, she pursued a policy of economic exploitation in her colonies. They were to provide raw materials for the factories of the metropolitan provinces, and the finished products of the factories were to be shipped back to the colonial people for consumption. Often the producers of the raw materials were required to sell their goods at prices far below, and to purchase the manufactured products of the Portuguese factories at prices far above, those to be obtained on the open world market.

Factors contributing to the rise of nationalist movements in Africa
(1) Widespread discontent among the people

In spite of the economic benefits which some Africans might have derived from colonial rule, ultimately these failed to satisfy the needs and aspirations of the majority. Even where Africans were allowed to keep their land and improve their standard of living by providing raw materials for European consumption, they were angered by the low prices paid them by the foreign firms. In other places, their lands were confiscated by their European masters, and many Africans were driven into the small, infertile and sometimes unhealthy reserves, as in Kenya and most other territories in East Africa. The Africans watched helplessly the exploitation of their natural resources by the alien imperialists; they felt the weight of unemployment, slave labour and heavy taxation – all of which featured prominently in South Africa. As a result of their experience under colonial rule, Africans came to believe that the early white missionaries in their midst taught them only how to say the 'Lord's Prayer' with the Bible firmly held to their chests, while their other white brothers robbed them of their wealth.

All the above factors combined with others to make the Africans dissatisfied. This widespread discontent was demonstrated in various ways. Africans began to realise the strength that they could draw from their ancestral history, and wanted to build a new and free future on the foundation of their pre-colonial past. Their desire was to remove the myth of white superiority and assert the natural equality of mankind, especially in respect of relations between the white and black races. This desire was expressed in the scholarly activities and achievements of men like E. W. Blyden, a West Indian of African descent who argued against the European belief that Africans had achieved nothing in the past until the arrival of the Europeans.[9] A spectacular demonstration of discontent by the rural population was the organised Cocoa Hold-up of 1937, mainly in the Gold Coast (Ghana), during which the cocoa farmers refused to sell their cocoa to the Europeans until the prices were increased.

Fig. 6.1 *Edward Wilmot Blyden*

The tendency to resist was shown not only in the economic but also in religious arenas. Many churches broke away from the missionary organisations. Although some still adhered to the orthodox doctrines of Christianity, they accepted only Africans as their leaders. The independent African church movements could not reconcile the Christian doctrine of brotherhood and equality with the discriminatory attitudes of the Europeans, many of whom were clergymen. The prophetic movements,[10] which also emerged as resistance groups, paid less respect to orthodoxy in their doctrines. They looked upon only African prophets as their leaders, and on African ideals as their yardstick.

(2) The Second World War and its effects

The Second World War and its aftermath contributed greatly to the emergent nationalist upsurge in Africa. The war acted as a catalyst, producing two processes: the emergence of a new radical leadership, and the creation of a large group of supporters for the new African leadership.

The Allied defeats in the early stages of the war at the hands of Germany and Japan and the German occupation of France indicated clearly that the colonial powers were not as formidable as was previously believed in Africa. The Africans appreciated now, more than ever, how much the Europeans depended on African troops and material aid. For instance, Nigeria contributed immensely to the ultimate victory of Britain and the Allied Forces during the Second World War (as they had done too in the First). Nigerians served in the armed forces, others toiled in the construction of airfields and roads for wartime communications and the production of vital raw materials. Although a relatively poor people, they also contributed money towards the war effort.

Furthermore, Africans, during the war, learned new technical skills, gained a wider perspective of world affairs, and met and exchanged ideas with Asians then engaged in the struggle to remove the European yoke. With this experience, the basis of European justification for continued domination of Africa was further undermined.

Allied propaganda during the war centred on the claim that they were fighting for freedom and the right of mankind to have a government of their choice. This was contained in the Atlantic Charter of 1944. After the war, the Africans became aware that the principle of self-determination as contained in the Charter was not meant to apply to Africa. Their political consciousness and nationalist sentiment were thus aroused and they started to think how best they could gain their freedom. The United Nations Organisation with its anti-colonialist, anti-imperialist and anti-racist policies also helped to keep the desire for self-government constantly in the minds of the Africans.

The war brought great hardship for the common people in Africa as a result of the new social and economic situations which it introduced. Essential consumer goods were scarce, and the countryside was depopulated; moreover there were problems of urbanisation, inflation and trade depression.

The African soldiers had fought side by side with their white comrades. They ate together, slept together in the bush; died the same way;

they received the same treatment and became accustomed to receiving regular food, medical attention, money and issues of clothing. In Europe some of the African soldiers experienced better social treatment than when in Africa. This all helped to remove the impression of white remoteness. Furthermore, the majority of the men who served and died during the war were colonial subjects, not citizens. Those who survived became much more disgruntled because their condition did not improve. They were still subjected to the humiliation of the colonial policies, which often meant trial without jury, sentence without trial, forced labour and heavy taxation. Little wonder that many ex-servicemen supported militant and radical groups in the struggle for independence after the war.

(3) The rise of nationalist associations

Before the Second World War, a number of significant organisations, which can be described as precursors of the nationalist movements, sprang up, especially in West Africa. Here we will examine those that emerged in British West African territories, where their activities were probably best organised.

(a) The Aborigines' Rights Protection Society (ARPS)

The ARPS was formed in 1897 at Cape Coast to protest against the Land Bill of that same year. In 1898, it sent a delegation of three prosperous merchants to London to protest against the bill on behalf of the natural rulers. The delegation met the British Prime Minister, Chamberlain, who finally decided to withdraw the bill. A jubilant ARPS therefore decided to form itself into a permanent organisation to protect the rights of the rulers and peoples of the Gold Coast.

(b) The West African Students Union (WASU)

It may be said that modern militant nationalism in West Africa was initiated by student organisations. One such organisation was the WASU, formed in Britain by a Nigerian, Ladipo Solanke, in the 1920s. The Union was endowed with a hostel in 1928 by Marcus Garvey, and it published a journal. This journal afforded great opportunities to nationalist writers. The WASU served until the 1940s as an important pressure group in the agitation against colonial rule, and as the training ground in militant nationalist politics for African youths studying in Britain. Its members became the more militant as a result of their experience and contacts overseas.

(c) The National Congress of British West Africa (NCBWA)

The NCBWA was formed in 1919 as a result of a meeting called in Accra by J. E. Casely-Hayford (a Gold Coast lawyer) in co-operation with Nana Ofori Atta and R. A. Savage. The first Congress, held in 1920, attracted delegates from many parts of West Africa. The Congress envisaged a larger and united nationalist forum for all the British West African territories. It demanded the introduction of universal adult suffrage; equal employment and promotion opportunities for both Europeans and Africans in the civil service; higher educational opportunities, especially the establishment of a West African University and a compulsory free education system; and finally, a clearer separation of the judiciary from the colonial administration.

A delegation of members of this Congress visited London to press their demands. Though it achieved little because of the negative attitude of the governors of the West African colonies to the Congress requests, nonetheless the Congress continued to meet, and it was perhaps partly as a result of its pressure that Britain accepted a limited franchise for the principal towns of West Africa and established Achimota College in 1920.

Ultimately, however, the Congress, like other political organisations before it, became conservative and started to compromise with the colonial administration. In 1930, when Casely-Hayford died, the Congress virtually passed away with him. The members quarrelled among themselves over leadership and offices. The British administrators also helped to liquidate the Congress by fanning the rivalry which existed between the traditional elite – the chiefs – and the new elite, the wealthy, merchants and educated elements.

It should be mentioned, however, that the main fault of the Congress was that it depended so much on the few educated elements to the total neglect of the illiterate masses, whose support was necessasry for its success and survival.

Fig. 6.2   *The deputation of the National Congress of British West Africa to London in 1920*

(d) The youth organisations

The emergence of youth organisations was a reaction to the conservatism of the older associations and politicians. The youth organisations wanted to involve many more people in their activities than had the older associations.

The Union of Young Nigerians was inaugurated under the leadership of Dr J. C. Vaughan, Ayo Williams and Ernest Ikoli for the purpose of informing the youth about conditions in their country. In 1932, Eyo Ita organised the Nigerian Youth League at Calabar. Its main objective was to forward educational reforms. Consequently, the West African People's Institute was established to prepare young men for self-supporting employment instead of dependence on foreign establishments for employment. In 1935, the Lagos Youth Movement was formed by Ernest Ikoli, Dr J. C. Vaughan, Samuel Akinsanya (now the Odemo of Ishara) and Chief H. O. Davies. This organisation agitated for higher education generally and protested against the alleged inferior status of the Yaba Higher College which it wanted to see raised to the status of a university. The name of the movement was changed in 1936 to the Nigerian Youth Movement. Throughout the inter-war period, the NYM tried to unite Nigerians, through ethnic co-operation, to educate the public in political consciousness, and to achieve complete autonomy for Nigeria. It called upon the colonial government to revise the Nigerian constitution and also agitated for social and economic reforms. The introduction of tribalism into Nigerian politics, however, brought about the collapse of this movement.

In 1938, the Gold Coast Youth Conference was initiated by Dr J. B. Danquah but, unlike the Nigerian Youth Movement, it was never organised as a political party. Its main objective was to create a forum through which the youths of the Gold Coast could meet and discuss national problems. In the same year, I. T. A. Wallace-Johnson formed the West African Youth League, otherwise called the Sierra Leone Youth League. This became the first effective political movement to enjoy wide public support. Its membership was made open to all sections of the community, so that it attracted supporters not only from the Colony area but also from other parts of Sierra Leone. It organised mass meetings, strike actions and trade unions, and in 1939 established *The African Standard* as its official newspaper. Gradually, the League was turned into a political party which sponsored candidates for elections. It is, however, interesting to note that in spite of its mass support and political successes, the League remained conservative. It concentrated on demands for constitutional rights of the people rather than complete independence from colonial domination

(4) The rise of political parties

Ultimately, between the world wars, a large number of political parties emerged in Africa. They included the Nigerian National Democratic Party (NNDP) founded by Herbert Macaulay in 1923, the Moroccan League (1926), the New Destour Party in Tunisia reorganised by Bourguiba in 1934, the Algerian Popular Party founded in 1937 by

Fig. 6.3 *I.T.A. Wallace-Johnson, founder of the British West African Youth League*

Messali after breaking away from the French Communist Party, and the National Council of Nigeria and the Cameroons, later called the National Council for Nigerian Citizens (NCNC)founded in 1944. Other important ones were the Action Group (AG) 1951, led by Chief Obafemi Awolowo, the Northern People's Congress (NPC) 1949, both in Nigeria, the United Gold Coast Convention (UGCC) 1947, led by Dr Danquah, and the Convention People's Party (CPP) in the Gold Coast organised in 1949 by the late Dr Kwame Nkrumah. In Sierra Leone, there was the Sierra Leone People's Party (SLPP) 1951; and in the Gambia the Progressive People's Party (PPP) founded in 1962. The Rassemblement Démocratique Africain (RDA), formed in 1946 primarily on the initiative of Felix Houphouet-Boigny of the Ivory Coast, eventually became the dominant political party of French West Africa. In East Africa, Jomo Kenyatta founded the Kenya African National Union; in Uganda there were the Uganda Nationalist Congress (1952) and Milton Obote's Uganda People's Congress; the Tanganyika African National Union was formed in 1954 under the leadership of Julius Nyerere. All these political parties developed as a result of the nationalist feelings and agitation which were widespread at the time. The willingness of the British and French colonial powers to concede some measure of self-government was also a contributory factor in the development of parties. The failure of such parties to emerge in the Portuguese territories at that time might lend some weight to the point made above.

Fig. 6.4 *Four of the nationalist leaders of Africa: Jomo Kenyatta, Kenya (above left); Julius Nyerere, Tanzania (above right); Kwame Nkrumah, Ghana (below left); Nnamdi Azikiwe, Nigeria (below right)*

(5) The roles of the African elite

The traditional elite of Africa were the rulers and the chiefs. Their attitude to European domination depended on the political situation in the different areas. There were great rivalries among the rulers, and these, rather than patriotism, dictated their attitude to European presence. By and large, many of the traditional rulers found themselves leading the resistance against the early European penetration and rule. Because many of them were stripped of most, or at times all, of their political powers and land, these allied with a new elite that was then emerging. This was the nationalist or educated elite. For instance, in West Africa, the Aborigines' Rights Protection Society, which protested against the Land Bill of 1897, was supported by chiefs and religious leaders; the National Congress of British West Africa was formed in 1919 in consultation with a traditional ruler of the Gold Coast (Ghana), Nana Ofori Atta; while in 1915 when Lord Lugard asked the Eleko of Lagos to persuade his people to pay the unpopular water rate, the Eleko refused after being advised by the new elite. Herbert Macaulay, a member of the new nationalist elite group, championed the cause of the chiefs and people of Lagos against the Lagos High Court ruling that the 1861 cession of Lagos to the British implied that all lands which were by then not privately owned should be Crown land. A test case was brought by Chief Oluwa, the Eleko, under the guidance of Herbert Macaulay. The Privy Council in London which heard this case ruled in favour of Chief Oluwa.

The co-operation between the traditional and nationalist elite mentioned above did not wholly remove the rivalry which existed between the two groups. The traditional elite wanted to retain a measure of authority in the political structure, and this they tried to achieve by compromising with the colonial regime after being defeated. In fact, the traditional elite were, in most cases, the first people to be mobilised initially as agents of colonial administration, and until a new elite emerged, there was little effort made to press for political independence. Because of the hard lesson they learned during the period of the so-called pacification, especially in the French African territories, they became sceptical about the radical attitudes of the new elite. The latter began to see the rulers as accomplices of the colonial regime, hence they (the rulers) as well as the Europeans became targets for anti-colonial campaigns.

In Africa, those who nursed the concept of a nation were products of the mission and government schools. Generally, many of them had received a relatively good Western education, some of them were part of the growing money economy, and a few were alert to developments on the national and international scene. It was this group which came to formulate the desire for the creation of African nation-states. The colonial administration, meantime, continually frustrated their aspirations. They lost many job opportunities, they were deprived from taking up senior civil service posts, they were paid lower wages than Europeans of equal or similar qualifications and experiences. The new elite therefore felt the need for political action, and it can be said that the economic disabilities and political insecurity of this new educated group were responsible for political activities in most of the African territories.

(6) The role of the press

The writings of educated men of African descent contributed greatly to the independence movements as their inspiration. Many of these writers began to deepen their knowledge of the traditions of their people in an effort to discover their cultural heritage. In 1903, Casely-Hayford published his *Gold Coast Native Institutions* and in 1911, *Ethiopia Unbound;* while John Payne Jackson, a Liberian settled in Lagos, edited the *Lagos Weekly Record* from 1891 to 1918. Also in Nigeria the following newspapers were started: *Nigerian Pioneer,* 1914; *Lagos Standard,* 1903; *Nigerian Chronicle,* 1908; and *Nigerian Times,* 1914.

The press helped to keep the elite in Africa in contact and united, though it was never profitable economically. The newspapers and journals especially were intended to educate the African masses and to influence public opinion, but only a few could read them. More seriously, only a few could afford even to buy them. Thus the practice of passing the same copy of a newspaper from hand to hand grew up, and few copies were actually sold.

A few of the newspapers that survived made a great impact on the political scene in Africa. In most of the territories, especially in British West Africa, the press was one of the most important elements in the birth and development of African nationalism. It was the watchdog of the colonial administration, exposing, as far as permissible, European oppression, domination and maladministration. It constantly reminded the British colonial rulers of their declared intention to grant independence to the Africans, and also kept Africans informed about events in other parts of the world. It is for these and other reasons that the Europeans tried to put obstacles in the way of the press. For instance, the *Gold Coast Independent,* which gave wide publicity to the grievances of the Ewe who were divided under French and British control, was banned in Togo by the French authorities. Again, the Convention People's Party's newspaper, the *Accra Evening News,* was banned by the British administration because of its radical views.

Paths to independence in Africa
British West Africa

Generally speaking, before the 1940s politics in British West Africa were dominated by the leaders who sponsored the conference of the National Congress of British West Africa held in 1920. These leaders were interested mainly in gaining an opportunity for increased participation in the government. They sought to achieve this through constitutional, non-violent means. Furthermore, they wanted the colonial government to transfer power to them, rather than to the traditional rulers, when independence was to be granted in th future. Lack of any consensus as to specific forms which demands for independence should take revived unhealthy competition and rivalries among the various groups, and from the 1940s onwards the nationalist leaders in British and French West Africa began to take different paths to independence.

In the Gold Coast, a new constitution was granted in 1925, which provoked strong opposition. It retained the three members of the 'educated' group, while it doubled the number of chiefs who sat in the new council. This issue continued for long to drive a wedge between the educated and traditional elite. The situation continued until 1947 when the United Gold Coast Convention, led by Dr Danquah, appointed Dr Kwame Nkrumah as secretary. Nkrumah's group appeared to favour radical and violent methods in the struggle towards independence, whereas Danquah's group wanted to pursue the same desire through moderate and constitutional methods. After a series of protests and boycotts, Nkrumah left the United Gold Coast Convention, and in 1949 founded the Convention People's Party (CPP). This party made a greater appeal to the masses for in spite of (or, perhaps, because of) Nkrumah's imprisonment as a result of a violent general strike and boycott organised by the CPP in 1950, the party still won the 1951 general election with an overwhelming majority. Nkrumah was invited from prison to become the Prime Minister. From this time onwards, power gradually passed into the hands of the African nationalist leaders of the CPP. The party was able to beat off all opposition including the challenge presented by the National Liberation Movement between 1954 and 1957. New constitutional changes were made in 1954, and the CPP's claim to be the successor of the British colonial rulers becme indisputable. Power was tansferred to it when the Gold Coast was granted independence as Ghana in March 1957.

Nigeria's strategy in the struggle for independence was not as radical as that in neighbouring Ghana. Its independence movement was spear-headed by the NCNC founded in 1944 and led by Dr Nnamdi Azikiwe. Although a group of young radicals – the 'Zikists' – attained temporary prominence in the late 1940s, the main leadership of this party adopted moderate methods to press its demands for self-government on the colonial administration. Other political parties later emerged, within the regional framework of the federal constitution; it was perhaps natural as well as unfortunate that these parties should have been largely based on ethnic support. The period between 1951 and 1958, when political activities were intensified, became one of adjustment and readjustment of ethnic interests among the three major political parties now based on the regions, the NCNC and the Action Group (AG) in the two southern regions, and the Northern People's Congress (NPC) in the north.

The necessity for readjustment became apparent when the ethnic minorities in each area began to assert their interests. So serious were these vocal minority groups that the issue formed an important, though unresolved, item for discussion during one of the constitutional conferences held on the future of Nigeria's administration. The strains and disunity which these rivalries produced brought about the compromise of 1954 reached through a new federal constitution.

This disunity had caused the Colonial Office to delay independence for Nigeria. Furthermore, the division created a situation where the south and north almost parted ways. The south attained a large measure of self-government in 1957, but the north was not considered to be ready for this until 1959. Hence, when independence was granted to Nigeria on 1 October 1960, it was to a precariously balanced coalition of disparate interests. Traces of this experience during the period of the struggle for independence were evident in the factors which led to military intervention in Nigeria's politics.

In Sierra Leone, the main rivalry was between the Colony – largely composed of Creoles – and the Protectorate, and this delayed constitutional changes in the period from 1945 to 1951.[11] However, the fact that many more people lived in the Protectorate than in the Colony meant that any party which gained and which effectively retained the support of the Protectorate would lead the country to independence, and would take over political control from the British. This party was to be the Sierra Leone People's Party which, emerging as the over-all winner in the election of 1951 and weathering the storms of economic crisis, strike actions, anti-chief riots, and a split in its own ranks between 1955 and 1958, was able to consolidate its position from then until independence was attained in April 1961.

In the Gambia, it was, again, the two world wars – particularly the second – which helped to speed up the attainment of independence. The agitation which followed the end of the Second World War led to the setting up of a Consultative Committee in 1953. In 1954, both the Executive and Legislative Councils established in the Gambia were made more fully representative of the people. The members were freely elected. Not until 1960, though, was a political party established, the People's Progressive Party led by Dawda Jawara. After the general election of May 1960, a coalition government was formed between Jawara's People's Progressive Party and the United Party of Pierre N'jie. Another election was held in May 1962; the People's Progressive Party won the majority of seats, and Jawara became the first premier of the Gambia. Full internal self-government followed in October 1963, and in February 1965, Gambia, the last of the British possessions in West Africa, was granted independence.

French West Africa

In French West Africa, it is difficult to identify independence movements until the very end of the colonial period. The assimilation and later association policies of the French in West Africa virtually removed any idea of self-government for the colonies. Kenneth Robinson has described the policies of assimilation and association as policies of identity and paternalism respectively. The policy of identity sought to establish in the colonies institutions identical with those in France, while the policy of paternalism sought to establish a special regime under French control for the mass of Africans who were regarded as subjects not citizens. In effect, therefore, what was emphasised by the French policies was equal treatment and opportunities for all the colonial peoples as French citizens, as well as the working out of the best form of association between French West Africa and France. Thus, the Rassemblement Démocratique Africain (RDA) (see page 91 above) envisaged close links with France instead of complete autonomy. However, by 1950 Houphouet-Boigny realised that the alliance with France had not even given his party a respectable position among the French colonial officials. Thereafter, he sought to establish a new form of association that would be acceptable to the French Communist Party as well as to his RDA.

The original motive for founding the RDA was the provision of a single political party for the whole of French West and Equatorial Africa. By the 1950s, however, the various territorial sections within this combination or group started to follow different paths. This tendency was especially pronounced after the 'Outline Law' (*Loi Cadre*) reforms of 1956 and 1957. The new law provided for the setting up of governments with limited powers in each territory. These were to be managed by the Africans themselves. This reversed the former French practice of treating the whole of French West Africa as a single unit.

The unity of the RDA was broken up as a result of differences of opinion and rivalries. Houphouet-Boigny advocated close links between each territory and France, while Sékou Touré of Guinea, much more radical in his approach to politics, favoured collective bargaining between all the French West African countries and France. Sékou Touré believed that by such bargaining the countries would win more concessions and privileges. Events in France also contributed to making any compromise more difficult to come by. In May 1958, General de Gaulle came to power. He favoured the creation of a new association – the Franco-African Community. De Gaulle gave the African peoples in the French colonies the chance to accept or reject the new union in the referendum of September 1958. All the other French West African countries except Guinea chose to join the community. Sékou Touré and his Guinea section of the RDA rejected the Community, and Guinea thus became fully independent on 1 October 1958.

The years immediately following Guinea's indepedence were very trying. The French administration, in retaliation, withdrew all technical, financial and administrative assistance to Guinea. The situation compelled Guinea to depend on a loan of 20 million naira (Nigerian) given her by Ghana under Kwame Nkrumah. Yet in spite of Guinea's bitter experience, her choice of independence dealt a blow to the attempt of France to preserve a union between herself and her African allies. The example became contagious, and by the late 1960s all the former French colonies had demanded and attained independence, making the Community a dead letter.

North Africa

From the nineteenth century onwards Egypt assumed the lead in the struggle for freedom in North Africa. Her geographical location and the Suez Canal made her a cross-road to the trade of the East, and this attracted early concentration of European interests in Egypt. Egypt thus became the first of the North African territories to be exposed to Western technological skills. Furthermore, her rapid economic development as the gateway to other parts of Africa and the modernisation process set in motion by her earlier rulers, especially Mohammed Ali (1804–49), contributed immensely to her leading position. The Pan-Islamic movements of Jamal al-Din al-Afghani and Mohammed Abdu strengthened Egyptian nationalis as well as affecting the attitude of all the Muslim states of North Africa. Initially, indeed, the nationalist movements in North Africa appeared to be based on religious patterns. For instance, until 1914, the Tunisian nationalist movement was almost entirely religious, while the Society of the Reforming Ulema, founded in Algeria by 1931, became an arm of the nationalist movement there.

The Egyptian nationalist movement passed through several stages before independence was won. In 1881, Colonel Ahmad Arabi led a revolt against the Turkish and European domination in Egypt. To suppress this revolt and establish a peaceful atmosphere for free trade, the French and British decided to co-operate in putting down the revolt, but in the event only Britain carried this out. By 1882 when the rebellion was crushed, the British refused to withdraw. The British occupations as well as their prolonged stay in Egypt fuelled nationalist sentiments. Men such as Mustapha Kamil, Mohammed Farid and Said Zaghlul, were turned into hostile nationalists as a result of the new policies introduced by the British. The British imposed the official use of the English language throughout Egypt; they monopolised the higher civil service posts, excluded the Egyptians from the operations of the Suez Canal Company, and declared a protectorate over Egypt. After putting down Mahdist rule in the Sudan in 1898, an Anglo-Egyptian condominium was imposed there, of which Britain was effectively in control. After the First World War of 1914–18, in which the Egyptians gave considerable aid to the British, there was a violent reaction. This was followed by the granting of qualified independence to Egypt in 1922.

Nationalist movements in North Africa followed similar patterns. In Tunisia, nationalist activities centred on a radical lawyer, Habib Bourguiba, who reorganised the Destour Party in 1934. He believed in political pragmatism and, appreciating the weakness of Tunisia, pursued a policy of modernisation. His foreign policy was one of friendship towards all. In 1955, he negotiated a form of independence for Tunisia, which became a sovereign state the following year.

In Algeria and Morocco, the nationalist movements were spear-headed by members of the educated class known as 'Effendiya'. In Algeria the educated elite that led the nationalist movement broke into two groups: the Extremist and the Tolerant factions. Al-Hajj Messali led the Extremist group, which demanded independence or nothing. In 1937, Messali broke with the French Communist Party and founded the Algerian Popular Party. This party was banned by the French in 1939, and in 1941 Al-Hajj Messali himself was given a sixteen-year gaol term. The Tolerant group was led by Ferhat Abbas. This group consisted of people who were Frenchified and who believed in the benefits of continued French rule provided that the Muslims were given equal rights as French citizens. However, this hope was shattered in 1938 when the European settlers succeeded in preventing the adoption of the bill that was to grant French citizenship to a select group of Algerian Muslims.[12] As these educated elements were rejected socially and politically by the settlers, they were driven into reasserting their Muslim identity in spite of their being Frenchified. In 1943, Messali again issued a manifesto demanding universal suffrage, a representative assembly and fundamental human rights. These demands led General de Gaulle to make a number of concessions in an ordinance of March 1944. The concessions united the nationalists for a while until an insurrection of 1945, which was ruthlessly repressed by the French, again divided them into two new groups: the Democratic Union of the Algerian Manifesto and the

Movement for the Triumph of Democratic Liberties. To break up the more hostile of these two groups, the French resorted to hand-picking representatives into the assembly. Those hand-picked became the 'yes men' of the French.

A critical look at the history of Algeria before independence was granted in 1962 throws some light on the eruption of violence there. The French brought together various divergent groups under a central political authority; the settlers treated all the indigenous people as different from and inferior to themselves. Apart from group rivalries, there wee also religious ones among the brotherhoods. Added to those problems was the effort of the white settlers in blocking many laws that would have improved the conditions of ordinary men. Furthermore, the Algerians saw that the taxes which they paid were used to provide amenities which favoured the white settlers. In Algeria, as in other states of the Maghrib, the French, from the 1850s onwards, embarked on a policy of cantonment for acquisition of land collectively owned by the indigenous groups. The Land Department restricted Algerians to a given section and distributed the remaining pieces of land to the white settlers. The implications of the land policy were that the land reserved for the Algerians was insufficient for their use; many were thereby forced to move into the urban areas in search of work, while many who could not secure jobs in the cities resorted to work on the settlers' farms. As a result, there was a violent reaction.

Although the Moroccan League and the Istigal Party, founded in 1928 and 1943 respectively, became avenues for the nationalist activities of the educated elite, the Sultan of Morocco, Sidi Mohammed V, who represented the traditional elite, openly identified himself with the nationalists' aspirations and demands. The Sultan made statements supporting the. nationalists, a move which greatly embarrassed the French authorities. He refused to sign any decrees considered offensive to the nationalists' cause and aspirations, and he joined in the demand for Morocco's complete independence. In 1953, the French deposed the Sultan, an action which forced the nationalist leaders to intensify their violent agitations against French rule.

From what has been discussed above, it is clear that independence movements in North Africa, generally speaking, followed violent paths. In Egypt the nationalist movement operated under great difficulties but nevertheless was able to do so openly. The French attitude to the nationalists in their North African colonies was in sharp contrast. Under the policy of assimilation or association, nationalist activities aimed at independence were regarded as illegitimate. Consequently, the French authorities employed various methods including exile, repression, imprisonment and press censorship, to discourage and suppress nationalist agitations. This policy soon turned independence movements in North Africa into an explosive force spreading quickly to other French colonies and resulting in a confrontation between a determined people and a reactionary colonial power. In Tunisia, Morocco and Algeria, violence became a main characteristic of the nationalist movements. A lesson from the situation in these colonies is that freedom has to be bought at a price, often in Bismarckian terms of 'blood and iron'.

East Africa

An important factor in the rise of the nationalist movement in Kenya was the racial conflct between the Africans, Asians and Europeans. In this, the numerically dominant group, the Africans, were at the bottom of the political and economic ladder in their own country. This was the begining of the Kenyans' frustration. Furthermore, in 1901, the British legalised the alienation of land in Kenya, whereby the most fertile areas were reserved for the European settlers. This land policy involved driving out the indigenous population from their homelands.[13] Apart from the emotional upheaval caused by such a land policy, economic frustration and social instability became widespread among the Kenyans. They were forced to take up wage-employment on European plantations and in other European establishments in order to be able to pay their taxes and indeed for their very survival. Every male over sixteen years of age in Kenya was expected to carry a registration certificate for identification; Kenyans were also discriminated against in the educational policies of the British authorities. Moreover, they were not able to compete on equal terms with the Asians in junior, technical and other economic positions.

The struggle for independence in Kenya falls into three phases. During the period before the Second World War, the first phase, the struggle was between the British settlers and the British Colonial Office. The Colonial Office supported the rights of the Africans on their own land, and this the British settlers considered as a threat to their own privileges and dominance. The settlers had already taken the best of the Africans' farm-land, and as a result of the temperate climate of the highlands of Kenya, they aimed to make Kenya, and indeed other parts of East Africa, their permanent home.

After the Second World War the struggle shifted from one between the British settlers and the Colonial Office to one between the Kikuyu, a major African group, and the white settlers. The impact of the two world wars increased the political consciousness of the Africans generally, and then, shortly after the wars, they began to challenge the claims to supremacy of the whites. In Kenya, the start of the struggle was marked by the formation of the Young Kikuyu Association by Harry Thuku. The climax of the organised efforts by the Kenyans to throw off the colonial yoke was the Mau Mau outburst in 1952. This movement centred on land agitation and it went on until 1959. The 'white highlands' became a symbol of white exclusiveness in a predominantly black African community. The other Kenyan groups, apart from the Kikuyu, played a subordinate role in this struggle, which was essentially a conflct over land. Land was of such great significance in this struggle because the white settlers, who were mainly farmers, believed that they had inherited the land they occupied, while the Africans claimed that the white settlers actually stole the land from them through the imposition of colonial rule.

Finally, during the period of militant protests the Africans were convinced that the white settlers would never return their land peacefully, neither would their rights be respected by the whites in Kenya. They therefore resorted to violent methods in their struggle. The Mau Mau movement was accompanied by the rise of radical political parties.

Many political, religious and secret associations performed various functions in the affairs of Kenya. These included the Kikuyu Central Association, the Kikuyu Independent Schools Association, the Kenya African Union, the Dini ya Jesu Kristo, and the Mau Mau movement. Of all these associations and movements, Mau Mau appeared the most militant. Its position was ambiguous and it is difficult to say exactly what it stood for because of the complexity of its structural organisation, leadership, membership and objectives. It combined religious with political activities. Mau Mau was predominantly a Kikuyu organisation and it gained little support amongst other groups in Kenya. It was the Kikuyu who had suffered most severely from the changes which had occurred with the coming of the Europeans. However, all Kenyans were overcrowded in the reserves allotted to them; they were given small wages for their services on European farms; they were not represented in the political bodies which made decisions that affected them; and they were discriminated against in other ways by the Europeans. All this combined to quicken the formation of various associations with the declared objective of winning independence for Kenya. The extremist factions of these associations demanded drastic measures against European dominance, and they received their main support from the secret society which emerged under the name of Mau Mau.

The aims of this society were to restore traditional customs and to unite the Africans in Kenya. They converted many, and a creed on the pattern of the Christian creed was drawn up which members were required to believe and to memorise. Oath-taking was an important feature of this society. In 1952, when the Europeans banned all legal outlets for the expression of grievances, Mau Mau intensified its activities in arousing the national feelings of the people in Kenya. The movement demanded the recovery of the land appropriated by the Europeans, the subjugation of foreigners, increased educational opportunities for Kenyans, and complete independence. Numerous revolts were supported and directed by Mau Mau despite the movement having been declared illegal. Generally, Mau Mau appears to have had a close, though informal, link with the Kenya African Union (KAU) founded in 1944 by Eliud Mathu, and led afterwards by Jomo Kenyatta.

As a result of the wisespread revolts in Kenya, the British authority declared a state of emergency which lasted from 1952 until 1959. Nevertheless, the revolts also forced some improvements. For instance, the Kenyans were given increased recognition in the civil service, a new programme of land allocation was adopted in order to encourage Kenyan participation in agriculture, and, by the Lyttleton Constitution of 1954, the Kenyans had direct representation in the Legislative and Executive Councils. Yet with all this, the colonial authorities insisted on a total ban on political activities among the Kenyans. At last, the different parties that had grown up merged into two after the Lancaster House Conference in London in 1960. These two parties were the Kenya African National Union (KANU) and the more moderate Kenya African Democratic Union (KADU), the latter favouring a federal system of government for the country with strong regions. In the event, KANU won the general elections of February 1961 and Jomo Kenyatta, who had been detained as a result of his participation in the Mau Mau movement, was released in July 1961 to form a government. Kenya thus became an

Fig. 6.5 *'General China', one of the Mau Mau leaders in Kenya, seen here in the courtroom at Nyeri while being tried by the British authorities*

independent country in December 1963, with a unitary system of government under the leadership of Jomo Kenyatta and his party.

In Uganda, Protestant groups helped the British to establish their colonial authority, and in 1900 when British imperial rule replaced British East African Company rule, Protestant African chiefs demanded a share of power in the new system. The result of the negotiations that followed was the Uganda Agreement of 1900. The Agreement regulated the powers of the Kabaka, and the relationship between the Ugandans and the British officials. The agreement virtually turned Uganda into a British protectorate under the Kabaka of Buganda as a constitutional monarch.

The British colonial system in Uganda introduced the principle of private and permanent ownership of land. Although the Land Law of 1908 tried to reduce the abuses of land allocation processes, the peasants were still forced to become tenants on the lands of the chiefly class. Until 1927, the British administration did not attempt to mitigate the peasants' hardships.

It appears that the initial political protests in Uganda were directed against the chiefs rather than the British. In 1919, for instance, the Young Baganda Association was organised to demand the involvement of groups other than the chiefly class in the administration. The protests shifted to ones between the Ugandans and the British, especially in the 1920s when the British started to advocate an East African federation, considered by the Ugandans as a threat to their country's internal autonomy. In the 1950s, the British revived the idea of federation and also tried to make the Uganda Protectorate a unitary state. The Ugandans, led by their ruler, Kabaka Mutesa II, resisted the attempts. The Kabaka was deposed in 1953, but restored in 1955 after a long period of negotiations.

The first nationalist party in Uganda was the Uganda Nationalist Congress founded in 1952. There was a series of splits within this party between 1956 and 1959. These resulted in Dr Milton Obote's faction emerging as a rival political party called the Uganda People's Congress. Other parties which sprang up included the Progressive Party and the Democratic Party. These parties disagreed on the future of traditional rulers in Uganda and on the form of government that was to be established on the attainment of political independence.

In 1960, the Uganda People's Congress secured, as a form of compromise, a quasi-federal constitution for Uganda. On 9 October 1962, Uganda became independent. This was followed by the working-out of a federal system of government that safeguarded the position of the traditional rulers. It needs to be mentioned here that the attempt made later to remove the rights and terminate the institution of the monarchy in Uganda contributed to the upheaval which led to the collapse of the Obote administration and the subsequent take-over of political power by the army.

After the end of the First World War, Britain was given the mandate to administer former German East Africa, except Rwanda and Urundi. The British area was renamed Tanganyika, and given a governor and an Executive council in 1920. The governors tried to restore trade and order as well as to establish a new administrative system. Sir Donald Cameron, one of these governors, revived tribal institutions as agents of colonial rule in an attempt probably to follow the spirit of the mandate and prepare the people for self-government in the future. However, the African population objected to equal representation with the officials in the Legislative Council and the nomination rather than election of such members.

In 1954, the Tanganyika African National Union (TANU) emerged under the leadership of Julius Nyerere, and in 1956 the inter-racial United Tanganyika Party was formed. The first elections in Tanganyika took place in 1958, and TANU won most of the seats. The party used the opportunity to request a speeding-up of the process of decolonisation. The next advance came in 1960, when another election was held. After this selection, Nyerere was appointed Chief Minister and was asked to choose ten out of the fourteen members of the Council of Ministers. Full political independence was won in December 1961, when Nyerere became the first Prime Minister of Tanganyika.

It should be added here that developments in Zanzibar in 1964 led to a union between Zanzibar and Tanganyika, and the name of the United Republic of Tanzania was adopted.

In the colonial history of Angola, the issues of Portuguese settlers and land acquisition were dominant. The 'ordinary African' in Angola was compelled by circumstances to serve as an unskilled labourer on the settlers' coffee and grains plantations. He received minimal wages for his services; he had no tenure of service. His cash crops were bought at very low prices, and he had no option but to accept in order to secure the cash required for the taxes imposed on him. Worse still, he might even be compelled to grow a type of crop required by the colonial masters.

Apart from the oppressed peasantry, there was in Angola the group of Western-educated Africans known as *assimilados,* who served as clerks and junior administrative officers under the Portuguese. Many of the *assimilados* were later dispossessed as a result of the influx of working-class Europeans during the 1940s. The expectations of these ambitious Angolans were considerably reduced, and fear of competition with the white settlers led to racial conflct. The situation deteriorated into open resistance against the political and economic policies of Portugal.[14] In the riots that erupted, both the white settlers and the *assimilados* were equally attacked, until these educated Africans became accepted as the leaders of the nationalist agitations. The Portuguese turned their attention to the *assimilados* whom they wanted to exterminate for their involvement in the nationalist movements. Many were arrested and imprisoned, and some were executed. The survivors were mainly those who escaped into exile, and these continued to make plans for resistance.

Portugal might have agreed to relax her economic and political domination but for the fact that she herself was not economically strong. However, because their neighbours had already been granted independence by their colonial overlords, the Angolans nursed the hope of similar fortune. Like the nationalists in Guinea-Bissau and Mozambique, they organised guerrilla resistance which at length forced Portugal to embark upon the process of decolonisastion. However, it was the army revolt in Portugal in April 1974 and the fall of the dictatorship that produced the *coup de grace.* Before the end of 1975 all the Portuguese colonies in Africa had gained their independence.

Central Africa

Not until after 1944 did the Congolese begin seriously to demand political independence. The Western-educated elements at first asked only recognition and improved status under colonial rule. Then in 1946 Joseph Kasavubu challenged the sale of land to the Church and Belgian companies by the colonial authorities in the Congo. A clear call for independence was to wait until late 1950s when an African press and African political parties began to appear.

All along, the Belgian educational policies never gave adequate attention to the Congolese. They were given education only up to the primary-school level. Until 1954 there was no university established in the Congo, and even when higher institutions were established they admitted only few undergraduates. Furthermore, the Belgians prohibited political associations and activities in the Congo until as late as 1959. Consequently, the Congo lacked a body of well-educated men who could give nationalist leadership.

The initial challenge to Belgian authority in the Congo started with the armed opposition organised by the powerful traditional states of the Congo, military mutinies, and the activities of religious movements. The Western-educated Congolese joined in this resistance in the late 1950s. From this period onwards, many Congolese groups, including the ABAKO under the leadership of Kasavubu, started to demand immediate independence. Events moved rapidly in the following years. Between 1957 and 1958 there was a series of elections into communal councils; there was also an escalation of inter-ethnic rivalries and hostilities; a few Congolese began to establish contact with other nationalist groups in Africa; and political parties began to appear. Following the 1959 Léopoldville riots, the Belgians started to consider the idea of negotiation because it was clear that the Belgian forces were finding it difficult to suppress the rioters. The date for the Congo's independence was set as 30 June 1960. A federal constitution was to be adopted and elections were fixed for May 1960. After several political party alliances, the ABAKO were forced to accept federalism; KONAKAT were encouraged by the settlers to demand a separate Katanga state; and the *Mouvement National Congolais* (MNC) led by Patrice Lumumba emerged as the most widely accepted political party. After a period of political compromise Lumumba became Prime Minister and Kasavubu the President of an independent Congo (now Zaire). But ethnic rivalries, personality clashes and entrenched Belgian interests were long to remain thorns in the flesh of the Congolese state.

The territories north and south of the River Zambezi followed different patterns of political development due to pressure from the white settlers in this area. Southern Rhodesia was granted responsible government in 1923 as a self-governing colony, and in 1924 the rule of the British South Africa Company was supplanted in neighbouring Northern Rhodesia and Nyasaland, which became Protectorates under the Colonial Office. Then in 1954, the federation of Rhodesia and Nyasaland was created. The Africans had not wanted this kind of union and this gave them a target for opposition, leading to the eventual dissolution of the federation. At last, following in the footsteps of Kenya, Uganda and Tanganyika, Zambia (Northern Rhodesia) and Malawi (Nyasaland) gained their independence in 1964 with Dr Kenneth Kaunda and Dr Hastings Kamuzu Banda as Prime Ministers respectively.

Rhodesia, formerly Southern Rhodesia, took the road of racial discrimination and white domination. The white minority government under the leadership of Ian Smith made a unilateral declaration of independence from Britain in 1965. British opposition to this rebellious act by her colony was hesitant and ineffectual, so that Rhodesian 'independence' remained virtually unchallenged until about 1975 when the black African nationalist guerrilla fighters started to threaten installations and security of life and property in Rhodesia with increasing ferocity. The nationalist fighters belonged to two Rhodesian political parties – the Zimbabwe African People's Union (ZAPU) and the Zimbabwe African National Union (ZANU.) – based in Zambia and

Mozambique respectively. By 1976 it became necessary for the white minority government to negotiate with the nationalist groups. Constitutional changes were made which allowed the Africans increased political participation but left much of the power in the hands of the whites. In 1979, developments which included nationalist guerrilla successes and international pressure finally forced Britain to work out a new constitutional framework with all the groups, re-establish her legitimate colonial authority and prepare the territory for independence based on majority rule. Robert Mugabe became Zimbabwe's first prime minister in 1980.

South Africa

The history of South Africa is one of a complex racial struggle. The complexity derives from conflct between the Dutch Afrikaners and the English, as well as between the Europeans and non-Europeans. In spite of their small number, the inhabitants of European descent remain politically dominant, while their isolation has produced an Afrikaner nationalism and apartheid (the doctrine of racial separation or apartness).

Following his expulsion from the South African Party at the end of 1913, General J. B. M. Hertzog formed the Nationalist (National) Party. He was succeeded by such avowed segregationists as Dr D. F. Malan, J. G. Strydom, Dr H. F. Verwoerd, and Mr John Vorster, who not only led their party but, in fact, as Prime Ministers, extended the frontier of apartheid and white dominance in South Africa.

A brief survey of the history of the people of South Africa might help to explain the character and nature of the political scene.[15] After the Great Trek of the 1830s, the Afrikaners saw both the Britons and the Africans as their rivals. The struggle was first against the Britons until the 1930s, when Afrikaner nationalism began to disappear as the feuds between the two white populations in South Africa also died out. Several issues, such as that of a *lingua franca,* as well as independence which had formed the main basis of the feuds and which led to the formation of the National Party by General Hertzog, had been settled. The Afrikaans language was accepted in 1925 alongside English as one of the country's two official languages, while with the passing of the Statute of Westminster in 1931 Britain fully acknowledged the national sovereignty of South Africa. Furthermore, the Afrikaner nationalists and the English-speaking South Africans had begun to work together politically. The National Party formed a coalition with the Labour Party. The Labour Party was an organ of the mainly English-speaking white workers. After the 1934 elections, the two parties merged into the United Party.

Contrary, however, to all expectations of unity, the months following the general elections of 1938 saw an astonishing revival of Afrikaner nationalist feelings arising from the centenary celebrations of the Great Trek, and a reflection on the devastations of the Anglo-Boer War of 1899–1902. The spirit of exclusive Afrikaner nationalism was thus rekindled. Cleavages between the English and the Afrikaners in South Africa had grown so greatly that when Dr Malan became the Prime Minister in 1948 it was no longer surprising that, for the first time in the history of the Union, a South African Cabinet was composed entirely of members of one of the white groups – the Afrikaners.

The cause of this revival can be traced to socio-economic conditions in the area. The economic inequality between the two white groups was never narrowed down: there were about twelve unskilled Afrikaner labourers to one non-Afrikaner white; the same ratio applied to the merchant class. The few Britons monopolised the exploitation of the gold and diamond industries to the exclusion of the Afrikaners; the Afrikaners were only employed in the lower-paid professions such as the civil service and teaching. Another grudge against the English-speaking section, which further explains why the Afrikaner nationalist 'gospel' was so popular at this time, was the tendency by the English-speaking whites to regard the Afrikaners as social inferiors.

The next stage of conflict was between the Afrikaners and the Africans. General Hertzog introduced discriminatory laws which included the Mines and Works Act of 1926, and the obnoxious colour legislation which established rigid inequality between the black and the white people in South Africa. In 1948, apartheid – officially approved racial and colour discrimination – became the official policy of the South African Government. Additional measures which were discriminatory in character were introduced. For example, the law requiring the people to carry identity cards showing race was enacted; the Population Registration Act ensured proper classification of races; mixed marriages were prohibited; the Group Area Act forbade Africans from living in white areas; an Industrial Relations Act prevented Africans from forming their own trade unions; the Native Law Amendment Act was intended to ensure that Africans did not overstay the length of time allowed them outside African reserves; the Industrial Conciliation Act and the Native Labour Settlement of Disputes Act prohibited mixed trade unions; the Job Reservation Act gave preference to the whites in some employments; while the Extension of University Education Act prescribed different types of university education for whites and blacks. Meanwhile, in 1951 the National Party had been formed by the union of the Nationalist and Afrikaner parties, and this has continued to provide the government of South Africa until now. Parliamentary opposition was provided first by the United Party, and when this broke up, the Progressive Federal Party.

The repressive acts that accompanied apartheid activated African nationalism. At the time when Hertzog was forming the National Party, Africans also were organising the Native National Congress (later renamed the African National Congress). The Congress aimed at uniting the various ethnic groups for the defence of their rights, privileges and freedom. Initially the Congress focused its attention on selected issues, the most important of which were the right of every adult to a vote, the land question (at this time, more than 90 per cent of all land in South Africa belonged to the minority white groups), the pass laws which imposed the carrying of identity cards, and the Master and Servant Act. In 1952, African nationalists adopted non-violent methods and passive resistance based on the philosophy of Gandhi. It was the Sharpeville shootings of 1960, which resulted in the killing of 60 and wounding of more than 180 people, and the declaration of South Africa as a Republic in 1961 that changed the Africans' tactics in their struggle. They now adopted a mixed policy of violent as well as non-violent agitation and opposition to white minority rule.

Three leaders have stood out in the Africans' struggle for majority rule in South Africa. They were Chief Albert Luthuli, Robert Sobukwe, and Nelson Mandela. Chief Luthuli, a Zulu, who won the Nobel Peace Prize in 1960, advocated passive resistance and respect for both the white and black races, but his uncompromising attitude and statements on matters affecting the interests of the Africans led to his imprisonment on several occasions. Robert Sobukwe was a militant nationalist who lost faith in the use of non-violent methods for African liberation. In 1959 he formed the Pan-Africanist Congress after breaking with the African National Congress. He advocated mass action based on good organisation. He was arrested for organising the Sharpeville demonstrations and was given a three-year term of imprisonment. Nelson Mandela, the third, was a lawyer who took over as President of the ANC after Chief Luthuli's death. Mandela operated from underground. He formed a military organisation known as the 'Spear' (Umkonto), which organised the sabotage of installations. He was later arrested, given a life sentence and imprisoned on Robben Island.

Today in South Africa, the independence struggle of the African nationalists is being suppressed by an uncompromising Afrikaner nationalism, symbolised by apartheid. The attempt by the South African government to establish the so-called independent 'homelands' or 'Bantustans' for the various black African ethnic groups as a way of breaking down African nationalist solidarity not only in South Africa but

Fig. 6.6 *Nelson Mandela, leader of the African National Congress, imprisoned on Robben Island, South Africa*

also in South West Africa or Namibia (a League of Nations mandated territory assigned to South Africa in 1919 but which she has refused to relinquish) can be seen as a political subterfuge to deny these people their South African nationality and make them foreigners in their own countries. The South West African People's Organisation (SWAPO), recognised by the United Nations Organisation as the legitimate representative of Namibia, has intensified its demand for full independence from South Africa. The wind of change which has transformed most of the continent from colonies to independent nations still blows, and yet the stubborn situation in South Africa may remain with us for quite a while. Even there, however, there are signs of changes: at least token reforms are being made in response to the black Africans' demand for equality, freedom and respect for human dignity, and to world pressure. The emergence of black consciousness – that liberating ideological–cultural force – provides the framework within which the black nationalists will henceforth articulate, define, integrate and co-ordinate their common struggle.

Notes

1   See Michael Crowder, 'Indirect rule: French and British styles', *Africa*, July 1964.

2   J. S. Coleman, *Nigeria: background to nationalism*, Los Angeles, University of California Press, 1958, p. 193; Michael Crowder, *West Africa under colonial rule*, London, Hutchinson, 1968, p. 428

3   For more details, see Michael Crowder, *West Africa under colonial rule*, pp. 174–97, 408; Joseph E. Harris, *Africans and their history*, New York, Mentor Books, 1972, pp. 165–6.

4   *Ibid.*, pp. 173–4

5   See S. A. Akintoye, 'The independence movement in the former Belgian Congo', *Tarikh* III (4), 1977, 52–4.

6   See Z. A. Marsh and G. W. Kingsnorth, *An introduction to the history of East Africa*, Cambridge University Press, 1965, pp. 87–109.*

7   P. J. M. McEwan (ed.), *Twentieth-century Africa*, Oxford University Press, 1968

8   Harris, *Africans and their history*, pp. 177–8

9   See G. W. F. Hegel, *The philosophy of history*, trans. by J. Sibree, New York, Dover Publications, 1956, p. 99; A. P. Newton, 'Africa and historical research', *Journal of the African Society* XXII, 88, July 1923, 268; Hugh Trevor-Roper, *The rise of Christian Europe*, London, Thames and Hudson, 1965, p. 9.

10 For more information on the independent church movements and the prophetic movements see J. D. Y. Peel, 'The Aladura movement in Western Nigeria', *Tarikh* III (1), 1969, 48–55; J. B. Webster, 'Independent Christians in Africa', *ibid*, 56–81.

11 Leo Spitzer, *The Creoles of Sierra Leone: their responses to colonialism 1870–1945*, University of Ife Press, 1975, pp. 196–215

12   See Jamil M. Abun-Nasr, 'The independence movements in the Maghrib', *Tarikh* IV (1), 1971, 61–3.

13   O. Adewoye, 'Nationalism in Kenya, 1920–1963', *Tarikh* IV (1), 1971, 30

14   David Birmingham, 'Portuguese role in Angola', *Tarikh* IV(4), 1974, 29–32

15   Freda Troup, *South Africa: an historical introduction*, Penguin Books, 1975, esp. chs 4–7

Questions for discussion

1   Would you regard the independence movement as more radical and violent in North Africa than in West Africa?

2   Assess the roles of the 'conservative' and the 'radical' elements in Nigeria's politics in the period before political independence.

3   The Second World War was a milestone in the Africans' struggle for independence. Discuss.

4   Attempt a critical analysis of European colonial policies in Africa.

Suggestions for further reading

Abun-Nasr, J. M. *A history of the Maghrib,* Cambridge University Press, 1971

Ajayi, J. F. A., and Crowder, M. *History of West Africa,* 2, Longman, 1974, chs 12–19

Balandier, Georges. 'The colonial situation', in *Africa: social problems of change and conflict,* Pierre van den Berghe (ed.), San Francisco, Chandler, 1965

Coleman, James S. *Nigeria: background to nationalism,* Berkeley, University of California Press, 1958

Coleman, James S., and Rosberg, Carl J. (eds). *Political parties and national integration in tropical Africa,* Berkeley, University of California Press, 1965

Crowder, Michael. *West Africa under colonial rule,* London, Hutchinson, 1968

Duffy, James. *Portugal in Africa,* Harvard University Press, 1962

Fanon, Frantz. *A dying colonialism,* Penguin Books, 1970

———. *The wretched of the earth,* New York, Grove Press, 1965

Gibson, Richard. *African liberation movements: contemporary struggles against white minority rule,* London, Oxford University Press, 1972

Hodgkin, Thomas. *Nationalism in colonial Africa,* New York, Oxford University Press, 1968

McEwan, P. J. M. (ed.) *Twentieth-century Africa,* Oxford University Press, 1968

Rotberg, Robert I. *The rise of nationalism in Central Africa: making of Malawi and Zambia, 1873–1964,* Oxford University Press, 1960

Wallerstein, Immanuel. *Africa: the politics of independence,* New York, Random House, 1961

7 Economic and social development in contemporary Africa

Toyin Falola

All countries in Africa today except South Africa belong to what is called the Third World, mainly in reference to economic and social development; they are often referred to as the 'underdeveloped', 'developing', or 'less-developed' countries. Compared with the developed countries, Africa is economically poor, and, in fact, eighteen of the least developed twenty-eight countries of the world are in Africa.

This chapter is intended neither to present an all-embracing theory of economic development nor to suggest a theoretical model which is applicable to all the developing African countries. The problems of underdevelopment, both practical and theoretical, are legion. They are more often than not debated in a subjective manner. Most of the current viewpoints on the subject are discussed in this chapter as objectively as possible without necessarily assigning to them any form of hierarchy of importance.

Characteristics of the developing African countries

A low life expectancy, poor and insufficient medical services, poor diet, hunger and starvation, a high birth rate, a high rate of unemployment, a low real income *per capita,* export of raw materials, inadequate economic infrastructure, a high rate of illiteracy, little urbanisation and a few other similar conditions have been described as the distinguishing characteristics of the developing countries of Africa.

Life expectancy

Life expectancy in Africa is less than 50 years (see Table 1, column 6). Many children and adults still die due to factors which can be controlled. Whereas life expectancy in the United States of America is about 73 years, that in Nigeria is 41. The difference in the death rate is significant, particularly in infant mortality. Although only about 20 die out of 1 000 before reaching the age of 1 year in the developed countries, an average of about 147 die in the less-developed countries of Africa (Table 1, column 5).

Medical services

These are poor and in many places virtually non-existent. Both the high

Table 1. Population data: selected African countries and developed countries, 1978

Region/ Country	Population esti- mate mid-1978 (millions)	Birth rate (per 1 000)	Death rate (per 1 000)	Rate of natural increase (annual %)	Infant mortality rate[1]	Life expectancy at birth (years)	Urban population (%)[2]	Per capita Gross National Product (GNP) (U.S. $)	Physical quality of life index[3]
Africa[4]	436·0	46	19	2·7	147	46	25	440	—
Egypt	39·6	38	12	2·5	108	53	44	280	42
Nigeria	68·4	49	21	2·8	157	41	18	380	25
Ghana	10·9	49	20	2·9	115	49	31	580	34
Ivory Coast	7·2	45	19	2·6	154	44	20	610	28
Sierra Leone	3·3	44	19	2·5	136	44	15	200	27
Senegal	5·4	47	23	2·4	159	40	32	390	24
Liberia	1·7	50	21	2·9	159	45	28	450	26
Ethiopia	30·2	49	25	2·4	162	42	12	100	19
Kenya	14·8	48	15	3·3	110	50	10	240	39
Tanzania	16·5	47	22	2·5	167	44	7	180	27
Zambia	5·5	50	19	3·1	159	44	36	440	30
Zaire	26·7	45	18	2·7	160	44	29	140	28
Un. Kingdom	56·0	12	12	0·0	14	72	76	4020	94
France	53·4	14	10	0·3	13	73	70	6550	94
W. Germany	61·3	10	12	−0·2	17	71	92	7380	93
Sweden	8·3	12	11	0·1	9	75	83	8670	97
U.S.S.R.	261·0	18	9	0·9	28	69	62	2760	91
Japan	114·4	16	6	1·0	9	74	76	4910	96
Australia	14·3	17	8	0·8	14	72	86	6100	93
Canada	23·6	16	7	0·9	14	73	76	7510	95
U.S.A.	218·4	15	9	0·6	15	73	74	7890	94
Europe[4]	480·0	15	10	0·4	20	71	65	4420	—

Source: 1978 World population data sheet (Washington, D.C.: Population Reference Bureau, 1978)
1 Annual number of deaths of infants under one year of age per 100 live births.
2 The percentage of the total population living in areas defined as uban by each country, usually towns of 20 000 and above.
3 Source: the figures in this column are taken from *Time Magazine,* 13 March 1978. They represent 'a measure of the effectiveness of social services'. They include life expectancy, literacy and infant mortality.
4 Figures for Africa and Europe include all countries in each of the two continents.

infant mortality and the low life expectancy are often difficult to check because of lack of medical facilities, personnel and public sanitation. Where medical facilities do exist, they are often unable to cope with the teeming population. In addition, they are not located close to all the villages, with the result that people have to travel long distances before they can receive medical care. In many parts of Africa, there is usually one doctor for more than 200 000 people; in Nigeria, Chad and Niger there is one doctor for 30 000, 73 460 and 56 140 people respectively, whereas in the U.S.S.R. the ratio is one doctor per 782 people, in the U.S.A. one doctor per 750, and in Israel, one per 452 people.

Diet

Hunger and starvation are still common in some parts of Africa; diets generally tend to be nutritionally inadequate. Starchy foods are supplemented with little or no protein. There is now a class of landless farmers, and many people are unemployed in the large urban centres. There is population pressure on the land – for example, in Uganda and parts of eastern Nigeria where population densities are very high. Emphasis is often on cash crops to the neglect of food crops. Most African countries can no longer feed themselves adequately, and food imports have been increasing steadily in recent years.

Birthrate

Birth rates in Africa are among the highest in the world (Table 1, column 2). Large families are the norm in African society. Traditionally, children are valued as economic and social assets to enhance the status of the family, to work on the farms or herd the cattle, and to provide security for parents in their old age. Even today many children are desired, even though they may be a drain on the limited financial resources of the family.

Employment

There is a high rate of unemployment. Many people are jobless especially in the urban centres, while many others are under-employed. This is why more and more people resort to begging as a 'profession'. Most unemployed people are unskilled, and this worsens their prospects of finding jobs where they can earn a steady income. Many young school leavers migrate to the cities and towns hoping to find jobs, but these are scarce. In frustration, they may turn to armed robbery, smuggling, crime or other socially undesirable activities to ameliorate their plight. Moreover, many African economies are not expanding rapidly enough to absorb the ever-growing pool of unemployed, and this situation leads to political and social unrest.

Income

The real income *per capita* is low, especially when compared to that of the developed countries. In Table 1, column 8, it is shown that the *per capita* gross national product in Africa averages $440; in Europe, by contrast, it averages $4 420. Broken down by country, the gap becomes more glaring: Ethiopia, for example, has a *per capita* GNP of only $100, while Sweden's is $8 670.

Exports

Unlike the industrialised world, African countries are primarily producers and exporters of raw materials and commodities. The economies of nearly all the African countries are tied to those of the European countries. Many are dependent on single cash crops for revenues, such as

Ghana, Togo and Benin, which depend largely on cocoa. Until very recently, Nigeria relied almost exclusively on cocoa, palm oil, ground-nuts, cotton and rubber. African producers of agricultural commodities are handicapped in the world market because they cannot control the prices for their commodities and they have little or no control over the natural factors that hinder productivity.

Economic infrastructure

The weak economic infrastructure, particularly the transportation and communication systems, must also be considered. Adequate roads have not been constructed to connect the major communities of the various African countries, and many of the existing road systems were designed to transport raw materials to the coasts, rather than to provide a network of intracontinental communications. The same could be said of the railway systems. Air terminals and sea ports are too few and inadequately developed to service the flow of goods and people. Communication is generally difficult; the postal system is often unreliable, and the tele-phone system suffers from frequent disruptions of service. All these are serious impediments to economic development.

Literacy

Another characteristic of the developing countries of Africa is the high rate of illiteracy. In many parts of the continent, a large number of people cannot read or write. Women and girls are disproportionately dis-advantaged in this respect. Formal education is not yet available to all. Only a small number of Africans are able to gain the few places in the universities, while many young people do not even attend elementary schools. In some African countries, the number of secondary schools is small and they cannot begin to accommodate all those eligible to attend. Lack of basic literacy and the inability to meet the educational aspirations of its youth affects the socio-political development of the continent. Participation in modern political activities is virtually restricted to those who are literate. Information on public matters does not spread to the whole populace. For instance, the *Daily Times,* which has the largest circulation in Nigeria, sells only around 400 000 copies a day. This is very small indeed when one remembers that the population of Nigeria is at least 68 million.

Urbanisation

Most people in Africa live and work in the rural areas. Figures in Table 1, column 7, show that the African urban populations constitute only 25 per cent of the total population; or, conversely, that 75 per cent are rurally based. Tanzania is about 93 per cent rural, although Egypt is only 56 per cent rural. Rural development schemes have not yet reached most areas, which still are without electricity, pipeborne water and other modern social amenities.

Other characteristics of underdeveloped countries

Underdevelopment is accompanied by dozens of other factors with which it is inextricably bound. Among them are the high proportion of the labour force which is engaged in agricultural activities, especially subsistence farming or herding. There are few industries, and in those that do exist low productivity is preponderant. There is an unfavourable balance of trade and lack of investment capital, production is low per man-hour. The poor are exploited. There is little time for leisure activities. Energy is consumed at low rate. Public utilities are scarce. The vast resources (both human and natural) are unexploited. There is a low rate of saving.

One view of underdevelopment has been expressed in these stark terms:

> the reality of poverty, hunger, disease and ignorance, of mendicity, raggedness and unhygienic surroundings. The squalor and promiscuity in which people live in African villages, the ugliness of underfed children, the shattered life of women who cannot leave their homes for lack of decent clothing, the destitution in which the aged die, the sufferings of the sick, the unbearable drudgery of farm work with primitive tools under the tropical sun and, above all, the humiliation attached in world consciousness to the colour of his skin, involving his culture and dignity as man.[1]

Given these characteristics, it is, therefore, not wrong to refer to most of the African countries as poor, less developed, underdeveloped, developing, emerging, low-income, transitional countries. It is ·by measuring development on the basis of the degree of education of the working groups; the amount of capital, including 'social capital' such as airports, hospitals, schools, roads, railways and so forth; capital per head; income per head; the percentage of resources yet to be tapped; savings. *per capita,* that the whole world has been classified into three main divisions. The 'First World' states comprise the advanced countries, notably the United States of America, Canada, New Zealand, the countries of Western Europe and Australia. The 'Second World' includes Eastern Europe and the U.S.S.R., while the 'Third World' comprises Africa, Latin America and Asia (except Japan), all of which share the characteristics briefly sketched above. Even within the so-called Third World there is a separating-out process whereby some countries fall back into a 'Fourth World' – that is the least developed countries of the less developed. As noted before, there are twenty-eight countries so designated by the United Nations, and eighteen of these (64 per cent) are on the African continent.

However, the concept of underdevelopment refers specifically to the economic and technological situation. It has nothing to do with the moral, cultural, physical, or mental development of the Africans. It is wrong to assume that because African countries are economically underdeveloped, they are therefore uncivilised. It is also wrong to describe their religious institutions as fetishes, their culture as primitive and their intelligence as undeveloped, and it cannot be convincingly shown that Africa has been the most economically backward continent from time immemorial. There was a time when most African countries were self-sufficient in their food and capital production. They even generated surpluses. In the fifteenth century European traders bought consumer good, cloth being the main item, from African manufacturers in places as far flung as Yorubaland, Loango, Mauritania, Morocco, Senegambia. Unemployment and the excessive rigidity in social stratification are phenomena which have accompanied European rule.

Obstacles to socio-economic development

Many inter-related factors hinder the socio-economic development of African countries. Certain problems are peculiar to some countries, although other countries have actually succeeded in overcoming a few of their problems. Some of the issues touched upon here involve a repetition of the issues discussed under the characteristics of developing nations. This is due to the inter-relatedness of cause and effect and of the 'vicious circle of poverty'.

Availability of natural resources

Availability of natural resources is an obvious factor affecting development potentials. In some parts of Africa, fertile land is scarce and over-farmed; rainfall is often inadequate or irregular, particularly in the Sahel where drought is a regular part of life. Many countries have no large supply of tapped or untapped mineral resources. Where the land is plentiful and fertile, it may be fragmented and shared among many family members because of the inheritance system of land tenure. This limits the exploitation of the land to its maximum potential. In addition, land is not effectively utilised because of bad management and lack of information about ways to increase yields. Many other factors affect the effective utilisation of lands for agricultural purposes. Most people are unwilling to surrender their lands for development purposes, since the family is the farming unit and it is primarily concerned with meeting its own immediate needs. Farming implements are outmoded and inefficient: there is a limit to what hoes and cutlasses can do.

Human resources

Human resources are also largely an untapped source. Not many people are highly skilled, and the few skilled personnel are often unwilling to work hard. There is a conspicuous absence of a capable entrepreneurial class which can train, motivate and mobilise human and capital resources for efficient production which, in turn, can lead to the benefit of all. A class of entrepreneurial industrialists has not emerged in Africa partly because of the shortage of capital and technological know-how, the stiff competition from foreign investors who dominate the economy, and African unfamiliarity with large-scale commercial enterprise.

Capital

Financial capital is very scarce. The majority of the African countries are very poor and they lack the financial resources with which to develop. The vital role that investment can play in economic development cannot be overemphasised: it increases the potential of the economy and the national income. It is difficult to accumulate money to invest in the developing countries. Many people are unable to save, yet it is savings that help banking institutions to grow and expand. Banks and banking are necessary if funds are to be obtained for development purposes; capital accumulation is necessary for economic development to occur. Society needs all these resources to increase its output, but many are lacking in developing countries.

Land use

Even where lands are fertile, one finds that they are inadequately and inefficiently utilised. The reasons for this are not unconnected with poor health, lack of education and ignorance of modern farming techniques. Although Africans are predominantly farmers and herders, they under-utilise their lands or overwork them with farming methods such as slash-and-burn cultivation which depletes the fertility of the soil. Overgrazing by the pastoralists results in deforestation and aggravates the hardship of their already difficult way of life.

Economic infrastructure

The inadequate economic infrastructure is another obstacle to develop-ment. Raw materials and finished products should constantly flow from the farms and factories to the households. This process accelerates economic development, but it is not efficiently carried out on the continent. Harbours, railroads, highways and bridges are essential if goods and people are to be transported from one area to another. Telephone and postal services are also crucial; their inadequacy imposes many barriers to economic development. Many agricultural products spoil because they cannot easily be transported from where they are plentiful to places where they are scarce. Mobility os labour is restricted.

Population growth

Population growth is a great obstacle to the social and economic develop-ment of developing countries. Birth rates are low in the developed countries but are high in the developing countries (see Table 1, column 2). It can be observed from this same table that the developing countries of the world have the highest rates of population growth (column 4). This, of course, has serious consequences for economic and social development. It increases rural poverty because population pressure on the land dimi-nishes the quantity and quality of land available to an individual. It encourages the drift from rural areas to the urban centres of persons in search of profitable employment. It has been pointed out that the developing countries are now witnessing an urban population explosion which must affect the availability and quality of education, health services and food supply. The pressure of population on food supply means that food production *per capita* in Africa is actually decreasing. Table 2 shows that from 1971 to 1976 food production *per capita* in Africa was lower than it was in the base period 1961–5. Rapid population growth has other effects on social development. It reduces the already low standard of living in the developing countries; although overall national income may increase, there are more and more mouths to feed. Fully 44 per cent of the African population is under the age of fifteen. Rapid rates of population growth also strain development planning, making realistic development programmes difficult to implement. Little investment is possible, and social amenities have to be shared by more and more people.

Table 2. Food production per capita in developing regions, 1971–6

Region	1971	1972	1973	1974	1975	1976
			(1961–5 = 100)			
Developing market						
economies	102	99	100	100	103	104
Latin America	103	101	101	103	102	107
Far East	103	97	104	99	106	105
Near East	103	108	100	105	109	109
Africa	99	95	89	93	93	94
Asian centrally planned						
economies	110	107	110	111	112	112
Total developing						
countries	105	102	103	103	106	107

Source: *World almanac and book of facts 1978,* (New York, Newspaper Enterprise Association, 1978), p. 130

Trained manpower

Another severe obstacle to economic development in Africa is the drastic shortage of well-trained technical, administrative and managerial manpower. During the colonial period the emphasis in the educational curriculum was on the liberal arts, to the exclusion of science and technology. Shortly after independence, the emphasis shifted to the provision of primary education, yet not every child has benefited from elementary education. A Kenyan Minister of Education has remarked:

> However hard we try, I do not think it is possible to enrol students in standard I at more than 4 per cent per annum. This means we are going to have millions of illiterate children, not because we want them to be illiterate children but because we shall not have schools in which to enrol them. This is a very unfortunate situation.[2]

Most African countries cannot provide the schools, teachers and educational materials needed by their citizens. The adult farmer and trader cannot be trained to write and read in order to facilitate the adoption of new techniques. The widespread illiteracy affects the quality of the working population. Training is necessary if the people in a country are to invent, operate, repair and manage machines. Education promotes health, understanding and appreciation of the needs of the community at large, and it raises the quality of human capital generally. It aids the innovations and inventions of new tools and commodities. A society cannot progress on the basis of a static and outworn technology; there need to be new inventions and new technologies if the productive capacity is to be increased. African countries have yet to witness the technological revolution that could lead to their economic take-off. It is pertinent to remark here that Europe would not have assumed the position it occupies today were it not for the radical departures made during the Industrial Revolution.

Attitudes to work

A peculiar problem of the developing countries is that many educated persons within them do not seem willing to work as productively in the national interest as they could do. Commenting on this attitude among the educated elite in the Nigerian political system, one writer observes:

> One major trend in the development of the Nigerian power elite was the increasing bourgeoisification of its members – their obsessive concern with acquiring wealth and the power which it could bring. Many of them were perceptive enough to realise that, in view of the general poverty in the country and the scarcity of capital, good connections with the governments and parties controlling them were indispensable if their ambitions for wealth were not to remain pipe dreams . . . . The essentially business attitude which most of the elite developed to the affairs of the nation meant that most of them devoted all their thinking and scheming to how well they could do for themselves from the material resources available to the whole populace.[3]

Public health

The quantity of labour is not enough to guarantee economic and social development. There is a great need for skilled and well-trained manpower. Poor health is a common phenomenon in most African countries. The medical and welfare services are inadequate and costly. Many children suffer from malnutrition and diseases with no causes other than poverty and lack of sanitation and hygiene. In urban centres such as Nairobi, Lagos, Accra, Entebbe and a host of similar places, many of the inhabitants live in poor and overcrowded houses, thus exposing themselves to further illness and delinquency. Drugs and hospital facilities are scarce. Public health programmes have not yet really tackled the major health problems. Malaria, polio, cholera, measles and tuberculosis still take far too many lives in these countries. Infant and child mortality are high due largely to poor hygiene in the home and lack of vaccination; malnutrition makes children more vulnerable to disease, with the result that many die of illnesses which for children in the developed countries are merely minor ailments. Poor health affects the quality of labour, since more time is lost through sickness and the effort expended is less effective. Nigeria, for example, loses over 21 000 man-hours a month for every thousand of the working population because of malaria alone.

Political stability

The disastrous impact of political instability on socio-economic development cannot be overemphasised, because a peaceful atmosphere is needed for economic development. National resources have yet to be fully exploited and justly shared. The African continent is yet to witness political stability.

Social factors militating against progress

Many things make our progress difficult. We have persistently refused to bury our differences, come together and make a deliberate attempt to forge a nation. Our own politicians want to operate within the system of modern politics without casting off their traditional gowns. Tolerance and the spirit of give and take cannot be found in the dictionary of governments and opposition parties. The opposition is seen as an enemy of the government and this breeds mistrust. Those who are in authority pamper their members with favours which non-followers are denied. Job allocation and award of contracts are tied to party functionaries or to the particular ethnic group from which the rulers come. The traditional ethnic groups still retain their individualities. Attempts to put an end to this have usually failed because the rulers only preach the message without reflecting on their decision-making or in the execution of their policies. Most African leaders still look on their own ethnic groups as a source of support. Thus many political parties follow ethnic divisions. Important issues are blurred by parochial considerations. The political leaders lack the self-discipline that could curb self-interst. They think and behave in terms of particular communities rather than of the over-all national interest. Some of them specialise in embezzling money without an atom of regard for public accountability. Hospitals, colleges, roads and industries are built not where they are most needed but where the rulers come from. These selfish leaders look on their country as created in their interest. They claim a perpetual right to rule for as long as they exist. They view general elections with disdain and as a sign of ingratitude. They are now life presidents and they live in costly presidential palaces. They believe that their exit means the collapse of the nation!

Added to this is the wave of coups and countercoups which has brought about an era of military rule in Africa. The reasons for and the impact of military rule are discussed in Chapter 9. Suffice it to repeat here that political instability stifles economic development and growth.

It is doubtful if the developing countries can progress without changing their current attitude to work and development. Most educated people have developed an aversion to work when it involves government or communal projects. The people do not identify themselves as part of the government; there is no 'we feeling'. There is an urgent need for governments to mobilise their people for collective efforts. Citizens have been led to believe that their respective governments can do everything for them. This is impossible. It is also important to revolutionise the work ethic; initiative, motivation and ambition should be encouraged. Certain societies, such as those of the Germans, Japanese, Americans and Chinese, possess an urge to work as part of their national ethos. Most countries in the developing world suffer from what has been termed the 'siesta syndrome' – sleeping away the afternoon – or the 'long week-end'. This attitude is rampant among the elite in the public sector who take little or no interest in their profession. This is less so in the profit-oriented private sctor and also among the generality of the unlettered and un-skilled masses who must work hard to make their living. The traditional work ethic is fast disappearing, a result probably of the impact of contemporary social attitudes and values among the literate urban dwellers. There is no short cut to development other than persistent hard work. The history of this century has revealed how the Russians, Chinese and Japanese suddenly appeared on the world map as industrialised nations.

A few of the African social and legal institutions tend to serve as barriers to socio-economic development. Personal and psychological factors, social and religious practices, numerous public holidays, tradi-tions, institutions and habitual ways of doing things all affect economic growth. In a few African communities, there is an excessive belief in divine intervention and in predestination in human affairs; this often obfuscates the perception of problems and their rational solutions. In others, children are expected to follow their family's occupation, and this makes it impossible for the labour force to undergo radical changes and adapt to current practices and procedures. Upward mobility of labour, which is crucial to development, is retarded. Legal institutions such as the land tenure system can adversely affect development and economic growth.

Impact of European countries on Africa

The impact of the European countries on the African continent is another major factor. The European involvement in the history of Africa is of great antiquity. Trade was at first the major reason for this contact. By the seventeenth century, the slave trade had become the most significant link between Africa and Europe and it grew in scope and volume in the subsequent centuries. This had serious consequences both for the domestic economies of African societies and socio-political structures. It drew Africa into the world economy not as producers or manufacturers but as appendages and suppliers of labour. The unprofitable trade diverted attention from the hitherto gradual development of socio-political and economic institutions to the unproductive endeavours of wars, raids and destruction. Then the replacement of trade in men with trade in products after the abolition of the slave trade in the nineteenth century only intensified the subordination of the African indigenous economy. It aligned the structure of production with the needs of the industrial economies of Europe and America. Many indigenous indus-trial activities, such as mining, smelting, smithing, weaving, dyeing and so forth, were progressively undermined because their products faced stiff competition from European goods. This tied the Africans to the Europeans since they now relied increasingly on European goods. The advent of the missionaries and their subsequent activities promoted the spread of Christiantity and Western education. This resulted in the emergence of a new African elite who were to further the interests of the various European countries. The situation later degenerated into the complete integration of Africa into the world economy from the beginning of this century when the whole of the continent was under colonial rule. The situation then turned from one of mere trading partners to one of unmitigated exploitation. European countries now controlled the transport and communication systems, and mobilised many of the African people towards attaining the maximum exploitation of their resources. Capital and raw materials were taken to the mother countries, financial resources were spent on things that could have contributed to the economic growth of Africa. Colonial rule was so successful that although nearly all African countries have now achieved political independence, they remain economically dependent on Europe. This unequal partnership in the global economy is a major obstacle to the socio-economic development of the African continent. A few of the dominant features of this neo-colonial dependence will now be briefly discussed.

The first is the problem of world trade. On a theoretical basis, international trade can enable the developing countries to have access to the necessary resources, human and capital, with which to develop, and they can concentrate on those that are profitable to them. However, practical experience has shown otherwise. The developed countries are in full control of the international arena. They dictate the prices of goods for raw materials and fix the prices for finished manufactured goods. This means that the developing countries have little control over the prices of their own goods and over the products they buy in the world market. In addition, the developing countries pay more and more for their imports and receive less and less for their exports. In the former Eastern Region of Nigeria, for example, a ton of specially graded palm oil was sold for N160 in 1952; eight years later the price fell to N95.50, while three years later it was sold for only N80. In the old Western Region, 90 000 tons of cocoa were exported in 1954 for N78 million in revenue. In 1962, only N66 million was received for 183 000 tons. This shows clearly that the developing countries are not sure of a steady income. While disadvantageous fluctuations in prices hardly occur for manufactured goods, they normally affect the agricultural products. The situation becomes difficult for the developing countries to overcome because most cannot themselves utilise their cocoa, coffee, rubber, timber, groundnut and cotton products; processing industries have not been developed locally. This reduces the chance of becoming self-reliant, a situation which the advanced countries exploit to their advantage by selling their finished products at increasingly higher prices. Many of the manufactured goods which are imported are of little relevance to the socio-economic development of the African people. Some are not even suited to the climatic conditions in the African countries, and some last only for a few years before they become useless due to lack of spare parts or relevant servicing skills. It has also been noted that outmoded goods are often dumped on Africa.

Prolonged foreign investment is another barrier to development. It curtails the growth of indigenous businesses and retards the development of local industrialisation. Foreign investment provides the opportunity to exploit the resources of the developing countries for the benefit of the industrialised countries. Because of the huge profits they usually make and repatriate, foreign firms deliberately endeavour to retain their position in the developing countries, and they have the backing of their home governments in this. Foreigners interfere in the national decision-making processes of African countries with a great deal of success, while they also influence governmental decisions that can affect them. They are able to exert their influence on the developing countries because of their access to ample financial capital, technical know-how, large markets and global market intelligence. Foreign investment is an extension of colonialism into the post-independence era because the main driving forces are still to have readily available markets where raw materials can be bought and at the same time finished goods sold.

The last point touches on the implications of foreign aid to these poor countries. Aid usually consists of financial, human and technical resources. The aim of the donor and recipient may not coincide. Whereas the developing countries think in terms of catching up, the developed countries often have in mind ideological considerations. Each of the advanced countries belongs to an ideological camp and their desire is not only to protect their interests but to gain allies. This means that strings (visible or invisible) are attached to this aid. It leads to complacency in many developing countries since it gives the impression that the solution to their ramified problems can be sought and paid for by the developed countries. Aid is at times for specific projects agreed upon in advance by both donor and recipient nations, and these projects may be unprofitable industrial or prestige projects. A notable example was the former Ghanaian President Kwame Nkrumah's misdirected N16 million for a building to accommodate the 1965 summit conference of heads of African states, which could hardly be justified from the point of view of Ghana's national resources and priorities.

Aid

It would, of course, be misleading to create the impression that serious and commendable efforts have not been made at national, regional and continental levels by Africans to come to grips with problems of developments. It would also, to be sure, be grossly incorrect to deny that external bodies have made contributions in kind and cash to the efforts to effect change in Africa. Progress has been made in every country on the continent since the era of political independence began about two decades ago. Much of the 1960s witnessed in several parts of Africa efforts at forging political integration in the various heterogeneous communities. The new sovereign polities have provided with varying degrees of success the socio-political framework in which to face the challenges, at times Herculean, of modernisation.

Contemporary African countries are at different stages of growth; this is inevitable because of the disparity in the natural and human resources available to each of them. They also face different challenges, ranging from drought and related ecological problems in the Sahel and elsewhere to migrants and labour, problems of rural development and a host of others. We must note the important role of regional and international organisation and foreign governments in providing both multilateral and bilateral economic assistance and technical aid and advice. At the international level, African countries, like other countries in the world, receive assistance from the World Bank, the Food and Agriculture Organisation (FAO), the World Health Organisation (WHO), the International Labour Organisation (ILO), the United Nations Development Programme (UNDP), and the United Nations Educational, Scientific and Cultural Organisation (UNESCO), to mention only the major ones. At the continental level, the Economic Commission for Africa (ECA) and the African Development Bank (ADB) are the primary promoters of economic advancement and social progress; at the regional level, too, there are organisations designed to foster the trade and economic growth of the member states, prominent among which are the Economic Community of West African States (ECOWAS) and the Customs and Economic Union of Central Africa (UDEAC). There are also organisations aimed at achieving more narrowly focused development goals, such as the sixteenth Permanent Interstate Committee for Drought Control in the Sahel (CILSS), the Lake Chad Basin Commission and so on. The *Ujamaa* system of communal villages in Tanzania which is ideologicaly motivated but rooted in African tradition is an experiment that should be watched for its potential in solving problems of rural development.

Even with all these efforts, laudable as they are, can we say that African leaders and governments are doing enough or doing the right things? What else needs to be done or to be emphasised?

Probable solutions

A comprehensive essay on the solutions to the problems of underdevelopment in Africa would need to take cognisance of each country's peculiar problems. Only guidelines of a general nature are suggested here. It should also be pointed out that this is a subject about which there is a great deal of controversy. It hinges much on ideological beliefs and different models of economic development. However, one fact worth emphasising is that the solution to economic emancipation should not be seen as residing in the hands of the advanced powers: foreign aid cannot solve all the problems. Self-help and self-reliance are the most crucial factors. The developed countries are conscious of the fact that any attempt to liberate the developing countries from their poverty is bound to affect their economic fortunes since they will lose considerable markets and areas for investment. On the other hand, it is pointed out that increasing the aspirations and purchasing power of the Third World will be a boon to the economies of the developed countries and that it is indeed in their economic interest to foster economic development. In any event, the unequal and asymmetric economic relationship between members of the Third World and the economically developed countries must change, otherwise the situation of dependence may remain indefinitely.

Both human and natural resources, however few, have to be fully exploited. To do this effectively, people have to be trained and effectively mobilised. Proper and widespread education and the awareness of a common goal furnish at least part of the answer. Under-education is a great handicap; so also is education not deliberatley designed to suit the purpose of each country. To imitate the educational pattern of the developed countries is to produce students who may not fit into the African programme for rapid development.

Agriculture has to be given priority. To concentrate on industrialisation to the neglect of agriculture is to complicate the problem, because the developing countries will then have to rely solely on the industrialised nations for the necessary equipment with which to take off and develop. The majority of the population still belong to the agricultural sector and the best way to raise their standard of living is to concentrate on agriculture. The establishment of big industries in the urban centres is capital intensive – that is, it can only absorb relatively few people; moreover, it may accelerate the drift to the urban areas with the result that the rural areas will suffer from neglect when it comes to the distribution of social amenities. Concentration on agriculture is likely to promote a more even economic development. The Chinese approach, which makes agriculture the foundation of the economy, should be emulated. Agriculture contributed immensely to the industrialisation of the United Kingdom, Australia, Japan and the United States.

It is true that there is a great need for financial resources, but the ultimate solution lies not in aid but in domestic saving and trade. Capital has to be created internally through voluntary and compulsory savings and by concentrating on what the people can produce to conserve capital and encourage investment. They have to rely less and less on imported food items and luxuries. Emphasis has to shift from prestige projects and wasteful spending to what can benefit the majority. Both the governed and the governors must be willing to make sacrifices by surrendering part of their conspicuous consumption.

It may be neccessary to adapt technological innovations from other parts of the world to local economic systems. This need not be expensive equipment but simple tools with which to make import-substitution a reality, especially in the realm of consumer goods.

On top of all this a peaceful political climate is essential, because without this efforts at development are likely to prove futile. Perhaps a blueprint is needed of goals that will command popular acceptance. This may make it possible to identify the wishes and aspirations of the people with the policies of their respective governments and may lead to the emergence of an informed public opinion among the citizens of the African states. If their governments really succeeded in building a public opinion solidly in support of their policies, African countries would gain the confidence to execute their economic and social development programmes and render services that would benefit the majority of their people.

Notes

1 Bede Onuoha, *The elements of African socialism,* London, Deutsch, 1965, pp. 24–5

2 'Going down to the people: barefoot doctors in conversation', *IDRC Reports,* Ottawa, International Development Research Centre, 4, (1), 1974, 7

3 S. O. Osoba, 'The Nigerian power elite, 1952–65', in *African social studies: a radical reader,* Peter C. W. Gutkind and Peter Waterman (eds.), London, Heinemann, 1977, p. 377

Questions for discussion

1 What are the characteristic socio-economic differences between advanced and underdeveloped countries? Illustrate your answer with concrete examples.

2 Can the developing countries ultimately become developed? What factors can bring this about?

3 Account for the economic underdevelopment of most countries in Africa.

4 To what extent can we blame the industrialised countries of the world for the underdevelopment of the African continent?

5 What are the social and economic implications of uncontrolled population growth?

Suggestions for further reading

Gill, Richard T. *Economic development: past and present,* Englewood Cliffs, New Jersey, Prentice-Hall, 1967

Goody, Jack. *Technology, tradition and the state in Africa,* New York, Oxford University Press, 1971

Gutkind, Peter C. W., and Wallerstein, Immanuel (eds). *The political economy of contemporary Africa,* Beverley Hills: Sage, 1976

Lloyd, Peter C. *Africa in social change,* Penguin Books, 1971

Myint, H. *The economics of the developing countries,* London, Hutchinson University Library, 1974

Narkse, Ragner. *Problems of capital formation in underdeveloped countries,* London, Oxford University Press, 1953

Onyemelukwe, C. C. *Economic underdevelopment: an inside view,* Longman, 1974

Rodney, Walter. *How Europe underdeveloped Africa,* Dar es Salaam, Tanzania Publishing House, 1972

Seidman, Ann. *Planning for development in sub-Saharan Africa,* New York, Praeger, 1974

Uppal, J. S., and Salkever, L. R. (eds). *Africa: problems in economic development,* New York, Free Press, 1973

8   Pan-Africanism and the Organisation of African Unity

S. O. Arifalo

How it all began

Pan-Africanism had its origins as a movement of intellectual protest against ill-treatment of blacks all over the world. It was initiated by the blacks of America and the West Indies whose ancestors came from Africa. In the words of Professor George Shepperson, 'Pan-Africanism was a gift of the New World of America to the Old World of Africa.'[1] It was an expression of the feelings of the people of African stock about their condition of helplessness and degradation.

Three inter-related factors lay behind the various resistance movements and organisations which attempted to restore the dignity and status of Africans in Africa as well as those of the diaspora, who have sought to rise from centuries of dehumanisation which began with the transatlantic slave trade. Thus the slave trade may be seen as the first factor in point of time. Hence, Pan-Africanism has been described as a delayed boomerang from the era of slavery. European colonisation in Africa was the second. Race-consciousness emanating from the first two factors was the third of the fundamental factors which propelled Africans at home and abroad to rebel against the conduct of the Western Europeans. Negatively, then, Pan-Africanism was a cry of revolt against slavery and racial discrimination. Positively, it stood for unity, solidarity and co-operation among the oppressed blacks of the world. Colin Legum summarises the situation this way:

> The emotional impetus for its Pan-Africanism concepts flowed from the experience of a widely dispersed people – those of African stock who felt themselves either physically through dispossession or slavery, or socially through colonialism, to have lost their homeland; with this loss came enslavement, persecution, inferiority, discrimination and dependency.[2]

At first the idea of Pan-Africanism was expressed in poems and songs popularly called 'Negro spirituals'. Before 1900 the movement remained a vague aspiration and a dream. But gradually it crystallised into a dynamic ideology for socio-politcal action.

The initiative was taken by Henry Sylvester Williams,[3] a West Indian who had come into contact with many West Africans in Britain during his undergraduate days and as legal adviser to West African chiefs coming to Britain over land disputes. It is thought that it was he who coined the word 'Pan-African'.

In the United States, one of the most articulate exponents of Pan-Africanism was W. E. B. Du Bois,[4] a black American. He played a major role in the Pan-African Conference of 1900 and continued his efforts to organise the leaders of the black world. A prolific writer, Du Bois edited *The Crisis* for nearly twenty-five years (1910-34). This was the popular journal of the National Association for the Advancement of Coloured People in the United States. Du Bois planned to educate the blacks about the hopeless conditions of the black world and to protest against white exploitation of the black people of the world. He convened four Pan-African congresses (1919, 1921, 1923, 1927).[5]

Another early leader of the Pan-African movement was Marcus Garvey,[6] a Jamaican. He held that the future of the blacks in the New World lay in their return to Africa. He appeared on the Pan-African scene in 1916. Garvey had travelled extensively in the West Indies and in Central and South America where he vigorously protested against white exploitation. He also spent two years in England agitating against racial injustice. Garvey believed that the blacks should move beyond self-help programmes and develop economic, political and military influence at an international level. He organised the Universal Negro Improvement Association, which had branches throughout the black world. The Association awakened black consciousness in many places. Garvey's newspaper, *The Negro World,* a weekly which was published in English, French and Spanish, reached out into West, Central and South Africa, where it made a great impact. Kwame Nkrumah stated that Garvey's philosophy and opinions influenced him more than anything else during his stay in the United States of America. Garvey organised many businesses and cultural and social groups in an attempt to make the black independent of the white. George Padmore also belonged to this group. Born in Trinidad, Padmore began his career in Pan-Africanism in 1934-5. With his dynamic personality he exerted a tremendous influence upon the young African and Afro-West Indian intelligentsia in the period between 1935 and 1958 by means of articles, lectures, contributions to discussions, and books. He has been described as 'the theorist, propagandist, organiser, co-ordinator and first amateur historian of Pan-Africanism'.[7]

The 1900 Pan-African Conference and the early congresses

The first phase of the Pan-African movement began in July 1900 at a meeting in London. It was presided over by Bishop Alexander Walters, with a Liberian ex-Attorney-General and Benito Sylvain, A.D.C. to Emperor Menelik of Abyssinia (Ethiopia), as Vice-Chairman.

Thirty-two delegates attended the Conference, representing the United States of America, Canada, Ethiopia, Haiti, Liberia, Sierra Leone, the Gold Coast (now Ghana), and most of the islands of the British West Indies. On the whole, Africa was poorly represented. Most of those who represented Africa were students living in England and they had not been delegated by anybody.

The aims of the Conference were:

(a) To bring into closer touch with one another the peoples of African descent throughout the world;

(b) To inaugurate plans to bring about a more friendly relationship between the Caucasian and African races;

(c) To start a movement looking forward to the securing to all African races living in 'civilised countries' their full rights and to promote their business interest.[8]

Although these aims were unobjectionable, they were limited in scope and had nothing to do with self-determination for the Africans then or in the future. The aims were assimilationist, and Africa did not seem to be of direct and special concern to the convenors of the Conference.

One important result of the Conference was the appeal 'To the Nations of the World',[9] written by Du Bois as Chairman of the Committee of Address. The appeal widened the original scope of the conference from Pan-Negroism to a Pan-Coloured Peoples' Movement in its declaratory part. In its practical part, in a memorial to Queen Victoria of England, it is strictly sub-Saharan in content, demanding no more than moderate reforms for Southern Africa, including Rhodesia. The appeal made little or no impression on the European imperialists who controlled the destiny of Africa.

Another practical result of the Conference was the transformation of the former African Association to a Pan-African Association with officers elected for the central body and for as many national or regional bodies as possible. The central headquarters was located in London.

These early efforts may seem premature, but a beginning had been made. The name 'Pan-African' was coined and given currency. For the first time, the various elements of nineteenth-century anti-colonial and anti-racial movements were brought together in a public demonstration. The symbolic value of Ethiopia, Haiti and Liberia as independent nations was recognised.

The First Pan-African Congress was held in Paris in February 1919.[10] Du Bois, who was in Paris to handle complaints of racial discrimination against American coloured troops stationed in France and to try to look after the interests of Africa in general during the peace conference after the First World War, had seized the opportunity to organise the congress. Fifty-seven delegates were present.

Although the immediate results were meagre, yet the Congress was important because for the first time French-speaking Africans and blacks from the Caribbean were brought together. However, this success was more apparent than real because most of the French-speaking participants were Caribbeans, and only Blaise Diagne, from Senegal, was an African. The French-speaking participants from the Caribbean identified themselves so much with French colonialism that they were thoroughly despised by the few African students and young African intellectuals who came to Paris from French-speaking Africa.

The Second Pan-African Congress was convened by Du Bois in 1921. It took place in successive sessions in London, Brussels and Lisbon. This time more than one-third of the participants came from

Fig. 8.1 *Founders of the Pan-African Congress movement: Henry Sylvester Williams (above), W. E. B. Du Bois (below)*

Africa itself. Forty-one out of a total of one hundred and thirteen members came from the United States and only seven from the West Indies. There were twenty-four Africans and Americans living in Europe at the conference.

As usual, the major resolution passed at the end of the conference was a 'Declaration to the World'. In it Du Bois made the memorable statement: 'The beginning of wisdom in inter-racial contact is the establishment of political institutions among suppressed peoples. The habit of democracy must be made to encircle the world.'[11] The resolution came out boldly for the recognition of the principle of racial equality, without denying any differences in the level of development. It went beyond the demands of the first congress by asking for sovereignty for Africans in their own continent.

The Third Pan-African Congress met in late November and early December 1923 in London and Lisbon. Its scope was much narrower than that of its predecessors. Eleven countries were represented. The African participants came mainly from Sierra Leone, the Gold Coast and Nigeria.

Reiterating earlier resolutions, the most important political demand was that Africans should be allowed to have a voice in their own government. It would appear that the enthusiasm which characterised the earlier congresses had evaporated. The apparent failure of this congress can be attributed to a number of factors. The organisation set up by the Second Pan-African Congress was suffering from a chronic shortage of funds. Du Bois and some of the officials of the movement were preoccupied with intrigues and quarrels over the printing of a constitution and the setting up of a permanent secretariat. There was also a failure in communication between the Francophone and Anglophone groups in the movement.

The Fourth Pan-African Congress took place in New York in 1927. It came about only because of the initiative of an organisation of black American women. Since there was no new idea or impulse, nothing really serious emerged from the Congress. Discussion centred on the history of Africa, educational problems in Africa, African arts and literature, and Christian missions in Africa.

The 1927 Congress closed a chapter in the history of Pan-Africanism. The movement fell into abeyance and did not regain momentum until the Second World War was about to end. The slump of 1929 destroyed the last chance to carry on. The great struggle for survival in the long years of depression, the rise of Fascism, and the coming of the Second World War in 1939 turned the attention of the blacks in America to other problems. And the young intelligentsia in Africa who were to continue the struggle afterwards were just growing up or studying in black universities in the United States of America.

It must be concluded that the Pan-African movement failed to make any significant contribution to the political education of Africans and peoples of African descent outside Africa. The practical achievements of the congresses were meagre and superficial. They failed to evolve a defined, self-sufficient ideology which might have helped to give Pan-Africanism greater intellectual discipline. Instead, the congresses were dominated to a large extent by emotional lamentations about the sufferings of black people all over the world. However, the movement was not wholly a failure. For the first time Anglophone and Franco-phone elements in Africa had co-operated, particularly in the 1919 congress. Geiss, a German historian of Pan-Africanism, sums up the movement thus: 'The most important result of the four Pan-African Congresses was perhaps simply the fact that they took place at all.'[12] Du Bois himself seems to have been of this mind. 'What has been accomplished?' he asked. 'This: we have kept an idea alive, we have held to a great ideal, we have established a continuity, and some day when unity and cooperation come, the importance of these early steps will be recognised.'[13]

The Fifth Pan-African Conference–Manchester, 1945

In October 1945, the Fifth Pan-African Congress convened in England at Manchester.[14] It was attended by ninety delegates and eleven observers. For the first time, it was a congress of Africa's young, promising leaders. It was the Second World War which had changed everything. The young Africans at the Congress were a collection of unknowns soon to win fame or notoriety and political power in their different countries. Among the delegates some stand out in bold relief: Wallace Johnson, Obafemi Awolowo, H. O. Davies, Jomo Kenyatta, Hastings Banda, Peter Abrahams, J. E. Taylor, Ako Adjei, Mrs Amy Garvey, Jaja Wachukwu, T. R. Makonnen, George Padmore and Kwame Nkrumah. For most of these their careers lay in the future. Many had to spend a time in gaol because of their political commitments. Some became political leaders of their countries.

The increased politicisation of the movement was reflected in the fact that for the first time three political parties were represented: the National Council of Nigeria and the Cameroons (NCNC), the Labour Party of Grenada, and the West Indies People's National Party, the last two from the West Indies. There were also three organisations equivalent to political parties: the Nigerian Youth Movement, the Nyasaland African Congress, and the African National Congress of South Africa. Also present for the first time was a farmers' organisation, the Gold Coast Farmers Association.

The Congress, as usual, passed resolutions dealing with various regions of Africa – Ethiopia, Liberia, South and South West Africa (Namibia) – and with allegations of colour discrimination in Britain and the West Indies. They were summarised in two short and pointed resolutions. The first was 'The challenge to Colonial Powers'. It was a compromise between the revolutionary impatience of Padmore and Nkrumah on the one hand and Du Bois's more cautious and non-violent approach on the other. The resolution says: 'The delegates of the Fifth Pan-African Congress believe in peace . . . Yet if the Western World is still determined to rule mankind by force, then Africans as a last resort, may have to appeal to force in the effort to achieve freedom even if force destroys them and the world.'[15] The second resolution was the 'Declaration to the colonial Workers, Farmers and Intellectuals'. It was drafted by Nkrumah. It expressed the yearnings of the Africans for independence and their opposition to imperial exploitation. The tactics recommended were strikes and boycotts, methods learned from the struggles against British rule in India.

Apart from the resolutions there were expressions of solidarity with others then fighting imperialism and colonialism, including the Vietnamese, the Indonesians and the Indians. The Congress also sent a message to the blacks in America supporting their struggles and affirming the link between those struggles and the liberation of Africa.

The 1945 Manchester Congress was another landmark in the history both of Pan-Africanism and of anti-colonialism. So far as Pan-Africanism was concerned, it was the first evidence of life after a lull of about two decades. Pan-Africanism had to a large extent emancipated itself both politically and socially. The days of dependence upon the thinking and direction of their European friends who had so often let them down were gone. Henceforth Pan-Africanism would not seek moral and political support from outsiders. The 1945 Manchester Congress did not ask for recognition or favours from the European powers. It unequivocally demanded an end to colonialism in Africa. It demanded social justice and rights. All schemes of half freedom were rejected. As Nnamdi Azikiwe later declared:

> The Congress . . . marked the turning point in Pan-Africanism from a passive to an active stage. The obvious transmutation in the character of the movement was precipitated by war. Those years brought a new kind of awareness to many old and young African leaders of the indignities suffered by the black man everywhere and especially in his own home in Africa. The time was ripe for positive action.[16]

The Manchester Congress gave an impetus to the efforts being made to achieve the goal of national independence. It served as a pacemaker of decolonisation in Africa and the West Indies. In the words of Peter Worsley:

> From then on, Pan-Africa nationalism was to spurt forward with such speed that the first comprehensive statement of its tenets, George Padmore's *Pan-Africanism or Communism?* only appeared a year before Ghana's independence.[17]

The masses were to be organised through trade unions and political parties. By those resolutions Pan-Africanism had reached the parting of ways with gradualism and resignation. Kwame Nkrumah, who was joint political Secretary of the Congress along with Padmore had this to say:

> We shot into limbo those African intellectuals who were gradualists, expressing the more total demand of workers, trade unionists, farmers and peasants who were decisively represented at Manchester and we breached imperialism's wall.[18]

The complexion of Pan-Africanism had changed for ever. From now on it was going to be African-based. African nationalism would replace Negro nationalism. From now on Europe would see so more Pan-African congresses. They would now be held on African soil.

Pan-Africanism in Africa

The next milestone in the history of Pan-Africanism was the 1958 All-African Peoples' Conference held in Accra, Ghana.[19] Between the Manchester Congress of 1945 and 1958 a lot of water had flowed under the bridge in Africa. Many historical events had enabled Pan-Africanism to expand its scope and assume a more continental outlook. These included the expansion of the Negritude philosophy; the Egyptian revolution (1952-3); the Algerian revolution, which began in 1954; the independence of Ghana in 1957; and the independence of Guinea in 1958.

It may be useful to make a brief comment on each of these developments. Léopold Sédar Senghor, President of the Republic of Senegal, the leading exponent of Negritude, has described the term as the sum total of the African social, political and cultural values of African civilisation.[20] In the past, the French had justified cultural assimilation on the erroneous premise that Africans had neither history nor culture of their own. Negritude is essentially a reaction against the French theory of assimilation. In 1947 Senghor and a fellow Senegalese, Alione Diop, founded *Présence Africaine,* a magazine devoted to the revival of African values. This philosophy of Negritude influenced African leaders like Nkrumah. The expansion of the Negritude conception through *Présence Africaine* was demonstrated in the Congress of African Writers and Artists held in Paris in 1956. The Congress itself broke the traditional language barrier between English and French-speaking Africa.

On 23 July 1952, a group of young army officers seized power in Egypt. They were led by Colonel Abdul Nasser, but used an older man, General Neguib, as a figure-head. The main preoccupation of the Egyptian Government under Nasser, who ousted Neguib in 1954, was not with Africa, but with Arab unity and solidarity: he did emphasise, however, that Egypt could not keep aloof from African liberation struggles. The emergence of Egypt as a radical force was a factor which affected French policy in North Africa. France and other Western European powers were embarrassed by the anti-imperialist propaganda which Egypt poured out through its radio and newspapers.[21]

The nationalist organisation in Algeria, the *Front de Libération Nationale,* began the Algerian rebellion in November 1954.[22] The Algerian revolution soon became a positive symbol of the Pan-African movement.

The independence of Ghana in 1957 had an electrifying impact throughout Africa. A modern Negro government, under a dynamic and charismatic leader, had emerged to demonstrate that, in fact, Africans could manage their own affairs. This is what Nkrumah had to say:

> Freedom for the Gold Coast will be the fountain of inspiration from which other African colonial territories can draw when the time comes to strike for their freedom.[23]

When Guinea, under the leadership of Sékou Touré, chose independence in 1958, France reacted immediately by withdrawing her civil servants and technicians and by stopping all economic aid to the country.

Nkrumah offered Guinea a loan of ₦20 million. Ghana and Guinea soon declared the formation of a Union.[24] This gesture of solidarity ended Ghana's isolated position in black Africa. (Guinea also received aid, probably of a more realistic kind, from Communist governments in Europe and Asia).

The All-African Peoples' Conference of December 1958 in Accra was unique in certain ways. The Conference of Independent African States which was held in April of the same year, also in Accra, was attended only by the eight independent states of Africa: Ethiopia (1040 B.C.), Liberia (1847), Egypt (1922), Libya (1951), Morocco (1956), the Sudan (1956) and Tunisia (1956). But the All-African Peoples' Conference was attended by delegates representing political parties, trade unions, women and youth organisations from twenty-eight African countries, most of which were still colonies. It was the first genuine all-African assembly, because Francophone black Africa was represented as well as the Arab lands of North Africa, the East African countries and the Congo (Zaire). It was organised by George Padmore, the West Indian who was then Nkrumah's adviser on African affairs.[25] The Conference also served to accelerate the movement towards independence in the Congo, from which three representatives, including Patrice Lumumba, had come. Before the Accra Conference Pan-Africanism remained in the realm of ideas and rhetoric. The conference placed itself in the Pan-African tradition and has been described as the Sixth Pan-African Congress. In the words of V. B. Thompson, the Conference 'was raising again the torch of Pan-Africanism which had been neatly hidden away from the Pan-African Congress in Manchester in 1945. It emphasised continuity.'[26]

The All-African People's Conference stated its aims and objectives as follows:

(i) To promote understanding and unity among people of Africa.
(ii) To accelerate the liberation of Africa from imperialism and colonialism.
(iii) To mobilise world opinion against the denial of political rights and fundamental human rights to Africans.
(iv) To develop the feeling of one community among the peoples of Africa with the object of enhancing the emergence of a United States of Africa.[27]

Even though the African leaders were agreed in principle on those aims and objectives, yet they differed in their proposed methods. By no means were all of them prepared for the submergence of the sovereignty of their countries. This problem was soon compounded by the Congo crisis. The year 1960 has been described as 'the year of Africa' because, at one great sweep, about half the continent became politically independent. However, it was also the year of the first of a series of major setbacks for Pan-Africanism. It was the year of the first Congo crisis, a crisis that split the continent into ideological blocs. The Congo became independent on 30 June 1960. Within a week of independence, the Congolese Army — the *Force Publique* — revolted, largely against the Belgian officers who were still in command and the Congolese Government which accepted the situation. In the confusion, mineral-rich Katanga Province under Moise Tshombe seceded. Belgian troops immediately invaded the Congo, ostensibly to protect Belgian citizens in the areas under the control of the Central Government, but the Belgian troops actually landed in Katanga Province. The Congolese Government thereupon appealed to the United Nations for troops, which were sent. The troops sent by the United Nations came in part from some African states. The United Nations command hindered rather than helped attempts by the Congolese Army, nominally under the control of the Central Government, to restore the authority of the Central Government in Katanga Province.

During the months of July and August 1960, law and order completely broke down in the Congo and confusion reigned supreme. Two factions of the Central Government emerged. One was led by the Prime Minister, Patrice Lumumba, and the other by President Joseph Kasavubu. Early in September Kasavubu dismissed Lumumba who challenged the legality of that action. The Congolese Army under Colonel Joseph Mobutu, who had ousted his superior officer, proclaimed its neutrality, but soon dismissed Parliament and arrogated power to itself in collaboration with Kasavubu.

Independent African states were divided over the question as to whether Lumumba or Kasavubu represented the legal Central Government in the Congo. Behind the constitutional problems of the Congo lay certain fundamental issues which divided Africa. On the one side were the African states who thought that the attainment of political independence was just a minor step in a more basic and revolutionary thrust for African liberation. This group of states advocated an organic political unification of African states. It believed that political independence had little meaning unless it was accompanied by 'economic independence'. Therefore, African states should totally reject neo-colonial links with their former colonial masters and the Western European capitalist states. This school of thought was led by Ghana and Guinea, who supported Patrice Lumumba. In the parallel debate on the Algerian war of independence, this group supported the cause of the Provisional Government of the Algerian Republic, known by its French initials as GPRA. The group was labelled 'the radicals'. It announced the formation of the Ghana–Guinea–Mali Union in April 1961. The union was designed as the nucleus of a West African and ultimately an African continental union. But the union was a fiasco, beset with problems which it could not solve.

On the other side were the African states who based their argument on a quite different premise. They held that because many African states were small and weak they needed assistance from the Western world in order to make economic progress. They advocated a pragmatic approach to African unity beginning with the co-ordination of effort in every field, including foreign affairs, economic development, health and education. They thought African political union to be a utopian goal. Instead of breaking economic ties with the West they wished to reinforce and expand them. This group particularly emphasised the need for the continued preservation of political sovereignty and condemned any outside interference in the internal affairs of their nations. It supported

136

Kasavubu and was conciliatory towards France in the Algerian liberation struggle. This group of states later became known as 'the moderates' and was led by Nigeria and Liberia.

The split between the African countries soon assumed institutional form when 'the radicals' (Ghana, Guinea, Mali, Egypt, Algeria, represented by the GPRA, and Morocco) held their conference in Casablanca in January 1961 and became known as 'the Casablanca Powers'.[28] The group adopted an African charter which advocated the creation of an African Consultative Assembly. It also decided on the creation of an African Political Committee, an African Economic Committee, an African Cultural Committee and an African High Command.

Shortly after the Casablanca Conference, in May 1961 'the moderates' held their own conference in Monrovia. The conference was attended by Nigeria, Liberia, Ivory Coast, Cameroons, Togo, Senegal, the Malagasy Republic, Gabon, Ethiopia, Sierra Leone, Somalia, the Central African Republic, Mauritania, Niger, Libya, Upper Volta, Tunisia and Congo (Brazzaville). The conference condemned South Africa for its racial policies. Referring to the Congo, the conference then condemned assassination as a means of attaining political power. The conference agreed that a commission of technical experts for the purpose of working out plans for co-operation in economic, educational, cultural and scientific fields should meet at Dakar, Senegal, within three months of the Monrovia Conference.[29] This group, which became known as 'the Monrovia Powers', accepted the basic principles of unity and stressed the right of the independent states of Africa to federate or confederate. In spite of the apparant similarities in the decisions taken by the two conferences, the cleavage remained.

The next attempt to find a concept of African unity acceptable to the leaders of the independent countries of Africa was in Lagos in January 1962. 'The Casablanca Powers' intimated their intention to attend but did not turn up after a meeting of their foreign ministers in Accra. The reasons given were that they had not been consulted as a group and that the Algerian Provisional Government had not been invited to the conference.[30] The delegates of the Sudan and Tunisia also walked out of the conference in protest against the non-recognition of and failure to invite the Algerian Provisional Government.[31] The Lagos Conference, attended by twenty-one independent African states, confirmed the decisions of the Monrovia Conference. These African states declared that they were all 'desirous that all African states should henceforth unite so that the welfare and well-being of their peoples can be assured' and were also 'determined to safeguard and consolidate the hard won independence as well as the sovereignty and territorial integrity of our states, and to fight against neo-colonialism in all its forms'.[32]

The Conference adopted, in principle, a charter for a proposed African United Organisation. The charter was to be submitted to all African governments for detailed study. However, the Conference deliberately refrained from formally setting up the organisation so that the countries not represented could still join as inaugural members at a later meeting.

Meanwhile the search for African unity continued. In 1963 the venerable Emperor Haile Selassie of Ehtiopia tried to bring together the heads of all independent African states and reconcile their divergent views on African unity. His diplomatic efforts proved an unqualified success because of three significant developments. The first of these was the internal reconciliation in the Congo. Lumumba had fallen into the hands of the Kasavubu government and in January 1961 was turned over to the Katangese authorities who murdered him. The Lumumbists then set up a rival government in Stanleyville. However, in August the two claimants to the Central Government in the Congo – the Kasavubu faction in Léopoldville and the Lumumbists in Stanleyville – agreed to a united government under Cyrille Adoula as Prime Minister. Thus Congolese sovereignty was re-established. The second was the Evian Accord,[33] which led to the independence of Algeria in July 1962. Thirdly, the Anglo-Nigerian Defence Pact which was signed at the time of Nigeria's independence was abrogated because it was regarded as a commitment detracting from Nigeria's sovereignty.[34] With the removal of these issues, the Addis Ababa Conference organised by Haile Selassie in May 1963 and attended by thirty-two African countries was able to give birth to the Organisation of African Unity (OAU). This brought together the two groups – the 'Casablanca' and the 'Monrovia' Powers.

The Organisation of African Unity (OAU)

The document signed at Addis Ababa on 25 May 1963 by the thirty-two heads of state was a medley of ideas and provisions borrowed mainly from the charters of the United Nations Organisation, the Organisation of American States and the Monrovia Powers. The preamble to the charter of the OAU reaffirms the principles of the United Nations and of the Universal Declaration of Human Rights. The purposes of the OAU are spelt out in its charter.

1. The Organisation shall have the following purposes:
   (a) to promote the unity and solidarity of the African states,
   (b) to co-ordinate and intensify their co-operation and efforts to achieve a better life for the peoples of Africa,
   (c) to defend their sovereignty, their territorial integrity and independence,
   (d) to eradicate all forms of colonialism from Africa, and,
   (e) to promote international co-operation having due regard to the charter of the United Nations and the Universal Declaration of Human Rights.
2. To these ends, the member states shall co-ordinate and harmonise their general policies, especially in the following fields:
   (a) political and diplomatic co-operation,
   (b) economic co-operation, including transport and communications,
   (c) respect for the sovereignty and territorial integrity of each state and for its inalienable right to independent existence,
   (d) peaceful settlement of disputes by negotiation, mediation, conciliation or arbitration,

(e) unreserved condemnation in all its forms, of all political assassination as well as of subversive activities on the part of neighbouring states or any other states,

(f) absolute dedication to the total emancipation of the African territories which are still dependent. [35]

The question may now be asked, how far has the OAU succeeded in fulfilling its purposes and principles? The OAU has been criticised and even derided by enemies of Africa. It has been said that the OAU can bark but cannot bite. The organisation is almost twenty years old. In that time much could have been achieved. But like any other human organisation it had its teething troubles. The degree of economic and organisational unity it has achieved is praiseworthy. It is true that it has failed to perform the miracle of forming a continental government. Therefore, in assessing the activities of the OAU we must bear in mind the great diversities in Africa: language, culture, history, level of economic development, social development, political and educational development. One must not forget the problems created by neocolonialism. Therefore there is need for understanding and for objectivity.

Failures of the OAU

The OAU has had many setbacks. Some are trivial, whereas others have had or still have important effects on African states. Ian Smith maintained for years his illegal white minority government in Rhodesia

Fig. 8.2   *OAU Foreign Ministers meeting in the Kenyatta International Conference Centre, Nairobi*

(Zimbabwe), and racial discrimination continues to wax strong in South Africa. The Government of South Africa continues to rule South West Africa (Namibia). There is apparent lack of unanimity among the African states on how best to deal with these and many other problems.

Let us look a little more closely at these issues. When in 1965 Ian Smith declared Zimbabwe independent of Britain (the Unilateral Declaration of Independence), the OAU members were unanimous in condemning this. However, while some African states felt that the initiative in dealing with the situation should be left to Britain, others called for military preparations and requested an emergency meeting of the OAU. At the end of the extraordinary meeting of the Council of Ministers which was held between 3 and 5 December 1965, it was announced that if the rebellion had not been crushed by 15 December, the African states would declare war on Ian Smith's regime, cut all economic exchanges and communication, and break off diplomatic relations with Britain.[36] Although the resolution to break off diplomatic relations with Britain if she did not crush the revolt was taken unanimously, reports from many parts of Africa shortly afterwards indicated reservations. Certainly countries had developed cold feet.[37] As a result of indecisiveness on the part of many OAU member states only ten finally carried out the resolution[38] and Britain remained unperturbed. The Zimbabwe question was raised at almost all subsequent meetings of both the Council of Ministers and the conference of Heads of State and governments, and resolution upon resolution was passed without effect.

The problem of Namibia places the OAU in a great predicament. Namibia, a former German colony, was, without consultation with its people, mandated as a trust territory to South Africa at the end of World War I. When the United Nations superseded the League of Nations in 1946, all other former trust territories came under the United Nations trusteeship system. However, South Africa refused to place Namibia under the United Nations trusteeship system. Since that time South Africa has tried to incorporate the territory into the Union of South Africa and has continued to propagate her apartheid policy there. Her blunt refusal to comply with the withdrawal of the mandate and her promotion of apartheid in that territory have caused widespread concern in Africa. Liberia and Ethiopia have jointly brought legal proceedings against South Africa before the International Court of Justice for violating the terms of the 1920 mandate by pursuing policies of apartheid and racial discrimination in the territory. When the court gave its ruling in 1966, it was to the effect that neither Ethiopia nor Liberia could be considered to have established any legal right or interest in the case.[39] Since then, although the United Nations has taken steps to bring Namibia under its direct supervision, South Africa has refused to comply with the decision. The Security Council brought a fresh action against South Africa before the World Court. The Court in its ruling in 1971 declared that South Africa was under an obligation to withdraw from Namibia. Yet South Africa remains as obdurate as ever. The much-talked about African High Command has not been formed to chase out the South African Government from Namibia.

The problem of South Africa itself remains unsolved. In an attempt to find a just solution the Pan-African Conference of May 1963 concentrated on the situation in South Africa. At the end of the discussions all independent African states which were represented agreed to co-ordinate and intensify their efforts to terminate South Africa's apartheid policy and wipe out racial discrimination in all its forms. This was a mere paper resolution. No effective action has so far been taken against South Africa other than launching ever-new appeals to the world powers, while some Western powers continue to supply arms to South Africa secretly in defiance of the United Nations embargo.

The Pan-African movement itself has not presented a united front over South Africa. There was the concept of 'dialogue' with South Africa which was propounded by Houphouet-Boigny of Ivory Coast and supported by Banda of Malawi and Busia of Ghana. Other African states vehemently opposed any compromise with South Africa. In recent times a South African Prime Minister, Vorster, paid secret visits to some African countries, and some African leaders have also visited South Africa. This situation tends to destroy attempts to bring about united action amongst African countries. As if these contacts with South Africa were not serious enough, some African countries have been receiving financial assistance from South Africa.[40] Since 1966 Malawi has been having secret contacts with the South African Government in an effort to secure a loan for some of her development projects.[41] Soon after a trade agreement was signed, South Africa offered financial and material assistance to Malawi for the installation of her radio transmitters. Malawi reciprocated by opening diplomatic relations with South Africa. South Africa later offered to make substantial contributions towards the building of Malawi's proposed capital at Lilongwe. In addition to this, South Africa's Industrial Development Corporation volunteered to construct a railway line linking Malawi with northern Mozambique. This project is said to have cost the corporation £6 400 000 (₦12 800 000). It is no surprise then that Malawi has persistently disagreed with the OAU stand on South Africa's apartheid policy. Other African states such as Gabon, Ivory Coast and Malagasy have also received substantial financial and material aid from South Africa.[42] This has weakened both the OAU and the resolution of some of its members.

Many of the young states of Africa have suffered from instability. A series of coups and counter-coups has taken place during the first decade of their independence. Nigeria has had three *coups d'états*. Dahomey (now Benin) probably holds the record of instability. Since 1960, when she became an autonomous state, there have been five constitutions, ten presidents – five of them civilian and five military – and six military take-overs.[43] Secessionist plots have caused serious civil wars in Zaire, Nigeria and Ethiopia.[44] This instability has made it possible for foreign powers to interfere in the internal affairs of African states.

Lack of funds is one of the most important reasons why the efforts to help the liberation movements in Africa have not yielded the desired results. The ₦4 to 6 million received annually from the OAU by liberation movements to purchase arms is inadequate, since their present requirements amount to about ₦500 million. Many of the OAU members are too poor to balance their annual budgets. Only a few OAU member states have honoured their pledges to provide the much-needed financial support for the liberation movements in Africa. It would appear that Zambia and Tanzania have been left to bear most of the burden of supporting liberation movements.

The OAU has been found wanting on other matters affecting the welfare of Africa. For example, the turn of events during the 1976 Angolan civil war exposed the fundamental weakness of the organisation. With forty-six member countries the organisation was unable to take effective steps to prevent a civil war that threatened to destroy not only one of the potentially wealthiest countries in Africa but also the solidarity of the organisation itself. This glaring impotence of the OAU encouraged non-African countries like Cuba and even South Africa to intervene in the war with impunity.

Certain aspects of the constitutional organisation of the OAU are defective. It has to rely on the willing co-operation of member states. No provisions have been made for sanctions to enforce any decisions or resolutions. Even the payment of contributions is voluntary. The OAU does not possess any sanction comparable to Article 19 of the United Nations Charter providing for the loss of voting rights by members who fail to pay their dues on time. Because of these shortcomings any member state of the organisation can defy any of its decisions with impunity. This partly explains why some members of the OAU publicly proclaimed their support of the Eritrean secessionists in Ethiopia while the majority was in support of a united Ethiopia including Eritrea. In the same way Tanzania violated the OAU principle of non-interference in the internal affairs of member states when it sent its 'Peoples Defence Force' (its army) to overthrow Idi Amin in Uganda. Paradoxically, on the same principle the OAU folded its arms while Idi Amin was committing atrocities in Uganda. One cannot but agree with Padelford when he writes: 'The instruments (of the OAU) are designed to promote cooperation not to exact it, to urge collaboration, not to punish for its refusal.'[45] The members of the OAU are now well aware of the urgent need for reform of its charter. At its 1979 Monrovia Conference it set up a committee to draft a Declaration of Human Rights which all member states would be compelled to ratify. The same committee was also to consider the much talked of Pan-African Defence Force.[46]

Achievements of the OAU

The most significant achievements of the Pan-African movement before 1963 was perhaps the spirit of mutual commitment which began to manifest itself in the political, social and cultural life of Africans. Any event which touched any part of Africa was viewed with concern by large sections of the African community. For instance, events such as the Italian invasion of Ethiopia in 1935, the trial of the leaders of Mau Mau in Kenya, the Suez crisis of 1956 and the Algerian war of independence all invoked interest in African countries which had no direct involvement. The murder of Patrice Lumumba in 1961 was received with dismay in many parts of Africa. Yet with the birth of the OAU in 1963 a new era began for Pan-Africanism. Deliberate efforts began to be made to bring about economic, political, social and educational co-operation. The spirit of brotherhood and friendship grew stronger.

In international relations, border conflicts have been causes of friction and even of wars between nations. Such conflicts have led to explosive situations in Africa, particularly over the boundaries inherited from the European imperialists. Boundary disputes have been the causes of wars between Algeria and Morocco and between Somalia and Ethiopia, and have led to a series of raids along the border between Uganda and Tanzania, Senegal and Guinea. It was also a boundary dispute that strained the relations between Niger and Dahomey. In almost all these cases the OAU stepped in to mediate between the warring parties. Its intervention led to the cessation of hostilities and to the normalisation of relations between the parties concerned. In fact the OAU has solved more border disputes in the last decade than the United Nations itself.

As far as mediation between African states is concerned, the OAU has performed creditably. Under the auspices of the organisation, President Hamani Diori of Niger successfully mediated in the dispute between Chad and the Sudan in 1966. President Mobutu Sese Seko of Zaire was delegated by the OAU to mediate in the dispute between Burundi and Rwanda. Mediation was also the weapon used in 1966 when some Guinean diplomats and students were detained in Ghana. President William Tubman of Liberia was called upon by the OAU to settle the serious dispute which arose from the detention of the crew of a fishing boat from the Ivory Coast who were charged with attempting to kidnap the deposed Ghanaian President Nkrumah in February 1967.

The Nigerian civil war (1967–71) brought about one of the most difficult problems ever faced by the OAU. The organisation saw the war as an African problem and treated it as such. During the war the organisation regularly preached unity and tried to mediate between Gowon and Ojukwu under the leadership of the Emperor of Ethiopia. It initiated peace meetings in Kinshasa in 1967, in Kampala in 1968, in Niamey in July and September 1968, and in Algiers also in September 1968.[47] Although the efforts of the OAU were as unsuccessful as those of other organisations, it was evident that African countries felt genuinely concerned. However, after nine months of fighting, President Kaunda of Zambia and President Nyerere of Tanzania stepped out of line by recognising the government of Biafra. They said that even though they believed in unity, a people should not be forced to remain as part of a political entity to which they did not feel loyalty.

In providing military assistance to one another, the OAU member countries were not found wanting. On 20 January 1964, the First Battalion of Tanganyika (Tanzania) Africa Rifles mutinied at Tolito, near Dar es Salaam. The mutiny began a chain of events which spread to Uganda on 23 January, and to Kenya on 24 January. The very existence of these states was then threatened. Because of the seriousness of the muntiny, the governments of all three countries appealed to Britain for military assistance. British troops were rushed in to take over from the soldiers who were demobilised immediately. This request embarrassed the OAU members who realised the implications of the presence of British troops in these independent African countries. The OAU Council of Ministers met in Dar es Salaam from 12 to 15 February, and adopted a resolution to replace the British troops with troops from African countries. Nigeria sent a battalion of five hundred troops, and Ethiopia sent airman. These forces were to stay in Tanzania until the crisis was over and a new Tanzanian army trained.

One of the most outstanding achievements of the OAU in the economic field has been the establishment of the African Development Bank (ADB) in 1964 with the government of twenty-two independent states as members.[48] It had a capital of some $300 million. Twelve years after its establishment, the capital stock has increased by more than 300 per cent and now stands at $960 million. Its membership increased from twenty-two to forty-six. The main purpose of the bank is to contribute to the economic and social development of its member countries both individually and severally. In order to achieve this objective, the bank encourages the investment of public and private capital in Africa. The bank uses its own resources to make or guarantee loans. It also encourages private investment in member countries. It encourages these countries to make better use of their resources by making their projects complementary and by providing technical assistance in the preparation, financing and implementation of development plans. It is also promoting an international private finance company which is to make capital, entrepreneurship and management expertise available to enterprises in African states.

Since the ADB began its operations in 1967 it has financed more than 110 projects in about forty African states. For instance, it has taken part in financing the 1 250-mile long railway which runs from Kampyo in Zambia to Kidatu and Dar es Salaam in Tanzania. In 1968 the bank approved three loans. These were loans for irrigation in Tunisia, for engineering studies and survey of water supply and a sewerage system in Uganda, and a sum of $408 000 to meet part of the cost of the construction of a fertiliser plant in the Ivory Coast.

The ADB mobilises funds from the international private sector for investment in Africa. Some of the projects involve tourism and the timber, textile and cement industries. In 1978 the bank also established a Special Relief Fund to channel aid to areas where disasters occur in Africa. As the most important development agency in the African continent, run entirely by Africans, the bank has initiated continental projects such as the African Re-insurance Corporation with an initial capital of $15 million, the Pan-American Telecommunications network and the Transcontinental Highway.

The ADB group financed seventy projects in 1978 at a total cost of about $425 million in some African states. Also in 1978, considerable sums of money were made available as loans for multi-national projects. These include the Liptoko Gourma telecommunications scheme, which embraces Upper Volta, Mali and Niger, the Accra/Abidjan highway, and the Ghana/Ivory Coast power interconnection. The ADB co-financed nine projects with the other major development and finance institutions to the tune of nearly $760 million in 1978. In the words of *West Africa*:

These records of solid achievements underline the fact that the ADB group is now playing effectively the most important role in the development of the African continent. It is no longer 'a paper and resolution' organisation but a strong pillar of African development process.[49]

Also in the spirit of the OAU, the Economic Community for West African States (ECOWAS) was formed in May 1975 in Lagos.[50] The basic aim of the Community is co-operation and development in all spheres of economic activity – industry, transport, telecommunications, natural resources, commerce, monetary and financial matters, and cultural relations. Sixteen West African states have signed the treaty establishing the organisation. General Ignatius Acheampong, then Ghana's Head of State, expressed the aspirations of the peoples of the West African region when he said:

> By our signature and subsequent ratification of the treaty (establishing the ECOWAS) we have raised in our citizens the vision of a vast, homogeneous society linked together by a complicated network of roads, connected by a direct, efficient and rational system of communications, enriched by a steady flow of commerce and sustained by common ventures in agriculture, industry, energy, mineral resources, and other fields of common activities.[51]

In 1977 the ECOWAS took a big stride forward by establishing the Fund for Co-operation and Development.[52] The fund was intended to finance projects in member states, particularly in the less-developed ones. Compensation to member countries which suffered as a result of the location of community enterprises or from measures of trade liberalisation is to come from the fund. It will also guarantee foreign investment made in member states in pursuance of the treaty provisions for harmonising the internal and external finances of the Community. The headquarters of the ECOWAS was established in Lagos, Nigeria, while that of the fund has been located in Lomé, Togo.[53]

Although the fund has yet to fulfil the aims and objectives of the founders, yet, with the appointment of Dr Romeo Horton, a Pan-Africanist and a renowned economist from Liberia, as its Director-General,[54] it holds much promise for the future advancement of West Africa.[55]

On the international scene the formation of the OAU has enabled African countries to speak with one voice on many world issues. OAU members of the United Nations Organisation have since its formation usually presented a united front on matters of mutual interest to Africa in that world body. Issues which might cause disunity among African states, such as the selection of officers to serve on United Nations' organs, are fully discussed well in advance, and suitable candidates to such posts as fall to Africa are nominated.

The OAU has brought many countries in Africa into closer contact than ever before. Hardly a month passes without an African cultural, economic or diplomatic delegation visiting another African country or an all-African regional conference of one kind or another convening in Africa. The All-African Cultural Conference in Algeria, the Festival of Black Art in Dakar in 1966, the All-African Trade Fair in Nairobi, the Second All-African Games in Lagos in 1973, and the Second World Festival of African Art and Culture (FESTAC 77) held in Lagos in 1977 may be seen as some of the positive achievements of the OAU – and of the Pan-African movement.

Although the organisation has not come to grips with the problems of Eritrea, the western Sahara, Namibia, the Chad Republic and the minority government in South Africa, and although there are still many areas of disagreement among African states, yet it has shown itself capable of doing great things for Africa. The quickening pace of regional economic groupings in different parts of Africa and the positive assertion of the African personality on the international scene are evidence of the Pan-African drive of which the OAU has become the expression.

Notes

1 George Shepperson, 'Notes on Negro-American influence on the emergence of African nationalism', *Journal of African history* 1 (2), 1960, 299-312

2 Colin Legum, *Pan-Africanism: a short political guide,* New York, Frederick A. Praeger, 1965, p. 15

3 J. R. Hooker, 'The Pan-African Conference 1900', *Transition* 36, 9 (iii) (Oct./Dec. 1974), 20-4

4 Robert W. July, *The origins of modern African thought,* Faber and Faber, 1968, pp. 405-06

5 Immanuel Geiss, *The Pan-African movement,* London, Methuen, 1974, pp. 135, 212, 235-58

6 *Ibid.,* pp. 263-83. John Henrik Clarke, 'Marcus Garvey: the Harlem years'. *Transition* 26, 9 (iii) (Oct./Dec. 1974), 14-18

7 Geiss, *The Pan-African movement,* pp. 353-4.

8 Hooker, 'The Pan-African Conference 1900, *Transition* 36, 9 (iii) 1974, 23

9 V. B. Thompson, *Africa and unity: the evolution of Pan-Africanism,* Longman, 1969, pp. 319-21

10 Geiss, *The Pan-African movement,* pp. 234-40

11 *Ibid.,* p. 244

12 *Ibid.,* pp. 261-2

13 *Ibid*

14 At the time, the journal *West Africa* ridiculed the idea of independence for African states in the following terms: 'Calling for national independence in its old sense of unfettered freedom of action is unreal. It is now a meaningless term. This kingdom (U.K.) has not got it' (*West Africa,* 3 November 1945, 1059). Reports of the proceedings of the Congress are on pages 1061-3 of the same issue.

15 Geiss, *The Pan-African movement,* pp. 406-07; George Padmore, *Pan-Africanism or Communism?* New York: Doubleday, 1955, p. 148.

16 *Africa* 25, Sept. 1973, 22

17 Peter Worsley, *The Third World*, London, Weidenfeld and Nicolson, 1963, p. 90

18 *Africa* 25, 22. George Padmore later wrote. 'At long last the die is cast and issue joined. From Manchester the African and other colonial delegates returned home to put their hands to the freedom plough and furrow the ground for the seed of liberty to grow' (*Pan-Africanism or Communism?* p. 148)

19 Thompson, *Africa and unity,* pp. 126-34

20 J. B. Webster and A. A. Boahen with H. O. Iodwu, *The revolutionary years, West Africa since 1800,* Longman, 1967, pp. 274-6.

21 Thompson, *Africa and unity,* p. 69

22 *Ibid.,* p. 81-4

23 Kwame Nkrumah, Speech at the Sixth Anniversary Convention of CPP of the Gold Coast, 1955, quoted in *Africa Tribune* I (2), Sept./Oct. 1955 and cited in Thompson, *Africa and unity,* p. 124

24 The Joint Declaration of the Ghana–Guinea Union was made on 1 May 1959. Mali joined in April 1961 when a Charter of the Union of African States was adopted by the heads of the three states – Modibo Keita (Mali), Sékou Touré (Guinea) and Kwame Nkrumah (Ghana). See Thompson, *Africa and unity,* p. 133; Sidney Tailor (ed.), *The New Africans,* London, Paul Hamlyn, 1967, p. 184

25 Geiss, *The Pan-African movement,* p. 354

26 Thompson, *Africa and unity,* p. 130

27 *Speeches delivered by Kwame Nkrumah and Resolutions of the first session of the All-African People's Conference, Accra,* 5-13 December 1955, p. 22

28 Conference of Heads of African States at Casablanca, 17 Jan. 1961, Casablanca, Morocco, printed in both French and English

29 Rémi Fani-Kayode, *Blackism,* London, V. Cooper, 1965, p. 38

30 *Daily Express* (Nigerian), 22 Jan. 1962

31 Thompson, *Africa and unity,* p. 168

32 Fani-Kayode, *Blackism,* Appendix II, p. 84

33 Alvin M. Josephy, Jr. (ed), *The Horizon history of Africa,* New York: American Heritage, 1971, p. 504

34 *Morning Post* (Nigerian), 22 Jan. 1962

35 Zdenek Cervenka, *The Organisation of African Unity and its Charter,* London: C. Hurst & Co., 1968, 1969. Appendix A. 'Charter of the Organisation of African Unity', Addis Ababa, may 1963, pp. 231-9

36 Adekunle Ajala, *Pan-Africanism: evolution, progress and prospects,* London, André Deutsch, 1973, pp. 221-2

37 On the eve of the deadline for the break, Abubakar Tafawa Balewa, the Nigerian Prime Minister, in an effort to prevent the disintegration that the diplomatic rupture might cause in the Commonwealth, decided to host a Commonwealth Conference in Lagos to discuss Rhodesia. This was a time when law and order had completely broken down in Western Nigeria and he was doing nothing about the situation. In the same way Kenya decided to raise the Rhodesian issue in the Security Council of the UNO without consultation with other members of the OAU

38 The countries are Algeria, Congo (Brazzaville), Ghana, Guinea, Mali,

Mauritania, Somalia, Sudan, Tanzania and Egypt

39 Ajala, *Pan-Africanism,* pp. 227-8

40 *Ibid.,* p. 240

41 *West Africa,* 6 June 1970, p. 602

42 Ajala, *Pan-Africanism,* p. 242

43 'Newsline', *Africa,* 99 (Nov. 1979), 10; 'The Record of Instability', *West Africa,* 6 Oct. 1975, pp. 1176-7

44 Emperior Haile Selassie of Ethiopia was deposed on 12 Sept. 1974, and the country has been under military rule since then (*Africa* 63, Nov. 1976, p. 39)

45 N. J. Padelford, 'The Charter of the OAU' in P. J. M. McEwan (ed.), *Twentieth-century Africa,* London, Oxford University Press, 1968, p. 477

46 *West Africa,* 30 July 1979, 1357: *New Africa,* 145, Sept. 1979, pp. 16-18

47 John de St Jorre, *The Nigerian civil war,* London, Hodder & Stoughton, 1972, pp. 191-2, 227-9, 366; Zdenek Cervenka, *The Organisation of African Unity and its Charter,* pp. 192-221

48 Ajala, *Pan-Africanism,* p. 134

49 *West Africa,* 21 May 1979, pp. 883-4

50 James O. Ojiako, *Thirteen years of military rule,* Lagos, *Daily Times* (Nigeria Limited) Publication, 1979, pp. 232-3; *West Africa,* 16 June 1975, 678-9. Members of the ECOWAS are Nigeria, Niger, Benin, Togo, Ghana, Ivory Coast, Liberia, Sierra Leone, Guinea, Gambia, Senegal, Mauritania, Cape Verde, Guinea-Bissau and Upper Volta (*West Africa,* 31 Oct. 1977, p. 2210)

51 *West Africa,* 2 Aug. 1976, p. 1091

52 *West Africa,* 13 Feb. 1978, p. 279; *Africa* 61, Sept. 1976, pp. 14-16

53 *West Africa,* 15 Nov. 1976, p. 1699; *West Africa,* 17 Jan. 1977, p. 95

54 *West Africa,* 13 June 1977, pp. 1139-41, *West Africa,* 17 Jan. 1977, p. 95

55 *West Africa,* 19 March 1979, p. 479

Questions for discussion

1 What led to the rise of the Pan-African movement?

2 What were the achievements of the 1900 Conference of the Pan-African movement?

3 Examine the role of Du Bois in the Pan-African movement.

4 The 1945 Manchester Congress was a turning point in the history of Pan-Africanism. Discuss.

5 Analyse the factors which transformed the Pan-African movement between 1945 and 1958.

6 Critically examine the problems which face the OAU.

7 Assess the achievements of the OAU.

Suggestions for further reading

Ajala, Adekunle, *Pan-Africanism: evolution, progress and prospects,* London, André Deutsch, 1973, New York, St Martin's Press, 1974.

Cervanka, Zdenek, *The unfinished quest for unity,* London, Julian Friedman, 1978.

The Organisation of African Unity and its Charter, London, C. Hurst and Co., 1969.

Fani-Kayode, Rémi, *Blackism,* London, W. Cooper, 1965.

Geiss, Immanuel, *The Pan-African movement,* London, Methuen, 1974.

Jorre, St John de, *The Nigerian civil war*, London, Hodder & Stoughton, 1972.

Josephy, M. Alvin, Jr. (ed.) *The Horizon history of Africa,* New York, American Heritage, 1971.

July, W. Robert, *The origins of modern African thought,* Faber and Faber, 1968.

Legum, Colin, Pan-Africanism: a short political guide, Westport, Connecticut Greenwood Press, 1977.

Padmore, George, *Pan-Africanism of Communism?* Doubleday, 1955.

Ras Makonnen, *Pan-Africanism from within*, Nairobi, Oxford University Press, 1973.

Tailor, Sidney (ed.) *The new Africans,* London, Paul Hamlyn, 1967.

Thompson, Vincent Bakpetu, *Africa and unity: the evolution of Pan-Africanism,* Longman, 1969.

Wallerstein, Immanuel, *Africa: the politics of unity,* Random House, 1967.

Woronoff, Jon. *Organising African unity,* Metuchen, N. J. Scarecrow Press, 1970.

Worsley, Peter, *The Third World*, London, Weidenfeld and Nicolson, 1973.

9 The military in contemporary African politics

S. O. Arifalo

The dramatic role which soldiers have played in contemporary African politics has so caught the imagination of journalists, observers, commentators and historians that they have tended to regard this phenomenon as something new in Africa. In this they overlook the fact that in many parts of pre-colonial Africa the military had always played a vital role in the political evolution of society. For instance, among the Bini, the Yaruba and the Kanuri in Nigeria, the Zulu in South Africa, military organisations not only guaranteed the security of the states against external aggression, but were also the ultimate instruments for making inter-state relations and obligations.

In pre-colonial Africa the possession of a strong army enhanced the prestige of the king at home as well as beyond his domains. The armies provided an instrument for the creation, development and expansion of states. In some cases the military leaders were appointed to govern parts of the kingdom.

When the European colonisers came to Africa their armies were the instruments that they used to conquer, expand and consolidate their hold on their territories. Britain used her military forces to conquer and establish colonies in such places as Nigeria, Ghana, Sierra Leone, Egypt, the Sudan and Kenya. The French did likewise in such places as Senegal, Algeria, Dahomey (Benin Republic), and Chad. In certain cases the commanders of such forces were appointed to govern the territories they had helped to conquer.

In this chapter an attempt will be made to analyse the various reasons for military intervention in contemporary African politics and to assess how the military have performed while in power. Because it is impossible to discuss every case of military intervention in Africa in a brief treatment like this, examples and illustrations will be drawn only from the French and English-speaking areas.

The military in contemporary African politics

On the attainment of political independence, the various African states inherited the colonial armies which henceforth formed the nucleus of their national armies. Although these colonial troops adequately served the needs of the colonial powers, they were not the best material for truly national armies whose officers and men would command the confidence of the people and their political leaders. Therefore, efforts were made in the various newly independent states to reorganise these armies to reflect the national image.

The imperial governments were the common enemies to the leaders of the anti-colonial movements in the various African states. With independence in the 1960s the focal point of unity began to fade away. Divisions among regional, ethnic, ideological and economic interests began to emerge. The leaders of the newly independent African states unleashed a revolution of rising expectations in the provision of social amenities without developing the available economic or natural resources to match the expectations. When the masses began to complain about the political, economic and social situations, especially unemployment in the urban areas, unprecedented inflation and declining food production many African governments reacted by silencing critics and ignoring or violating their nations' constitutions. Single-party governments, either *de jure* or *de facto,* began to emerge in many African countries. Such governments were kept in power by the use of the armed forces. The armed forces became steadily more reluctant to be manipulated in this way by inept and corrupt political leaders. They appeared (at least to themselves) to be the only organised group capable of taking over the government from the political parties.

Between 1960 and 1966 there were military coups or mutinies in fourteen African states. The first military coup in West Africa took place in Togo on 13 January 1963. In the same year the governments of Dahomey, Burundi and Congo Brazzaville were toppled. The year 1964 witnessed army mutinies which rocked Kenya, Uganda and Tanzania. On 18 February 1964, the Gabonese army overthrew Léon M'Ba's government in a bloodless coup only to have the coup reversed by French paratroopers. The next spate of military take-overs occurred in rapid succession as civilian governments collapsed like houses of cards − in Zaire on 25 November 1965; in Dahomey on 29 November 1965, 22 December 1965, 17 December 1967 and on 26 October 1972; in the Central African Republic on 1 January 1966; in Upper Volta on 3 January 1966; in Nigeria on 15 January 1966, 29 July 1966 and 29 July 1975; and in Ghana on 24 February 1966, 5 July 1978 and 4 June 1979. By 1975, twenty-one of the forty-one independent states were being ruled by military or civilian-cum-military groups. The potential power of the gun is everywhere in Africa a disturbing reality.

Nigeria

We now examine the reasons for military intervention in contemporary African politics. In such countries as Ghana, Congo Brazzaville and Nigeria, the military intervened ostensibly in order to displace governments which were notorious for their corruption and inefficiency. Although Nigeria provides an exceptional case since it was not just subjected to a single-party government or dictatorship, it was not without some degree of truth that Ojukwu, the 'Biafran' secessionist leader, described the period of civilian regime there as wasted years of helplessness, incompetence, abuse of office and gross disregard for the interest of the common man. This view was shared by many Nigerians at the time, especially in the south, and this partially explains the popularity of the first coup. Nzeogwu, one of the leaders of 15 January 1966, stated

Fig. 9.1   *The role that the armed forces have played in the recent history of African countries is illustrated by the number of army officers who have come to power: above left, General Murtala Mohammed (Nigeria, 1975); above right, Flight-Lieutenant Jerry Rawlings (Ghana, 1979); below left, Colonel Gadafy (Libya, 1969); below right, General Idi Amin (Uganda, 1971).*

The achievements of military leaders in politics have varied. The period of office of General Murtala Mohammed was one of stability and economic advancement in Nigeria, and under his rule the foundations were laid for the return to civilian government in 1979. By contrast, General Idi Amin's rule in Uganda became a ruthless dictatorship during which the Ugandan economy all but collapsed. Armed force was needed to overthrow him before civilian politics could be restored.

the aims of the coup as follows:

> Our enemies are the political profiteers, the swindlers, the men in high
> and low places that seek bribes and demand ten per cent, those that
> seek to keep the country divided permanently so that they can remain
> in office as Ministers and VIPs of waste, the tribalists, the nepotists,
> those that make the country look big for nothing before the inter-
> national circle, those that have corrupted our society and put the
> Nigerian political calendar backwards. We promise that you will no
> more be ashamed to say that you are a Nigerian.[1]

The chance for the first coup in Nigeria came when the political
leaders had lost the confidence of the masses through their attempt to
cling to power at all costs. The events which brought matters to a head
were the disputed census figures of 1963, the Federal elections of 1964
which were nearly deadlocked over allegations of irregularities, and the
'rigged' October 1965 election in the then Western Region which led to a
breakdown of law and order there.

The coup of 29 July 1966 in Nigeria was a counter-coup or a
retaliation. The 15 January coup itself had been marked by ethnicism
and partiality as certain political leaders from the north, mid-west and
west – in particular, Alhaji Sir Abubakar Tafawa Balewa (the Prime
Minister), Alhaji Sir Ahmadu Bello (Premier of the Northern Region)
and Chief S. L. Akintola (Premier of the Western Region) – were
assassinated whereas the premiers of the Eastern and Mid-Western
regions were spared. It was hardly a coincidence that the two premiers
who were not killed, Dr M. I. Okpara and Chief Dennis Osadebay, were
Igbo, the group to which Major Nzeogwu belonged. In the same way it is
possible that Nzeogwu was betrayed by his colleagues. The northerners,
having lost many of their leaders during the coup, saw the whole exercise
as a plot against their interests, and the coup of 29 July 1966 was
therefore designed to adjust the balance.

The July 1975 coup in Nigeria was similar to that of January 1966 in
one significant respect. It was designed to remove an administration
which was stigmatised as corrupt and inefficient. Speaking over the radio
on 30 July 1975, the new Head of State, General Murtala Muhammed,
said that General Yakubu Gowon, the former Head of State, was
deposed because, despite the resources available to the country, the
aspirations of the people were not being met. Other reasons for Gowon's
removal included disregard for responsible public opinion including that
of intellectuals and traditional rulers, his inaccessibility to the people, his
insensitivity to the yearnings and feelings of the people, and the
indecision and indiscipline of his administration.[2]

Ghana

The purpose of the coup of 24 February 1966 in Ghana, according to
General Ankrah, was to 'banish privilege, overlordism, political
opportunism, wasteful pompousness, and incompetence', and thereby
restore to the people of Ghana the blessing of 'liberty, justice and human
dignity.'[3] We could also add to this list differences and competing

153

ambitions. It is significant to note that specifically military grievances, which were not noticeable in the Nigerian coups, also seemed to have played some part in both the 1966 and 1972 coups in Ghana. These were the decision to introduce new methods of training for officers, the retirement of some officers, cutbacks in the amenities and services for the armed forces, rumours and threats of the possibility of sending the troops to fight in Zimbabwe after the Congo experience, the establishment of the powerful, better equipped, better paid and more trusted President's Own Guard outside the regular army, the by-passing of General Otu (the most senior officer) by his subordinates in advising the President[4] and interference with the professional autonomy of the army. About the plight of the regular army under Nkrumah, General Ocran writes:

> One day, they were to pay for their electricity, the next day they were to lose their training allowance, the following day they were to lose their travelling facilities. We wondered what was happening to us.[5]

There were also complaints about torn uniforms and boots and about salaries introduced in 1957 which meant little in 1965 owing to inflation. As Robert Pinkney has pointed out, many of the complaints of the soldiers were common to many sections of the community.[6] The soldiers were not the only group of people wearing ragged clothes in Ghana nor were the officers the only people whose pay had been seriously affected by inflation.

Ignatius Acheampong's intervention in Ghana on 13 January 1972 was to a large extent an 'officers' amenities' coup. This is not to say that all was well with K. A. Busia's government. The impact of the dramatic fall in the price of cocoa on the world market in 1971 was handled in a careless manner. The country's international indebtedness was rising and the rescheduling of old liabilities offered only temporary relief. Busia's 1971 budget banned the import of cars and television sets, while the cedi was devalued by 48.3 per cent. The budget also reduced defence expenditure by 10 per cent. Therefore top on the official list of the reasons for the coup was the reduction in the defence budget, the cutbacks in the armed forces and the civil-service fringe benefits, and the erosion of the purchasing power of salaries resulting from the devaluation of the cedi. Thus the grievances of the armed forces had again precipitated a coup in Ghana.

Acheampong himself was removed by General Fred Akuffo in a bloodless coup on 5 July 1978. Here is what Akuffo said:

> Broadly speaking (the coup) was to remove the ominous tendencies of the former Head of State and to re-establish the principle of collective responsibility. Besides, under his leadership, the position of the Head of State which should have been a driving force for uniting our people, has been shaped into a wedge dividing our people. This state of affairs had to be rectified.[7]

This should be taken as an official justification of the coup. The real motive of the young officers was the feeling that the economy of the country was in confusion, that the Union Government referendum had been a failure, and that the government was not paving the way for a smooth transition to civilian administration. In addition, it appears that the people had lost respect for the armed forces. Some senior officers in the army felt that Acheampong had been acting in a dictatorial manner and without adequate consultation with his colleagues.

That was not to be the last coup in Ghana in the decade, for on 5 June 1979 there was yet another coup. An Armed Forces Revolutionary Council (AFRC) replaced Akuffo's Supreme Military Council. The Chairman of the AFRC was Flight-Lieutenant J. J. Rawlings. Rawlings accused the senior army officers of reducing the affairs of Ghana to a shambles. He described the coup as a 'cleansing exercise' necessitated by the shameless acts of the military men who had ruled Ghana since 1972. The coup was well received in many quarters in Ghana. This was so because the ills which Akuffo had promised to remove were still very much in evidence. Acheampong had not been tried for his alleged offences. Senior military men who had been in government or in civil positions were vying with alien or local businessmen in the building of big houses and in the possession of businesses and fleets of vehicles. Akuffo spoke much about the need for accountability. He dismissed many members of the Supreme Military Council who had lost public trust, but he never prosecuted anyone.

The Sudan

In such countries as the Sudan and Sierra Leone, the army initially intervened as an 'umpire' to mediate between two warring political parties or to prevent the country from disintegrating. Here we are referring specifically to the first military coup in the Sudan. In August 1955, a few months before independence, southern Sudanese troops rebelled amid rumours that when independence was achieved the Moslem northerners would lord it over the southerners. Thereafter there was civil strife and bloodshed. The southerners began to demand either complete autonomy or some kind of federation. Then in 1958 there was a revolt of the army in the north, and in order to avoid chaos General Ibrahim Abboud was invited to intervene by the Prime Minister. In 1964, however, Abboud bowed to growing popular demands for a return to civiliam administration and the politicians were reinstated. Long-standing differences continued to impede economic and social progress, and in 1969 the army resumed power under Colonel Gaafar Mohamed Nimeiri. Muhammed Omar Beshir described the situation under the civilian regime as follows:

> The parliamentary regimes of 1965 to 1969 were characterised by chaos, intrigue and lack of purpose. The successive Governments representing the traditional parties and groups failed to carry out what they set out to do. Crisis followed crisis and their impotence became obvious.[8]

Nimeiri predictably blamed the depressed economic situation on colonialism and declared his willingness to expand trade with the socialist and Arab countries.

Sierra Leone

In Sierra Leone, after the bitterly contested and controversial elections of May 1967, the opposition African People's Congress (APC) apparently defeated the ruling Sierra Leone People's Party (SLPP). When the leader of the APC, Siaka Stevens, had been sworn in as Prime Minister, Brigadier David Lansana quickly intervened. He was removed within two days by his own junior officers, and military rule was established. A National Interim Council was later established which prepared the way for the return to a civilian administration in April 1968.

Benin

In Dahomey (called the Republic of Benin after 1975) and Togo, the military became involved in politics for reasons little different from those in other West African countries. Dahomey is reputed to hold the unhappy record for Africa of having had the largest number of coups since it became independent in August 1963. The following is what one writer had to say about Dahomey in 1975:

> A rough calculation shows at least six coups, six constitutions and eleven governments since 1960, not to mention a number of interregna, abortive coups and plots, strikes, scandals, abortive elections and a near civil war.[9]

The problems of Dahomey centred on regional and conflicting ethnic interests. Migan Apithy, Hubert Maga and Justin Ahomadegbe rose in succession as leaders of ethnic, regional or sectional interests. Following a week of trade union strikes and massive demonstrations in the coastal areas of the country, the first Republic fell on 20 October 1963. President Maga was forced to resign from office by the army. General Christophe Soglo was made provisional head of state while a new constitution was being drafted.

The immediate cause of Maga's fall was corruption in the civil service and other agencies of the government, wasteful expenditure on a sea-front palace and other grandiose but unjustifiable buildings. As if this was not provocative enough, the workers were being asked to bear the brunt of the consequent austerity measures in pay cuts and in the loss of fringe benefits. After the elections, Apithy and Ahomadegbe were declared President and Vice-President respectively.

The Second Dahomey Republic under Apithy and Ahomadegbe lasted until November 1965 when feuding between the two incompatible leaders and their followers virtually paralysed the day-to-day administration of the country. During this period, the country's financial and economic situation was going steadily downhill in spite of draconian austerity measures. Clashes between Apithy and Ahomadegbe reached a crisis when they failed to agree on the appointment of a judge to head the country's Supreme Court. Again, as popular and massive demonstrations were staged in the coastal towns, Soglo stepped in and handed over an interim government to Tahiron Congacou, Speaker of the House. Congacou's inability to resolve the constitutional deadlock and the strong opposition within the army itself to a return to civil rule led Soglo to step in for the third time, this time taking over power himself. He then banned political parties, dissolved the municipal councils, suspended the constitution, and set up a military government with himself as Head of State. The new government announced that its aim was to establish a new style of politics under which men would unite around a programme rather than around personalities. Even though Dahomey was to experience two further brief periods of civilian rule – Dr Emile-Derlin Zinsou's military-sponsored administration (1968–69) and a rotating three-man Presidential Council (1970–72) – the 1965 military take-over marked the end of the Dahomean attempt to follow constitutional government and the emergence of the military as the dominant factor in the political life of the country.

On 26 October 1972, there was yet another coup in Dahomey. This time the plotters were headed by Colonel Mathieu Kerekou. In his maiden broadcast to the nation Kerekou recalled the bloody events that marked the presidential and legislative elections of March 1970. He said that the elections were undemocratic because of pressure, violence, and the glaring malpractices engaged in by the candidates and their supporters. The military Directorate had been forced to intervene and nullify the elections.

Kerekou castigated the Presidential Council and its government which, he said, had been divided and undermined by their own contradictions and condemned to inertia, demonstrating daily their 'congenital deficiency, their notorious inefficiency and their unpardonable incompetence in the handling of state affairs'. His broadcast contained some of the most virulent indictments ever made against any civilian regime by the military in an African state.[10]

Zaire

The revolt of the army in Zaire in 1960 was brought about by the troops' belief that their position as a corporate body was being threatened. Independence, which had promised life more abundant, had only brought them disillusionment. They resented their unchanged lot in the new nation – their long years of service without promotion or substantial pay rises. Mobutu Sese Seko on assuming office as President of Zaire in 1965 said that the army intervened to save the country from anarchy and chaos. From that moment onwards Mobutu firmly established his personal control over the government not only as a military dictator but also as head of a bureaucracy made up of diverse ethnic groups in the country. He disliked the politicians and saw the army as the last hope of the country. He accused the political leaders since independence of destroying the country by their intrigues, ambition and personal rivalries to the detriment of the ordinary man.

Uganda

The situation in Uganda in 1970 was similar to that of Zaire in the sense that the Ugandan army, as a result of the attempts of Milton Obote (the

Ugandan Prime Minister) to alter its political image, believed that its corporate existence was being threatened. In Uganda the personal element as a factor in coups in Africa was perhaps most clearly evident. The failures and the inadequacies of the civilian government enumerated by Idi Amin's 18-point justification for his coup do not fully explain the causes of the coup or of its timing. Ethnic unrest, a depressed economy and official corruption had not been the preserve of the civilian government; military officers and Idi Amin himself had shared in them. A more cogent reason for the coup was Amin's personal fear that he was about to be dismissed. It has been alleged that he was involved in the misappropriation of defence funds, that he disliked Obote's ideological pronouncements, and that Obote telephoned from Singapore to have him detained just a few hours before his coup.

Libya and Morocco

The circumstances in such countries as Libya and Morocco bring out other causes for military intervention in politics in Africa. In general, there has been no serious political ideology propounded by military leaders in Africa. But this is not the case in Libya and Morocco. Apart from the usual general excuses for staging a military coup, there has been the additional factor of 'Arab socialism' and the call to abolish the monarchical system of government, even though the officers concerned had personally sworn oaths to defend that system. Colonel Qaddafi overthrew the monarchy of King Idris in Libya in 1969 and proclaimed adherence to the Arab socialism of Algeria and Egypt, while the unsuccessful attempt to overthrow the regime of King Hassan of Morocco in 1971 was partly motivated by Arab socialist leanings.

Foreign involvement in African coups

One putative factor which has not been easy to confirm is the extent of foreign involvement in the coups of Africa. The February 1966 coup in Ghana and the Ugandan coup are cases in point. Nkrumah might have had his own faults at home, but he was in the vanguard of the fight for the total liberation of Africa from foreign domination. The claim by General Kotoka, one of the coup-makers in Ghana, in an interview with the West German television network to the effect that the army decided to depose Nkrumah because he wanted to send troops to fight in Rhodesia (Zimbabwe) has aroused a suspicion of British interest in Nkrumah's downfall.[11]

The circumstances surrounding Idi Amin's coup in Uganda in 1971 are dubious. At the Commonwealth Conference in Singapore at the time of the coup, Milton Obote was busy attacking Britain for selling arms to South Africa. British resentment of Obote's position is possibly demonstrated by the allegation that Edward Heath, then British Prime Minister, who had got wind of the impending coup in Uganda, deliberately instructed British Intelligence agents not to inform Obote of this in advance.[12] When the coup was announced many Western European countries followed the British lead in recognising Amin's government.

Whatever their motivations or local circumstances, military takeovers in Africa have been strikingly similar, at least in terms of their methods. The radio station, the television house, the major telephone offices, the important government buildings and the airport have been the main targets of the coup-makers.

From the foregoing it can be seen that the failure to achieve the expected rapid development after the attainment of independence, mismanagement and financial extravagance, corruption in high and low places, political schism, inter-ethnic rivalries, the attempt by political leaders to stay in power for life, cutbacks in military budgets, slow advancement for military officers, threats to the corporate existence (and perquisites) of the army, and disagreement over ideology and foreign vested interests have all combined to create the environment in which coups can be successfully carried out.

An assessment

In Africa today (excluding South Africa) there are only five countries where the governments allow an offical opposition or the expression of alternative views to their policies. Eighteen states are under direct military rule. Three states, Egypt, Algeria and Zaire, have decreed that they are civilian regimes; the others operate one-party governments. However, the flood of military take-overs which overtook so many African countries appears to be a clear reflection of the dangers inherent in the seizure of absolute power by civilian politicians which leaves the aggrieved disillusioned and with no alternative but to encourage a violent change of government. Even with the military, one coup makes another one likely as discontented officers may well try to emulate their colleagues. However, it would appear that nobody learns from the mistakes of the past.

How far have the military succeeded in solving the social, economic and political problems in the various African countries where they have taken over political power? A. R. Zolberg has this to say: 'A military takeover and rule by officers never constitutes a revolution in Tropical Africa, but rather a limited modification of existing arrangement.'[13] In some cases the military rulers succeed in restoring the state they had taken over to the conditions existing before the breakdown of constitutionalism and economic chaos. The soldiers rarely indeed produce revolutionary or durable changes in the internal political structure in their states. As Robert Pinkney has pointed out, when a change of administration is brought about by force of arms, those effecting the change have not normally had the time or the will to draft manifestos. They are primarily concerned with ensuring the successful acquisition of power, and what to do with the power is a secondary consideration.[14]

Togo

Nevertheless, when one looks at specific cases one notices marked differences in the performance of the military. When Olympio was assassinated in Togo in 1963 the coup-makers had no definite programme for the country. With the exception of a few narrow and short-term demands, the coup appeared to have been purposeless. Of course the three former sergeants who led the coup were rewarded by being promoted to senior positions in an enlarged army.

Eyadema's first two years in office were devoted to the consolidation and assertion of army rule. During this period also constant allusions were being made to the eventual return to civilian rule. Special committees were set up to draft a new constitution, to suggest means of achieving national integration and providing guidelines for the return to civilian rule. On 13 January 1969, Eyadema officially announced that the military had completed its task of effecting national reconciliation and had no further justification for remaining in power, the partisan politics could resume, but that the army would reserve the right to judge the capability and the determination of the political leaders to operate above vain political squabbles. In what looked like a spontaneous reaction, the people of Togo in their thousands took to the streets and pleaded with the Togolese leader and his colleagues to stay in office. Some observers have alleged that the whole affair was stage-managed.[15] On 17 January 1969 the military-backed cabinet revoked its authorisation of a return to partisan political activities saying that it was bowing to the wishes of the people.

In September of the same year Eyadema declared that he had endorsed the proposal to create a national political party which would embrace all Togolese. Not long after that he announced the formation of his Rassemblement du Peuple Togolais (RPT). A consultative assembly declared in November 1969 that the party was organised 'to direct and control the life of the nation in its political, economic and social aspects'. The participation of the army in government was to be expressly recognised and Eyadema was invited to remain as Head of State. The founding of the RPT was intended to obliterate the image of a military government in Togo. In January 1977 Eyadema replaced the last soldier in his cabinet with a civilian, and he has remained Commander-in-Chief of the Togolese Army ever since.[16]

In his political activities, Eyadema has been greatly helped by the increasing earnings from the Kpeme phosphate industry which he nationalised in January 1974. Large budgets have also helped him utilise government patronages to pre-empt potential Ewe opposition elements, to please the army, and to make the first serious efforts to develop the north of the country; here such social amenities as schools and hospitals have sprung up, and road construction has been undertaken to link Upper Volta with the port of Lomé.

Togo's budgets have been balanced without the imposition of additional taxes, although expenditure on social services has shot up by about 230 per cent. Workers were granted a 10-per-cent increase in 1975. During the period between 1978 and 1979 Togo recorded a harvest surplus and the overall state of the economy looked healthy. In December 1978 the Togolese Minister for Planning and industrial Development, Koudjolou Dogo, released figures which showed that

Togo's gross domestic product has risen from CFA50 000 millions in 1968 to CFA 160 000 millions. Income *per capita* over the same period went from CFA27 000 to CFA62 000.[17] This economic development has been attributed to the relative stability which the country has enjoyed under Eyadema. Togo's success story, to be sure, has been greatly aided by increases in the world prices of phosphate, cocoa and coffee and by good harvests from the farms.

From 1977, Eyadema, like Mobutu Sese Seko, began introducing new nationalistic policies. These included a cultural 'revolution' which made it compulsory for public officers to exchange their Christian or foreign names for indigenous ones; Eyadema himself changed his name from Etienne to Gnassingbé. Names of towns have also been affected by this policy.

Eyadema's prestige has been enhanced by the apparent improvement in the standard of living of the people. His name is constantly eulogised by the press and his subordinates. In almost every street in the capital there is a portrait of the President, and the masses are exhorted to sing his praise. But beneath this ostensible stability and popularity lies a latent opposition. Part of this can be traced to the D'Souza and Olympio families who ruled the country before Eyadema took over in 1967. The RPT claims to have welded together the forty ethnic groups in the country. Time has to show the durability of this unity. Togo under Eyadema may enjoy relative stability as compared with many African countries, but a military regime, no matter how benevolent, is a far cry from a democratically elected one.

Benin

In Benin, formerly Dahomey, too, the military has been an agent of stability. The present regime has been the most durable administration the country has seen since independence. Kerekou's Marxist-Leninist orientation was solemnly proclaimed on 30 November 1974. An administrative reorganisation of the country was undertaken in an attempt to decentralise the decision-making process, to give local administrative units a greater degree of autonomy, and to promote or encourage active peasant participation in the economic development of the country. Local 'revolutionary' bodies were then set up to spearhead the envisaged transformation of society. In 1975 Kerekou announced the four golden rules of the new ruling Mouvement du Solidarité Dahomienne: the submission of the individual to the organisation, the minority to the majority, the less important to the more important, and the part as a whole to the Central Committee.[18] One observer thinks that the President forgot to add 'that as President of the Central Committee, these four rules mean submission to the will of Lt Colonel Kerekou'.[19]

As a corollary to the declaration of the country as a Marxist state, Marxism has been made a compulsory subject in schools and has to be studied by all citizens. Nationalisation of certain industries and some institutions, including schools, was announced by the government. Some observers think that the purported nationalisation was a mere farce since the scale of the nationalisation of industry was no greater than in many other African countries where Marxism has not been adopted. The industries which had been nationalised are being run by the kind of state agencies which in the past have proved to be inefficient and corrupt.

Communism as an ideology has not taken firm root. Private traders are still riding high in the country. Cotonou's notoriety as a haven for currency traffickers and smugglers remains unchanged. Cigars, cigarettes, spirits of all sorts and high-quality textile materials are sold to smugglers from neighbouring countries.

An agricultural reform programme was launched in Benin in 1977. This was ostensibly designed to create a network of socialist farming co-operatives and to redistribute incomes in relation to each individual's work. To achieve this objective the government created the Groupment Révolutionnaire à Vocation Rurale (GRVC). In 1978 seventeen such groups with a total membership of 1 925 were reported.[20] The campaign for food production is aimed at getting every Béninois to devote part of his leisure to farming. Government propaganda is relayed to all parts of the country. So far a modest achievement has been recorded. Rice production increased from 5 223 tonnes in 1972 to 17 458 tonnes in 1977, while maize production went up from 216 703 tonnes to 234 457 tonnes in the same period.[21] This development has not greatly affected the economy of the country.

Sweeping changes in nomenclature and the establishment of new committees like the Military Committee for the Revolution and the National Consultative Committee cannot be equated with real social change in the country. Since the declaration of Benin as a Marxist state many educated Béninois have left the country. Neither the country's ethnic cleavages nor its chronic economic problems have been cured. The country still has to rely heavily on French financial support. Within the army itself tension and ideological differences are rife and often lead to abortive coups. One must agree with Samuel Decalo when he writes:

> Despite the superficially sharp divergences of Kerekou's policies from those of previous leaders, civilian and military, the concrete domestic reality is systematically similar.[22]

Uganda

The performance of the military in Uganda was a source of embarrassment to many Africans. Idi Amin has been accused of murdering up to 300 000 Ugandans and foreigners. Widely respected men like the Chief Justice of the country, Benedicto Kiwanuka, the Vice-Chancellor of Makerere University, Frank Kalamuzo, the Governor of the Central Bank of Uganda, and the Mayor of Kampala all disappeared. The death of the Anglican Archbishop of Uganda, Janan Luwuum, and two cabinet ministers in mysterious circumstances in 1977 was part of the general wave of killings in the country. The Archbishop himself summarised the situation in a letter to the President shortly before he met his end:

This brain drainage of our country, the fear and the mistrust make development, progress and stability of our country almost impossible. The gun which was meant to protect Uganda as a nation, the Ugandan as a citizen and his property is increasingly being used against the Ugandan to take away his life and property.[23]

Having appointed himself president for life, Idi Amin installed sheer force as the basis of power and politics in Uganda. Almost everyone was regarded as an enemy, real or imagined, by Idi Amin. Thousands of Ugandans fled their country.

Islam acquired a new importance in Uganda under Idi Amin. There were only 500 000 Muslims in Uganda, but Amin favoured this minority group in appointments to key and sensitive posts in the civil service and in the army. He planned to turn Uganda into an Islamic state, and attacked Christian fund-raising events for the 1977 centenary of the Ugandan Church. Many Christians missionaries were deported from Uganda.

On 4 August 1972 Amin announced that God had directed him to order the community of 50 000 Asians out of Uganda within ninety days.[24] These Asians almost totally controlled the country's commerce, factories and plantations. They also controlled many other professions. They were an easy target for Amin because they were not generally popular with the Ugandans. So on 8 November 1972 all Asians, including those carrying Ugandan passports, were sent out of the country with only $100 personal allowance. This expulsion, far from benefiting the generality of Ugandans, only enriched Amin's friends and the soldiers, who looted the property left behind by the expelled Asians. The soldiers were then let loose on society to carry out arrests indiscriminately and to detain innocent citizens at their own discretion. They looted property without let or hindrance. An acute shortage of food developed. While the ordinary Ugandans had to queue for their daily rations, army officers lived well in rent-free houses and drove expensive cars. Each battalion had a well-stocked depot which supplied the needs of the soldiers. They did not even spare Uganda's famous wild life, which they decimated, selling the meat in Uganda and smuggling the rhinoceros horns, skins and elephant tusks to neighbouring countries.

Idi Amin's rule could not continue indefinitely. On 11 April 1979 thousands of Ugandans were in the streets to celebrate the end of a nightmare, for on that day an invasion took place by an army from Tanzania and by the Ugandan National Liberation Front, a group of exiles led by sixty-seven-year-old Yusuf Kronde Lule.[25] This had been the country which Winston Churchill once described as the 'pearl of Africa' because of its beauty, its fertile land and economic potentialities. Amin left the country in turmoil, its economy devastated, and the population fractured by ethnic rivalries.[26]

Ghana

Whatever may be the failures of the military regimes in countries like Ghana, Zaire, the Sudan and Nigeria, the situation is not as disturbing as that of Uganda. In the Sudan, Zaire and Nigeria the military regimes have achieved some measure of stability and national unity.

Before General Acheampong was overthrown in Ghana in 1978 he had advocated a Union Government, by which he meant 'a national government formed by all sections of the community, the civilian population, the army and the police'. This innovation was rejected by the professional bodies, who wanted a government popularly elected on the basis of universal adult suffrage and upon the principles of freedom of association and expression.

In spite of this objection, Acheampong was determined to implement the proposal. He repudiated more than £35 million of debts owed to British firms by Nkrumah's government and devalued the cedi by 44 per cent. The problem of shortage of consumer goods, the two-way smuggling, corruption and inflation remained largely unresolved. However, the Acheampong government had some success with its 'Operation Feed Yourself' programmes, which reduced Ghana's dependence on imported food.[27]

When General Akuffo took over power in 1978 he said that the proposed Union Government would be scrapped and replaced by an interim National Government, which would hold office for at least four years. There would be free elections but on a non-party basis. This was only a slight modification of the Acheampong plan, except for the non-participation of the army and the police. The Ghanaian Bar Association again strongly criticised the new proposals. It said that parliamentarians elected on an individual, no-party basis would have no acceptable nation-wide objectives and could not therefore implement any electoral commitments. In spite of this criticism the Supreme Military Council appointed a Commission to draft the constitution for the Third Republic.

People's confidence in the military administration was shaken by the military attempt to seek civilian scapegoats for Ghana's chronic economic problems. For example, when the Chief of Defence Staff Lieutenant-General Joshua Hamidu assured Ghanaians that the government would effect the repatriation of timber, cocoa and mineral export earnings which had been lodged in foreign banks, he did not mention any military involvement in this massive misappropriation of public revenue;[28] but he specifically mentioned the Lebanese, Syrians and Asians and a few Ghanaian lawyers as being the offenders. Military institutions were unaffected by the findings of the various enquiries. It is true that Acheampong was later cashiered, disgraced and confined to his village, but he was not then tried for his alleged offences.[29] All this increased the disillusionment of the ordinary Ghanaian.

Prices of foodstuffs soared, and the department stores were almost empty. In the rural areas commodities like soap and toothpaste were scarce. Ordinary Ghanaians continued to suffer while the top military men were feeding fat on the meagre resources of the state. If the masses of people were too cowed to react to what was happening in the country, the Bar Association behaved differently. In its resolution passed at the 1978 Annual Conference in Kumasi they came out boldly to say: 'Ghanaians are witnesses to the incompetence of the military adventurers, their rapacity, corruption and ineptitude.'[30] This was the background to the Rawlings coup of June 1979.

After the general elections and what he called a 'house cleaning exercise', Flight Lieutenant Rawlings' Armed Forces Revolutionary Council (AFRC) handed over power to the civilian government of President Hilla Limann on 24 September 1979. It was a unique event in Africa for the armed forces to seize power, allow elections to take place within fourteen days, and then turn over power to a civilian government, having spent only 124 days in office.

Rawlings saw his action as giving birth to a new national consciousness in Ghana, and held that the people would never again condone the corruption of their rulers or tolerate the plundering of the poor by a callous and unscrupulous rich few.[31] If this apparent change of heart should remain permanent and not just be the result of the fear of the gun, he believed, then something worthwhile had been achieved. The coup was followed by a drastic reduction in the prices of commodities. Some traders who were found selling above the controlled prices were publicly flogged. Some culprits were made to parade the streets with placards showing their misdeeds.[32] This resulted in changes in many areas, including low prices where the goods were available and low rents and fares for the working classes. The fear of public flogging or of facing the firing squad restored, at least temporarily, public honesty.

But Rawlings' coin had another side. Ghana's tradition of passing through political turmoils without great loss of life was broken as eight men, including three former military heads of state, Generals Acheampong, Akuffo and Kwesi Afrifa, were executed, having been found guilty of robbing the state by the 'Peoples' Court'.[33] Discipline in the army and police had been seriously damaged. The AFRC was shouting most of the time about a revolution, but in fact it did not offer any coherent solution to Ghana's economic problems. Dr Hilla Limann put it thus:

The army cannot manage anything, they can only destroy, they can't build. Those of them who are normal know that they don't have any magic solution to our problems.[34]

The Sudan

The Sudanese Fourth Republic began under the rule of General Nimeiri in 1969. On taking over power in the Sudan, Nimeiri banned all political parties and demonstrations, in the same style as other military regimes in Africa. The Sudanese Socialist Union, the only party which emerged, gradually extended its influence over the country. President Nimeiri's task of uniting the country was not easy, but he not only ended the seventeen-year-old bloody civil war between the north and the south, he also carried out far-reaching measures of reconciliation and rehabilitation. In 1977 Nimeiri declared a general amnesty for Sudanese exiles, appealing to them to return home and contribute to the national development effort. As a result of this appeal, more than a million people returned to resume their normal life in the Sudan.

Under Nimeiri the south was granted its autonomy, with the defence and foreign affairs remaining the prerogative of Khartoum. The south has its Peoples' Assembly at Juba, its capital. The President of the regional assembly. Abei Alier was made Vice-President of the Democratic Republic of the Sudan. Major-General Joseph Lagu was converted from an Anya-Nya rebel to being Inspector-General of the Sudanese Army and a confidant of President Nimeiri. Although the policy of the Government has considerably lessened tension, the relative unity and stability achieved in the country in recent years remains precarious as a result of further (though abortive) coups and rumours of impending coups.

In an attempt to revolutionise the economy of the country Mimieri launched a six-year development plan. He negotiated a $260 million loan from the Internatioanl Monetary Fund to help pay for essential imports.[35] Cotton production, the mainstay of the country's economy and its major foreign-exchange earner, was declining owing to a number of factors including falling prices in the world market. The Sudan, like most other African countries, has been bedevilled by inflation, low wages and shortage of basic commodities. Corruption and misappropriation of public funds have not been eradicated in the country.

Nigeria

The military regimes in Nigeria did achieve some measure of unity and stability, after a bloody twenty-month civil war. The disorder in the then Western Region, which had been the immediate cause of the crisis in Nigeria in 1966, was quickly brought under control. The Tiv riots were also effectively checked. The ban on some newspapers in the different regions was lifted. Areas where the former government refused to commission completed projects as a punitive measure had their projects commissioned immediately. This partially explains why the advent of the military regime was welcomed by the major political parties, cultural organisations, university students, youth organisations and traditional leaders.

General J. T. Aguiyi-Ironsi's problem was how to reconcile his vision of 'One Nigeria' with ethnic loyalties and sensitivities, particularly of the Hausa-Fulani in the north. Ironsi's apparent lenient treatment of the coup-makers of 15 January 1966 was construed as condonation of the coup and the murders of the country's leaders. His 'Unity Decree' Number 34 further compounded the problem. Thereafter nearly every attempt he made for the reform of the administration was interpreted as a grand design for Igbo domination of the country. The killings of many Igbo in the north between July and October 1966 made the attempted secession by the Igbo and the subsequent civil war virtually inevitable. As Gutteridge puts it:

> The January plotters claimed to stand for 'One Nigeria', the participants in the July coup asserted the danger to the nation of Igbo domination, and eventually the secession of Biafra was attempted on the grounds of escaping Northern domination.[36]

General Yakubu Gowon was faced from 1967 with the problem of the civil war in Nigeria. He was committed to the task of keeping Nigeria one and united. He quickly created twelve new states out of the former four regions in the country. Then at the end of the civil war he implemented his humane 'three Rs' – reconstruction, rehabilitation and reintegration.[37] To this end he issued a nine-point programme,[38] which included the implementation of the Second Development Plan, the eradication of corruption in the country, the reorganisation of the armed forces, the creation of more states, the preparation and adoption of a new constitution, the organisation of national political parties, the transfer of power to a popularly elected civilian government, the organisation of a new national census and the introduction of a new revenue allocation formula.

Of these rather ambitious nine points only four were actually attempted. The Development Plan did not achieve much. Unemployment and underemployment worsened. Agricultural production stagnated. The First Progress Report on the Plan accepted the shortcomings in the following terms:

> Serious underlying and long-term manpower problems continued to manifest themselves. A rapidly expanding labour force continued to strain the job creating capacity of the economy and there was evidence that in some areas urban unemployment was growing in seriousness.[39]

Education accounted for ₦77.8 million or 13.5 per cent in the Development Plan. Medical and health facilities improved, if one judges by the number of medical officers which increased from 1455 in 1962 to 3112 in 1972. A better system of revenue allocation was introduced, and the armed forces were said to have been reorganised.

The census of 1973 was a disastrous failure mainly as a result of rivalry between the states and consequent inflation of the figures. The result was rejected by many sections of the Nigerian community, who saw the census as cutting down their share of the national 'cake'. Cowon's promise to consider the creation of more states in the country was not fulfilled. The drafting and adoption of a new constitution, the organisation of national political parties and the election of a popular government remained mere paper proposals. Under Gowon, corruption and indiscipline seemed to increase all over the country and the regime failed to come to grips with rising inflation, the chaos at the Nigerian ports, the poor distribution arrangement of petroleum products throughout the country, and the confusion and alleged corruption surrounding the planned Festival of Black and African Arts.[40]

When General Murtala Mohammed took over power in July 1975 he quickly responded to the national mood of frustration and the general disillusionment that had been created when Gowon retreated from his promise to hand over power to a civilian regime in 1976. There was a massive purge in the civil service and other public institutions,[41] the results of which can be at best described as mixed. However, more important, in response to popular demand Murtala's government quickly set 1 October 1979 as the firm date for return to a democratically elected government. To this end Murtala inaugurated the Constitution Drafting Committee. The creation of seven new states also helped to lessen tension in the country and reduce the fear and suspicion of minority groups being dominated by the larger groups. (There seems to be no end to the demand for the creation of more states because there are groups who will always believe that they are minorities.) Murtala took drastic steps to decongest the Nigerian ports. He also set up a panel on the re-siting of the federal capital which eventually led to the choice of Abuja to replace Lagos.

Big strides towards the return to civilian administrations were made when the new regime promulgated local government reforms and local government elections, the first since the coup of 1966, were held. Unfortunately many of the local government councils did not make the desired impact – for example, with regard to rehabilitation of their roads.

After the assassination of General Murtala Mohammed in the abortive coup of 13 February 1976, Lieutenant-General Olusegun Obasanjo, Chief of Staff at the Supreme Headquarters, picked up the mantle of leadership and continued where Murtala Mohammed had left off. The government emphasised reform of the system of education in the country, launching the (perhaps over-ambitious) Universal Free Primary Education scheme (UPE). Existing universities were taken over from the respective state governments and six new universities were opened, although without giving full consideration to their staffing and financing. The regime also abolished payment of fees in secondary schools and universities throughout the country.

The government realised the critical need to provide sufficient food for the ever-increasing population in the country and launched the 'Operation Feed the Nation' (OFN) programme. This was only a qualified success, but it can at least be said that the programme did alert the nation to the serious need for self-sufficiency in food production. In addition, the military took measures to curb secret societies, corruption (by setting up an investigatory bureau), and inflation (by means of Price Control Boards), but none of these met with much success. On the other hand, General Obasanjo's government saw an impressive amount of physical development such as the Murtala Mohammed International Airport, a couple of local airports, the new port at Tin Can Island (Lagos), the building of many housing units in Lagos and some state capitals, the Ogorode Thermal station, the Lagos–Ibadan Expressway, roads, bridges and flyovers. But the award of government contracts at highly inflated prices had the effect of widening the gap between the rich and the poor and increased the incidence of corruption.

The major improvement in the economy of the country took place for a reason unconnected with any action of the military government. It was the so-called oil boom. Increases in military budgets, the staging of events like the Boy Scout Jamboree, Sports festivals, the Festival of Black and African Arts (FESTAC) and trade fairs, tended to wipe out the increase in economic productivity. The lot of the ordinary citizens did not improve appreciably. The crime wave in the country, which had been increasing since the end of the civil war, was not effectively deterred by the Armed Robbery Decree which stipulated death by firing squad for those found guilty of armed robbery. The country continued to face the problem of constant electric power failure, insufficient technical knowhow, inadequate water supply and bad road links. In general, these, then, were the conditions in the country when General Obasanjo handed over power to the elected representatives of the people on 1 October 1979.

Zaire

When General Mobutu took over power in Zaire in 1965 he was reported to have told a foreign journalist in Kinshasa: 'I want to make the Congo a country that the world will no longer laugh at.'[42] In the first five years of his rule political parties were banned. His own Popular Revolutionary Movement (MPR) was allowed to function as a national movement but not as a political party. The 1967 Constitution named Mobutu as President for seven years in the first instance, and he was given full powers to operate a presidential system of government.

In his search for unity and stability in Zaire Mobutu reduced the number of the provinces in the country from twenty-one to twelve. He imposed on the people a harsh and repressive regime. No opposition was tolerated. He made a ritual of public executions of former allies and colleagues who dared to oppose him. Many of the Zairean dissidents who sought refuge in foreign lands were lured back only to be executed. When university students demonstrated against his economic policies, soldiers were ordered to open fire on them and about fifty were reported killed.[43]

For some time Mobutu achieved a measure of success in the economic sphere. The currency was stabilised. Agricultural production went up. However, prosperity was limited to the elite, military and civilian. The ordinary citizen might be grateful for the temporary peace and stability in the country, but the economic boom was passing him by.

Mobutu had placed a high priority on education at every level. At independence in 1960 Zaire had fewer than thirty university graduates. Today there are over 7 000 graduates of universities and other institutions of higher learning. More and more Zaireans are being trained in all fields of national life to take over from foreigners.

These achievements were soon interrupted by a rebellion in Shaba Province, formerly known as Katanga. Mobutu was forced to call on foreign troops to fight the rebels. By the time the rebellion was quelled the economic position of the country had deteriorated drastically. *West Africa* of 30 May 1977 reported that Zaire was in debt to foreign banks to the tune of some $3 billion and that inflation was running close to 80 per cent.

Yet whatever might be the shortcomings of Mobutu and the problems facing the country, law and order has been restored to a country whose name was only recently synonymous with disorder and chaos and was virtually written off as impossible to govern. With Sam Uba we may conclude of Mobutu: 'A Machiavelli and a Bismark rolled into one, he has at least destroyed the cruel slander that Zaireans are ungovernable.'[44]

Conclusion

In sum, then, the military regimes in Africa have made little headway in their apparently half-hearted attempts to wipe out corruption, tribalism, nepotism and inefficiency. Corruption remains a hard fact of life in spite of the military rulers' pleadings, sermons, threats, admonitions and warnings. The reason is that some of the soldiers themselves became even more corrupt and nepotic than the discredited civilians. The soldiers, in some cases, had access to more money than the civilians. Their governments necessarily relied on the same civil servants, public officers and agencies to perform the functions for which the politicians had been removed. Mistresses and contact men still remained as channels for distributing government favours and patronages.

With a few exceptions, there has been no concrete evidence of any sincere desire by military regimes in Africa to bring about fundamental social and economic changes. Many of the military regimes have proved themselves incapable of achieving economic revolution or social restructuring in their countries. At best they have applied palliatives to chronic economic problems. Too often the military have seized power with 'virgin' political minds.[45] Perhaps, to expect soldiers to effect a transformation of the societies they take over is to overestimate their political acumen. To be a good military commander is not the same thing as being a good political leader.

With a few exceptions like the Sudan, Zaire and Togo, military regimes in Africa have been unable to achieve stability in their countries, and even there they have achieved only a relative stability. In Congo Brazzaville, Burundi, Uganda and Ethiopia, the military have been a positive agent of instability. In these countries, disappearances, mutinies, abortive coups and assassinations have almost become the normal way of life.

Thus the military take-over 'as a cleansing experience, a rite of purification, or an act of self-sacrifice and deliverance by dedicated military men',[46] is largely an illusion. It is obvious that the performance of the military does not differ significantly from that of their civilian predecessors. The replacement of civilian regimes by military governments has not led to the disappearance of the major problems which brought down the civilian politicians. A gramophone record made in Ghana in 1968 summarised the position: 'The cars are the same, only the drivers are different.'[47] Be that as it may, the extra-constitutionality of military regimes and their control over arms have enabled them to perform certain feats. The creation of new states and the take-over of state universities in Nigeria by the Federal Government, the overthrow of Nkrumah's authoritarian and one-party regime in Ghana, the deposition of Emperor Haile Selassie in Ethiopia are examples. It is one thing to seize power; it is quite another thing to know how to use it to the advantage of the people. As Gutteridge has pointed out, the soldiers often intervened as a 'corrective' measure, but almost invariably without any clear-cut policies. Very few of the regimes had or have a defined ideology. High-sounding words and phrases used by the military have become mere slogans. Solutions to social, economic and political problems have continued to elude them. The armed forces themselves have lost their traditional discipline. We may conclude our assessment of the role of the military in contemporary African politics with these pungent remarks by A. Aforka Nweke:

All these weaknesses, coupled with internal cleavages within the leadership group, proliferation of largely uncoordinated advisory committees, centralisation of power and decision-making to the disadvantage of the out-laying local communities, and the eagerness to use force to elicit compliance, make military rule in Africa a very doubtful substitute for government by elected civilian politicians.[48]

Notes

1 Text of a speech read over Radio Kaduna on 15 January 1966, cited by Ruth First, *Barrel of a gun*, Penguin, 1970, p. 285

2 James, O. Ojiako, *Thirteen years of military rule, 1966-77*, Lagos *Daily Times* Nigeria Limited Publication, 1979, pp. 79-82

3 General J. A. ANkrah, 'The Future of the military in Ghana', *African forum* II (1), Summer 1966, p. 5.

4 A. A. Afrifa, *The Ghana coup of February 24, 1966,* London, Frank Case, 1966, p. 102

5 Major General A. K. Ocran, *A myth is broken,* Longman, 1969, p. 43

6 Robert Pinkney, *Ghana under military rule, 1966-1969,* London, Methuen, 1972, p. 3

7 'Interview with General F. K. Akuffo', *West Africa,* 7 August 1978, p. 1525

8 Muhammed Oman Beshir, *Revolution and nationalism in the Sudan,* London, Rex Collins, 1974, pp. 81-2

9 'Benin, record of instability', *West Africa,* 6 Oct. 1975, p. 1176

10 *West Africa,* 6 Nov. 1972, 1479

11 Adekunle Ajala, *Pan-Africanism, progress and prospects,* London, André Deutsch, 1974, p. 248

12 *African diary,* XIV (1), Jan. 1976, pp. 7747-8

13 Cited by W. F. Gutteridge, *Military regimes in Africa,* London, Methuen, 1975, p. 183.

14 Pinkney, *Ghana under military rule,* p. 1

15 *West Africa,* 18 Jan. 1969; *New Africa,* 140, April 1979, pp. 31-32

16 *New Africa,* 137, Feb. 1979, p. 26

17 *Ibid.*

18 *West Africa,* 22/29 Dec. 1975, p. 1593

19 *Ibid.*

20 Dominique Legarde, 'Benin's push for prosperity', *West Africa,* 15 May 1978, p. 921

21 *Ibid.*

22 Samuel Decalo, *Coups and army rule in Africa: studies in military style,* New Haven and London, Yale University Press, 1976, p. 83

23 Henry Kyemba, *The state of blood,* London, Corgi, 1977, p. 274

24 *Ibid,* pp. 56-7

25 *Newsweek,* 23 April 1979, p. 8

26 *West Africa,* 23 April 1979, p. 699

27 *West Africa,* 22/29 December 1975, p. 1559

28 *Ibid,* 11 June 1979, p. 1011

29 *Ibid.*

30 *Ibid,* 9 Oct. 1978, p. 2017

31 *West Africa,* 1 Oct. 1979, p. 1783

32 *New Africa,* 145, Sept./Nov. 1979, p. 27

33 *New Africa,* 144, Aug. 1979, pp. 16-17

34 *Sunday Times* (Nigerian), 20 March 1980

35 William Ndebe, 'A question of credibility', *Africa,* 99, 1 Nov. 1979, pp. 45-6

36 Gutteridge, *Military regimes in Africa,* p. 117

37 Guy Arnold, *Modern Nigeria,* Longman, 1977, p. 23

38 Ojiako, *Thirteen years of military rule,* pp. 70-71

39 A. Aforka Nweke, 'Military rule in Africa', *Africa,* 34, June 1974, p. 68

40 Supo Ibikunle 'A post mortem on military control of Affairs', *The Daily Times,* 1 Oct. 1979

41 Ojiako, *Thirteen years of military rule,* pp. 89-92

42 Cited by Sam Uba, *Africa,* 30, Feb. 1974, p. 13

43 *Ibid,* p. 14

44 *Ibid,* p. 15

45 Ibrahim A. Gambari in a review article, *New Nigerian, 4 June 1979*

46 Kenneth W. Grundy, *Conflicting images of the military in Africa,* Nairobi, East African Publishing House, 1968, pp. 22-3

47 Cited by Gutteridge, *Military regimes in Africa,* p. 78

48 Nweke, 'Military rule in Africa', *Africa,* 34, June 1974, p. 68

Questions for discussion

1 Examine the role of the military in pre-colonial African politics.

2 'The Republic of Benin is Africa's "Enfant terrible".' Discuss.

3 Examine the circumstances which led to the overthrow of Kwame Nkrumah in Ghana.

4 What brought about the first miltary coup in Nigeria?

5 Compare and contrast military rule in Uganda and Zaire.

6   Account for the military involvement in the politics of Morocco and Libya.

7   'Political power comes out of the barrel of a gun' (Mao Tse-Tung). Discuss

8   What are the characteristics of military rule in Nigeria?

9   Assess the character and achievements of military rule in the Sudan.

10 'A military take-over and the rule by officers never constitute a revolution in Tropical Africa, but rather a limited modification of existing arrangements' (A. R. Zolberg). Discuss.

Suggestions for further reading

Afrifa, A. A. *The Ghana Coup of February 24, 1966,* London, Frank Cass, 1966

Austine, Dennis, and Luckham, Robin (eds). *Politicians and soldiers in Ghana,* London, Frank Cass, 1975

Decalo, Samuel, *Coups and army rule in Africa: studies in military style* (New Haven and London, Yale University Press, 1976)

First, Ruth. *The barrel of a gun: Political power in Africa and the coup d'état,* Penguin, 1970

———, *Libya, the elusive revolution,* Penguin Books, 1975

Grundy, Kenneth W. *Conflicting images of the military in Africa*, Nairobi, East African Publishing House, 1968

Gutteridge, William F. *Military regimes in Africa,* London, Methuen, 1975

———, *The army in African politics,* London, Methuen, 1969

Kyemba, Henry, *State of Blood,* London, Corgi, 1977

Lee, J. M. *African armies and civil order,* New York, Praeger, 1969

Luckham, Robin, *The Nigerian military,* Cambridge University Press, 1971

Mazrui, Ali A. 'Soldiers as traditionalisers: military rule and the re-Africanisation of Africa', *World Politics,* 28 (2), Jan. 1976, pp. 246-72

Nweke, A. Aforka, 'Military rule in Africa', *Africa,* 34, June 1974, pp. 66-8

Ocran, A. K. *Politics of the sword,* London, Rex Collins, 1978

Oyediran Oyeleye (ed.). *Nigerian government and politics under military rule 1966-1979,* London, Macmillan, 1979

Panter-Brick, Keith (ed.). *Soldiers and oil: the political transformation of Nigeria,* London, Frank Cass, 1978

Pinkney, Robert *Ghana under military rule, 1966-1969*, London, Methuen, 1972 1972

Price, Robert M. 'Military officers and political leadership: the Ghanaian case', *Comparative politics,* 3, April 1971, pp. 361-79

Sylvester, Anthony, *Sudan under Nimeiri,* London, The Bodley Head, 1977

For pre-colonial and colonial warfare, see (for West Africa):

Crowder, M. *West African resistance,* London, Hutchinson, 1971

Smith, Robert, *Warfare and diplomacy in pre-colonial West Africa,* London, Methuen, 1976

10 African languages and literature in today's world

Adebisi Afolayan

Introduction

After brief preliminary comments on language and literature and their general significance to man, attempts will be made in this chapter to put two views to the reader. First, the reader will be called upon to consider the view that although deceptively simple, the situation in Africa today in respect of language and literature is complex and at times confused. Secondly, it will be suggested that the positive development of Africa demands her outgrowing her colonial heritage and radically cultivating and utilising her abundant resources in language and literature.

Preliminary comments on language and literature and their significance to man

Language is generally conceived today as a unique human property, marking man out from all other creatures. Man has been described as a thinking as well as a social animal; and these two attributes have combined to make him a talking animal. Language essentially has both individual and social aspects which are immortalised in these two statements of the seventeenth-century English dramatist, Ben Jonson: 'Language most shows a man; speak, that I may see thee,' and 'Speech is the instrument of society.'

In its individual aspects, language is the means of identifying entities, categorising objects and concepts, perceiving ideas and things, grasping the abstract, the concrete as well as the supernatural, and thinking about anything in whatever form. Language is more than the mere dress of thought. As Edward Sapir has remarked, 'Thought may be a natural domain apart from the artificial one of speech, but speech would seem to be the only road we know that leads to it.'[1] Thus from the individual point of view, the significance of language in this day of science and technology is clear for all to see. The tongue or the pen is often mightier than the sword, the machine-gun or the bomb; and thought obviously lies behind every creative activity and technological discovery and advance.

The statements from Ben Jonson about the social aspect of language already indicate that what we know as the human society today, rural or urban, literate or pre-literate (or non-literate), traditional or technological or modern, has been made possible through the instrumentality of language in its spoken or written form. Language makes it possible for men to communicate, even to transmit knowledge across space and time. It is the means of socialisation. It enables us to pool our various kinds of knowledge, skills and abilities together and subsequently organise the community intricately on the principle of a division of labour. Unfortunately, however, language can also play a divisive role in human society. It is the most suggestive index of the groups and sub-groups within society and contributes to the politico-social problems of sectionalism and divisiveness.

Literature, as described by Raymond Cowell in *The critical enterprise,*[2] is an exploration of the relationship between the 'word' (spoken or written) and the 'world'. It relates 'language style' to 'life style'; therefore it is a record of language in use, seen from the personal and the social points of view. The individual expresses through language his joys and sorrows, his expectations and disappointments, his plans and achievements, his judgements and his reflections on things physical or philosophical, temporal or eternal. His expressions are ordinary or heightened; simple or difficult; pithy and aphoristic or diffused and discursive; poetic or dramatic; realistic or exaggerated, and easily forgotten or memorable. Whenever man has something significant to say about any of his preoccupations, and he says it effectively, literature is in the making. Ideas and concepts together with the sayings that accompany them become the corporate property of the community. Such ideas may be social, cultural, political, religious, moral, artistic or scientific. They in turn constitute the contents of oral traditions, stories and folklore, the components of oral literature. When digested, abstracted, expanded, given a perspective and an interpretation and reduced into writing in some recognised form, they, together with other written artistic creations, become the written literature of the people. Such literature usually takes the form of poems, essays, short stories, novels and plays.

Therefore literature is a work of art expressed in words to mirror life and to be perceived intellectually to uplift the mind and the soul. As a work of art, it has aesthetic values for man, exuding beauty and thereby giving him satisfaction and pleasure. As a mirror to life, it instructs man in the ways of the world, making life more intelligible to him. As an intellectual exercise, it uplifts the mind and the soul of man, showing him how to live better, die better and leave the world a better place. Finally, being all three things (a work of art, a mirror to life and an intellectual exercise) rolled into an indivisible whole expressed in words, literature has humanising, unifying, consolidating and even revolutionising effects on man and society. It electrifies the man producing it, is communicable, and indeed is communicated across time and space to another man or a group or to innumerable groups of men who upon receiving it in its correct form can be charged or electrified as the producer has been.

In some, language has been shown to be a defining property of man and an instrument of society, whereas literature, as a work of art expressed in words to mirror life, can be seen as the joint product of man and society. Language and literature are therefore essential components of any culture. Although related, they are two different entities.

Theoretically language can exist without literature, but literature cannot exist without language. However, because man is always impelled to give expression in words to his feelings, desires, wishes and judgements, wherever language is found literature is bound to accompany it.

Languages of Africa
Indigenous and foreign languages

There is a dichotomy among the languages of Africa. Generally, there are two kinds of languages in any given African country. Some are foreign to the community, whereas others are indigenous. Usually, those that are foreign are fewer in number than those that are indigenous.

This concept, however, is too simple, and for two main reasons. First, there are languages that are strictly neither foreign nor indigenous in the sense above, pidgins and creoles. Secondly, from the functional points of view, the distinction between the foreign and the indigenous is blurred.

Pidgins are simple languages developed and used for limited communication between two sets of people with different languages. For example, pidgin English in West Africa is a simple language developed from English under the influence of local West African languages and Portuguese for a restricted purpose, initially for commercial transactions among English traders and coastal West African peoples and later for communication among the various peoples of the local multilingual West African communities. On the other hand, creoles are pidgins that have become so rooted that they become the mother tongues of some people just as indigenous languages are. Such are Krio of Sierra Leone in West Africa and Swahili in Tanzania, Kenya and Uganda in East Africa; but whereas the process of creolisation is full and complete for Krio, it is not yet so with regard to the use of Swahili by every socio-cultural group everywhere in East Africa.

The languages that are foreign subdivide into two groups from the point of view of function and usage or social role. Some of them are used in conducting everyday life, whereas others are used only for restricted purposes.

Languages that are used for some aspects of everyday life but which are not the primary languages of the people are technically referred to as second languages. In most African countries, these second languages were introduced into the countries by the former colonial masters. Thus they are generally modern European languages. Four of them are most commonly used: English, French, Spanish and Portuguese. Of these four, the two most dominant are English and French. Consequently, the Anglophone countries and the Francophone countries together include most of the black African countries.

As languages of the former colonial masters who have been involved in the demarcation and the evolution of the various countries into single political units, these languages have remained as the official as well as effective national languages of the various countries. There are, however, exceptions to this pattern, such as are found in East Africa, particularly Tanzania and Uganda. Uganda, for example, has declared English as its official language but Swahili as its national language. On the other hand, Swahili is both an official and a national language of Tanzania, with English as the second official language. Even then, there is a great difference between the situation in Tanzania and Uganda in respect of Swahili. Although it is effectively used and developed in Tanzania, its use remains largely as a statement of intent in Uganda, largely because of the different stages of creolisation of the languages in the two countries. In Tanzania it is largely a creole but in Uganda it is largely a pidgin or even, for many people, a foreign language.

Some of the languages foreign to African countries can indeed be technically referred to as 'foreign languages'. They are so called because they are used only for restricted purposes. These purposes include the reading of books and journals, moving about in foreign lands on visits and excursions, and learning at particular institutions or levels of education for the purpose of performing specialist duties, such as those of foreign representatives, interpreters and translators. In this regard, other main non-African languages such as German, Russian, Chinese, Italian and Japanese are used. Similarly, many indigenous African languages such as Arabic, Hausa, Swahili and Yoruba are also so used.

The languages that are indigenous to each African country are very many. As a result no single black African country is without indigenous languages that are unknown to numbers of her citizens. Consequently it has been difficult to choose any of them for adoption as the national or official language of the state or country. The exception referred to earlier, the Tanzanian experience, has been possible because of the existence of Swahili which is generally a creole and, in some places, a pidgin, which has evolved from Arabic and indigenous local languages through very early commercial activities within the area. But generally in independent black Africa, there is the characteristic language limitation to the freedom of each community as a political entity. This language situation therefore poses one of the greatest political problems to each black African country.

At this point, it is necessary to refer to the special positions of three languages which are indigenous to some African countries. These are Arabic, English and Dutch (which has developed into Afrikaans). Arabic is the language of Arab countries in North Africa populated by non-black people. As a language, it has permeated most African countries – at least as a foreign language of religious liturgy; it is the language of Islam and the Koran. The translation of the Koran into local African languages is but a recent development. Arabic is a strong element within Swahili.

English is in a stronger position than Arabic in Africa, largely because, as has been mentioned earlier, it is a second language in Anglophone countries, while it is a foreign language in other black African countries, particularly the Francophone ones. Moreover, in Zimbabwe, South Africa and Kenya it is the mother tongue of the white citizens of these countries.

The history of Dutch in Africa is even more interesting than that of

English. Like English, its main speakers are the white citizens of South Africa, and it has therefore qualified, as English does in this respect, to be referred to as an indigenous African language. It has, however, taken a more interesting step in developing into the genuinely indigenous African form that is now known as Afrikaans. Thus in South Africa alone, we have three kinds of mother tongues (first languages); various local black African languages, English as the mother tongue of some white citizens and Afrikaans (Dutch) as the mother tongue of the most powerful white citizens. It is interesting to note that both groups of white citizens together form a small minority of the total population. This linguistic fact is an important element in the evolution of the apartheid policy of that country.

Equally important is the fact thay many indigenous languages of black Africa are also used as second languages by other citizens both within and outside the political or even socio-cultural units in which they are found as mother tongues. Most prominent among such languages are Hausa of the West African Sudan, Swahili of East Africa, and Yoruba of the Guinea Coast. However it must be noted that every major indigenous African language really serves as a second language because of the social, political and commercial interactions among the various peoples. In any case, with such an increase in these interactions as one would expect, there would be a corresponding increase in the use of such major languages as second languages.

The language situation depicted above puts the black Africans at a great disadvantage. Their indigenous languages tend to be local. Pan-Africanism therefore has to be promoted and conducted in a non-black African language. Even national integration, development and welfare can only be maintained through those languages that are foreign to the individual country. To cap it all, for the citizens of these countries there exists the wrong equation of formal education with the knowledge of a foreign, generally European language. The citizens cannot be physicists, technologists, doctors or engineers unless they first acquire one modern non-African language or another as a prerequisite. Their own languages are often neglected and written off as 'useless vernaculars'. Yet often they are able to attain only a degree of proficiency in these languages to a level which is often ludicrously exaggerated or overrated by them.

Thus it can be seen that, although language is the unique property of all human beings, its manifestations vary widely over the world in general and Africa in particular. Consequently, while language identifies Africans with the rest of humanity, languages differentiate Africa from any other continent, particularly with intricate multilingualism.

Categorisation of African languages

Many African languages, however, are wrongly labelled in the same way as the various ethno-linguistic groups using them. Labels such as 'dialects' and 'vernaculars' are freely used to refer to the languages, while the ethno-linguistic groups are generally called 'tribes'.

Those labels, to start with, are ordinary English words, and there seems to be nothing unusual about their use. However, behind them and their use is a great deal of linguistic politics over which protesting

Africans are often accused of being unjustifiably touchy. Perhaps the best approach to the understanding of the political aspect is to accept the argument of the so-called objective users of the terms and examine the ordinary meanings of them as given in a standard dictionary. Here then are the entries for those words in the *Oxford Advanced Learner's Dictionary of Current English:*

dialect: form of a spoken language, way of speaking, used in a part of a country or by a class of people: e.g. the Yorkshire dialect.

vernaculars: adj: (of a word, a language) of the country in question; the newspapers in India, those in the various languages (except English) of India; a vernacular poet, one who uses a vernacular language; noun: language or dialect of a country or district: the vernaculars of the USA.

tribe: 1. racial group, cap. one united by language and customs, living as a community under one or more chiefs: the Indians of America. 2. (botany, zoology) group of plants or animals, usu. ranking between a genus and an order. 3. (usu. contemptous) group of persons, etc. of one profession.

From an objective examination of those entries, it seems clear that the adoption of 'dialect' and 'vernacular' as labels for African languages and of 'tribe' as the label for the ethno-linguistic groups speaking the languages is pejorative. Many of the different local African speech-forms are indeed languages. Reference to them as dialects makes the erroneous assumption that all Africans speak the same language, most likely a barbaric one, and that the differences between their forms of speech are simply dialectal. The same kind of assumption of similarity of grouping, behaviour pattern and social development lies behind the use of the term 'tribes'. It is often not realised that what are often called tribes are in fact nations. In many cases, each group may number as many as 10 millions, comparable to that of many recognised European countries. 'Vernacular' may appear a more objective term, judging from the dictionary entry; but two other contexts of using the term point to its pejorative connotation. First, some centuries ago, when Latin was regarded as the language of scholarship and civilisation (consequent upon its being the language of the Roman empire that included Britain as one of her provinces), English was regarded as vernacular. Thus there seems a long tradition of master-servant relationship in language designation. The conquering or imperial people use a language, but their subject people use a vernacular. Thus although English is the language of the people of England, it is not, following a strict application of the dictionary entry above, referred to as vernacular there. In contrast, Hausa, which is the language of Kano state and other areas of Nigeria, is a vernacular in Nigeria. The objection may be raised that the term 'vernacular' is also used to describe English in England. This is true, but that brings us to the second relevant context of using the term. It is used together with 'English' to form a compound label 'vernacular English', which refers to a kind of English that stands in contrast with another kind labelled 'standard educated English'. The context thus seems to point to the pejorative connotation of the term.

It is therefore pertinent to assert the desirability of discontinuing the use of 'dialect' and 'vernacular' as labels for distinct African languages. No African language is more primitive or less developed than any modern European language. What is more, any of these languages is capable of being used as the medium for scientific or technological discussion, learning or teaching. Every one of them has the phonological and morphological resources for expansion to meet any new demands made upon it. Besides, it must be remembered that languages freely borrow necessary items of vocabulary from one another. No language in the world today has not so borrowed from another. What is more, such borrowings can be kept for ever and even legitimately converted into the personal property of the borrowing language. Indeed, most scientific and technological terms are international. There should therefore be no reason for looking down upon any African language as incapable of being used in the worlds of science, commerce, industry, technology or the humanities.

A common colonial experience in Africa makes the language situation unique and rather complex. In most cases, the delimitation of the boundaries of each country was carried out arbitrarily by the various European powers. Many ethno-linguistic groups sharing the same language and culture are often separated among different countries, and those with different cultures and languages are often merged with the fraction of a dismembered group. Such a colonial experience is added to the unusual multiplicity of languages in each African country as well as to the accepted social superiority of the foreign European language used in those countries. Quite often this results in form of psychological reaction which makes the African look down upon his own language. There are many African scholars, doctors and engineers today who stoutly oppose any attempt to educate their own children in their mother tongues even at the primary school level. They are so much carried away by the scientific or technological superiority of the Europeans or Americans that they identify this superiority with their language. They therefore refuse to accept the fact that the majority of African children can expect only primary education and that it is necessary to give them the education that will equip them to live most efficiently. The fact that the majority of African children still live all their lives in their locality amongst speakers of the same local languages often comes to such people as a shock. Neither do they realise that only a privileged few with secondary or tertiary education can play a useful role at the national and international levels.

Language groups in Africa

Although the languages of Africa may number hundreds or perhaps thousands, from the typological point of view they belong to only a small number of language groups. As given by Greenberg, all the languages of Africa (and he lists as many as 730) can be assigned to only four large families; these are Congo-Kordofanian, Nilo-Saharan, Afro-Asiastic and Khoisan.

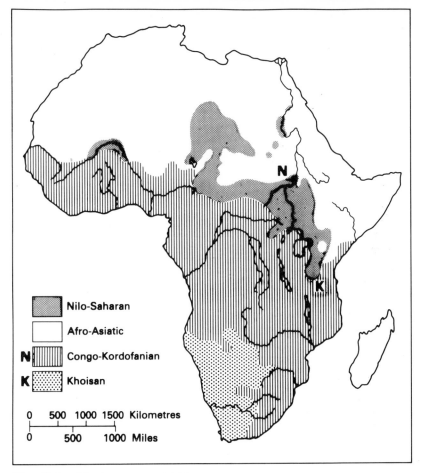

Map 10.1   *The languages of Africa*

The small number of language families in Africa has a number of effects, potential and actual. One major outcome is the ease with which regional varieties or dialects of the various European languages used in Africa tend to develop. For example, as was noted by Peter Strevens in his paper, 'Pronunciation of the English Language in West Africa':

> There are differences of detail at the local level, but broadly speaking, those pronunciations spoken in Northern Nigeria, Northern Ghana and Sierra Leone form one type: the pronunciation of English in the Southern part of Nigeria and the southern part of Ghana forms another; that of Freetown . . . forms a third. However, the Freetown pronunciation is at once so restricted in distribution and so exceptional in other aspects that it falls into a category different from that which comprises types 1 and 2.[3]

This observed emergence of a category of West African English is not surprising. It arises from the relatedness of the local languages and an important linguistic fact of bilingualism which has been aptly observed by Strevens in the same paper as follows:

> The fundamental issue is that in speaking a foreign language, we commonly use, not the sounds of that language, but those sounds of out mother tongue which we imagine to be equivalent to the sounds of foreign language; and quite apart from the quality of the sounds in isolation, we follow the rules of our own language, and not of the foreign language, in joining sounds together in connected speech, in stress, in rhythm, in intonation.[4]

Language and politics

Another result of the small number of families into which the languages of Africa divide is the general similarity of language problems in Africa. Of course, this is also contributed to by the similarity of the socio-economic background of the various African peoples. All black African countries fall within the category of 'developing nations', a euphemism for 'under developed countries', and the common lack of a high standard of socio-economic development provides comparable kinds of background within which language problems develop.

These problems are largely of two kinds, political and educational, and they may be restricted by national boundaries or by continental limits. Generally the educational problems are restricted within each country. The presence of economic blocs such as the Economic Community of West African States (ECOWAS) and even the existence of the organisation of African Unity (OAU) often makes political problems continental or international.

Within each country, the political language problems are of two kinds. There are those problems that deal with identification and development of local indigenous languages for use within the country. The second kind concerns the specification of official and/or national language or languages. At this juncture, it may be necessary to draw attention to the distinction between 'official' and 'national' languages. Basically, official languages are those used for transacting official business or businesses of a given community, locally, nationally or internationally. In contrast, a national language is one adopted by a particular community as the symbol of its national integration, development and independence. Very often, the same language or languages play these two roles, the exception in Africa being East African countries such as Tanzania, Kenya and Uganda where a distinction is made. As was noted earlier, the presence of Swahili has made this distinction reasonable as well as possible.

On the continental plane, the basic political problem is the adoption of a single language or a number of languages for the purpose of transacting political and economic business among African nations. Indeed, this problem can be analysed into three separate issues. There is the question as to whether to pursue a policy of monolingualism, bilingualism or multilingualism for the continent. Then there is the question whether an indigenous African language, a number of indigenous African languages, a modern European language, a number of modern European languages, or a mixture of indigenous African languages and modern European languages should be chosen in pursuance of the policy of adopting one, two or more languages. Thirdly, there is the question of which particular language or languages, indigenous or foreign, is to be chosen and adopted. Unlike the situation within each country where there is usually one modern European language available, on the continental plane a number of modern European languages are available for possible adoption. At least two are very widely used in the continent, English and French. Similarly, all the indigenous languages of the continent are potential candidates for adoption. Undoubtedly, the adoption of a single language would be advantageous. Undoubtedly, too, the policy that seems most consonant with the unification of Africa is the evolution or adoption of a language indigenous to Africa. However, the possibility of success of such a policy is remote indeed. Languages are related to the emotional feelings of their users and coercive efforts to make people give up their own languages for others usually fail. More important still, even peaceful and willing adoption of a single language over the continent of Africa requires for its success such massive political, administrative and educational efforts that can be neither initially supplied nor progressively sustained now or in the foreseeable future.

Educationally, language problems are even more serious because the language or languages used for education condition the effectiveness of educational plans and activities. Furthermore, solutions to educational language problems should contribute to those for political problems. Yet the importance of language problems is often not recognised. Formal education in Africa is widely equated with knowledge of a modern European language, and the problems of education are therefore not seen in their stark reality, neither identified nor tackled as they deserve.

The fact that similar language problems are widespread in Africa gives rise to the possibility of adopting similar solutions in at least some of the different African nations. What kind of language policies have a chance of meeting with success? Although both political and educational language policies derive their power from politics, there is a measure of difference in the involvement with politics of the two kinds of language policy. The political language policy derives its power essentially from politics, whereas the educational policy derives much of its justification from education. Although language specialists could be called upon to advise on the two kinds of policy, it is the educational one in which his expertise can more easily be utilised dispassionately. This is because of the fundamental differences in the nature of the starting points of the two kinds of policy. For the educational policy, the starting point is the determination of the basic goals of education in terms of the answers to three questions:

(1) education for whom and at what level?
(2) education for what purpose? and
(3) education in what manner or through what language medium?

In contrast, the starting point for a political language policy is the determination of the type of political structure or nation-building model the country wants. Thus it can be seen that the basic question here is political, rather than educational.

The political language policy attempts to identify the different languages being used by the citizens of any given country, to ascribe to the various languages certain functions within the bodies politic of the country, and finally to designate one or more of them as the official and/or national language or languages for conducting the official and national and international policies of the country. As has already been noted, such a policy may be based on languages foreign to the country. When that is done, the policy is said to be exoglossic. On the other hand, the policy may be based on languages indigenous to the country, and when that happens, the policy is said to be endoglossic. Also, as has been suggested, since such policies are often based on considerations of national pride, prestige and autonomy, it is desirable that the policy is endoglossic.

Opinions are often divided as to how to establish whatever the chosen policy is, particularly the endoglossic. Some people have argued that, given the right atmosphere, such a policy may be legislated upon or decreed with success. Others, however, would feel that the method of legislation or decree may be inadequate to create the required atmosphere or climate. Doubts about the efficacy of coercion make others advocate the alternative procedure of evolution rather than revolution. The policy of evolution usually assumes that the success of a political policy largely depends on a successful implementation of a purposive educational policy designed for it. This means that the educational policy is made the midwife to the political policy.

In answering the three basic educational questions posed for an educational policy, certain considerations are particularly applicable to the African continent. The socio-economic conditions in various African countries indirectly affect the success of any educational programme and also considerably increase the costs of making such programmes successful. For primary education, for example, it is not enough to get school buildings, to provide adequate teachers, and to have qualitative teaching materials in the right numbers. In order that primary education become effectively universal, roads have to be developed to make the schools easily accessible to all children, particularly in the rural areas. When it is remembered that many African countries are within the equatorial forest, the difficulty of this requirement is the more easily appreciated, for unless the roads are very strongly built, they will be waterlogged for the greater part of the year. Similarly, the various villages and hamlets will have to be supplied with good housing, water, and light in order that teachers may reside there and serve the school and communities effectively. It is because of a lack of amenities that teachers in schools in the rural areas of Africa often live in nearby cities from which they commute to their work. Since it is not uncommon that officials of the Ministry of Education often find it impossible to visit such schools regularly, there is usually no way of maintaining standards in such schools today.

The influence of socio-economic conditions on the effectiveness of educational programmes is not restricted to primary education. Secondary and tertiary levels are also affected. Take, for example, the need for boarding facilities. Largely because of lack of suitable amenities such as light, water and comfortable sitting and sleeping furniture in the average African home, in order to guarantee effectiveness of education at the secondary and tertiary levels, boarding schools, hostel accommodation or residential halls for students have to be provided. Undoubtedly, such requirements greatly increase the cost of education, particularly as colleges and universities tend to increase their student-population as education develops. The answer to problems of this kind seems to lie, therefore, in the rapid overall socio-economic development of the African countries.

Another consequence arising from the same economic constraints is that primary education is terminal for most citizens of developing African countries. There is hardly any African country today that can guarantee secondary and tertiary levels of education to as much as 30 per cent of her population. These facts together influence the answer to be given to the question of 'education for what purpose' in Africa. Normally, the two basic goals of education are self-fulfilment and usefulness to the community. Given the situation just depicted whereby the majority of citizens have only primary education, it is wise to assume that such primary school products make their contributions to the development of their countries mostly at the local levels, in local languages and mostly among speakers of the same language. Similarly, it can be reasonably assumed that it is from the products of secondary and tertiary education that those who should contribute to the development of their communities at the national and international levels will come. If these assumptions are right, then the situation requires a new dynamic educational language policy on the part of Africans in order that Africa may emerge as a developed continent rather than remaining a developing one.

The first important step towards such a policy and its effective implementation is the realisation that it is time to do so. The countries of Africa must take a new look at this fascinating yet melancholy linguistic situation and decide that indigenous local African languages deserve as much planning, cultivating, inproving and developing as are taking place in the fields of economics, science and technology, for African languages are indispensable to the emergence of a truly African culture.

The next important step is to follow up the realisation with resolute planning and action. This step includes maintaining, reinforcing and enriching (including codifying and elaborating) the local indigenous languages. Even if and when it is conceded that appropriate European languages may be adopted to supplement the indigenous local African languages, then that adoption must be oriented towards specific and original African aspirations and goals.

It remains for us to say what we consider the essential ingredients of such a new dynamic policy. First, local indigenous African languages, and not European languages, must be made the real instruments of both government and education. In politics a progressively endoglossic policy should replace the erstwhile exoglossic policy. In education, the indigenous local African languages should, to start with, become the media of basic or primary education and then progressively become the media of secondary and even tertiary education. It is, for example, hard to defend the use of modern European languages for the teaching and examination of indigenous African languages at the undergraduate and even postgraduate levels, as happens today. How, for example, can the style and flavour of African literature written in indigenous African languages be effectively conveyed through the medium of European languages with any measure of authenticity? It is our considered view that Africans will make their own contribution to science and technology only when original African thought, ideas and methods of production, based on African culture and rooted in its own ecology, can emerge. That is why the proclaimed transfer of technology from Europe and America has never succeeded. The trouble is that what is involved is more than a mere transfer; it is a transplant. For a transplant to succeed, the receiving body must be conducive to transplantation. What is more, a transplant is never as authentic, effective and durable as a natural cultivation. Surely, the natural cultivation of authentic African culture, science or technology requires the indigenous African language as its vehicle or tool? Mere transfer of technology can never rise above technological colonialism. Therefore, when and where modern European languages must supplement the indigenous African languages, their international functions must be clearly distinguished from the local and national. It is not linguistic jingosim to insist that in local and national life they can be adopted only so far as such adoption is compatible with the specific aspirations and goals of the local African peoples. Their international functions are a different matter.

There is no doubt that there are many problems to be solved in pursuing effectively the type of policy just suggested. However, what is important is to realise that these problems are surmountable. Experience has shown that the most difficult problem to overcome is that sense of psychological defeat that most Africans bring to the consideration and implementation of such a policy. Once there is the necessary political will the problems can be progressively solved. It will then become possible for black Africa to pursue not only progressively endoglossic policy within each country, politically and educationally, but also a pan-African political language policy centred upon some indigenous African language.

Literature of Africa

The current language situation depicted in the preceding paragraphs is indicative of the state of literature in Africa. Generally, the indigenous languages of the black citizens of Africa support a mainly oral literature in its rich diversity. Written literature — technically a redundant term necessitated by the existence of oral literature — has only relatively recently been developed in these languages. It is interesting to note that those languages among them that are not restricted within the confines of only one single political unit or country — in short, those that tend to be international — are the ones that have the longest tradition of established written literature. Such are Swahili of East Africa, Hausa of the West

African Sudan and Yoruba of the Guinea Coast. In contrast, the languages of whites in Africa enjoy long traditions of written literature, although they tend to be less rich in oral tradition.

Now, let us attempt a deeper analysis of literature in Africa from the conceptual point of view. The notion of literature earlier given emphasises its two component aspects, the 'word' and the 'world' (see page 175), or more precisely, 'life style' and 'language style'. A clear understanding of literature in Africa therefore requires an examination of the 'life style' and the 'language style' of the continent. What then are these two styles of Africa?

The two styles can be conceived as the form and the content of literature. After a look at both the 'life style' and the 'language style' of Africa, we shall examine the kinds of literature that have emerged from the correlation of the two styles. Finally, we shall make suggestions concerning the future development of literature in Africa.

In order to think adequately about the 'life style' of Africa it seems necessary to recognise three different categories. These are: the 'life style' of black Africa, the 'life style' of non-black Africa north of the Sahara, and the 'life style' of non-black Africa south of the Sahara.

The most striking characteristic of the 'life style' of black Africa is its being predominantly non-literate, rural and agricultural. As such, each black African society is usually marked by its cultural artefacts, rich traditions of religion, and intricate organisation and administration of the community, often expressed in colourful dance, music, poetry and story-telling. Often such traditional materials are misunderstood and written off as primitive or superstitious. In reality, such materials include historical facts, incidents and even judgements enshrined in otherwise simple traditional stories, particularly those of official or court poets and story-tellers. Similarly, traditional medical and other scientific concepts and practices are recorded in such stories or poems, while philosophical and sociological concepts exist in large numbers. Gone are the days when certain scholars could say that Africa had no history or that the African was incapable of conceiving the idea of the soul or of God, thanks to the uncovering of rich oral deposits of traditonal wisdom. One of the most elaborate and best recorded is the Ifa corpus of the Yoruba-speaking people of Nigeria and Dahomey (now the Republic of Benin). Others, less well known, abound in the different African communities, and the duty of every community is to ensure that they are preserved and analysed, described and utilised.

The next significant characteristic of the 'life style' of black Africa is the presence of aspects of foreign 'life style', those of the non-black people from outside Africa and also those of the non-black neighbours north of the Sahara. The non-black people from outside Africa are Europeans, Americans and Asians. The northern neighbours are Arabs and Arabised Berbers who also regularly visited the east and west Sudan from early times, and also settled on the coast of East Africa.

Understandably the 'life style' of black Africa is different from that of the non-black people. While black Africa, as has been earlier described, is largely non-literate, rural and agricultural, Europe or America, for example, is literate, urban and industrialised. Consequently, as a result of the contacts between the black Africans and these non-black people, certain new aspects of 'life style' were injected into the manner of living of black Africans. The aspects of foreign life style thus introduced into black African 'life style' came through three main areas of human endeavour: trade, religion and social life. Through legitimate trade new items were introduced to change the pattern of living. Through the illegitimate trade in human cargoes, black African life was debased and then, later, returning freed slaves brought back new ways of life. Through religion literacy was introduced as a positive contribution, but a discontinuation of traditional morality and values occurred as a negative effect. Similarly, changes in clothing, food, housing and the introduction of technological gadgets brought both blessings and woes to black Africans. Consequently the 'life style' of black Africa has become characterised by a great deal of ethical and cultural diffusion.

The nadir of the negative influence of black-non-black contact in Africa has been reached in the colonialism exercised by Western Europeans. Although most of Africa is now politically independent, there are still pockets of European domination in southern Africa and, worse still, there is to be found everywhere a great deal of economic as well as intellectual subjugation of black Africa to exploitative non-black visitors and so-called friends. Indeed, the colonial mentality of many educated Africans is the worst legacy bequeathed to black Africa by colonialism.

However, the rejection of things black and the corresponding adoption of things white have never been wholesale, total or without resistance. What is more, in recent times the situation has been interestingly complicated by the resurgence of black African arts, ethics and culture. Certainly, it is true to say that the novels, poems, plays, and music of black Africans today, in the east, west or south of the continent, celebrate or at least record these various ethical and cultural situations.

Now let us turn to the 'language style' of black Africa. As is to be expected from the language situation earlier depicted, there are four possible major kinds of 'language style' to be found, namely, the spoken indigenous African language, the written indigenous African language, the spoken European language, and the written European language. However, not all four serve as carriers of different kinds of literature. This lack of one-to-one correspondence between the number of 'language styles' and the number of literature varieties arises from the nature of correspondence between literature content and 'language styles'. As has been noted, the content of oral literature generally consists of traditional materials that have become the corporate property of the community. Consequently oral literature is usually carried by the local indigenous language that is associated with the traditional body of materials. Thus the spoken European language in black Africa does not have any identifiable oral literature; what is found is usually an aspect of written literature, a sort of oral literature in transition. Comparable to the written literature, such oral literature many derive from two different sources or 'life styles', the local African and the foreign European.

There are then only three identifiable kinds of literature in black Africa: oral literature in the local black African language, written literature in the local black African language, and written literature in a modern European language. Oral literature in a modern European language exists only for the minority white citizens of black African countries who have such a language as their mother tongue. Since such a language is also the language of the home country of the former colonial power and since we have identified oral literature with the local language, for brevity we shall henceforth refer to the three kinds of literature as oral literature (always implying it is in a local language), written literature in local languages, and written literature in the language of the former metropolis.

These three kinds of literature together constitute 'African literature'. Thus African literature is not just one single phenomenon or entity, and its three facets are differentiated in language style, content and future expectation.

Oral literature seems to be the most predominant kind of African literature. This is predictable since, as has been earlier noted, the black communities of Africa are predominatly non-literate, rural and agricultural. As is generally known, preliterate or non-literate societies are usually noted for their memory and artistic creations and embellishments in the process of retelling or reciting traditional material. Although the content of oral literature is traditional material, the fact that its language is the local language in which every one is creative and the fact that the society is itself changing, make oral literature dynamic rather than static. It is subjected to contemporary influences in both content and style and its future lies not only in its dynamic creativity but also in the transition of a great deal of it into written literature.

Written literature in local languages is the least known and the least plentiful of the three kinds of African literature. The sparseness of this kind of literature may appear strange. The explanation is found in the neglect of local African languages and the corresponding undue emphasis on the language of the former metropolis in the education of the African, as has been earlier noted. But there is little doubt that this type of African literature is bound to increase in volume as the result of the progressive transition of black Africa from the predominance of oral literature to that of written literature. Indeed, it is this aspect which calls for the concentration of national efforts in the development of African literature for these major reasons. In the first place, written literature in local languages provides a greater opportunity for the development of literary talent than does written literature in the language of the former metropolis. As has been suggested, primary education is terminal for the majority of African children and primary education should therefore be given in the local languages. One important reason for the adoption of local languages as the media of primary education that has not yet been mentioned is the goal of permanent literacy. Certainly permanent and functional literacy can be more easily attained in the local languages than in foreign European languages. For one thing, there is greater motivation for the use of local languages among such people. Since the percentage of people that will be literate in local languages will be at least three times and may be even as much as ten times those literate in the modern European languages in each country, a far wider reading public can be foreseen.

The second major reason for concentrating on local languages is the possibility of attaining higher critical literary judgement and output on the part of the writers. Most people have their natural roots in oral literature and a large part of developed written literature is likely to be closely related to oral literature. Undoubtedly the various oral literatures are available in local languages. Therefore, the literary raw materials available for use are in local rather than modern European languages. First concentrating on the development of literary skills through the use of local language should therefore promote greater transference of literary skills and judgements in the handling of written literature in modern European languages later by those who would need it. Once an African child is able to assess what makes a good play, a good novel or a good poem in his own local language, it would be relatively easy for him to see what makes a good play, poem or novel in a modern European language if and when he encounters that literature.

Finally, it is through such a development that African literature can be most enriched. Besides being the most vigorous and effective medium of reflecting the contemporary ethical and cultural diffusion prevalent in Africa, the promotion of written literature in local languages provides the best channel for making European, American and even other African literary values and ideas available to an increasing number of black Africans by means of translations.

What has been most commonly equated with African literature is written literature in the language of the former metropolis. This is largely because written literature in black Africa has been generally promoted as part of literature in the various modern European languages. This development has had two consequences in the literary world and they are bound to be taken further in the future.

First, until perhaps fifteen years ago no one would have dreamt of including black African literature written in the various languages of the former metropolis within the purview of literary, academic discipline related to such languages, but it is today widely recognised and incorporated. Certainly, in its future development the discipline will also include works originally written in local African languages but translated into languages of the former metropolis. It would seem true to say today that it is the African literature written in the language of the former metropolis that most easily captures the contemporary African situation of ethical and cultural diffusion.

The other consequence of the development of African literature in modern European languages is the change in the coverage of texts designated originally as literatures in those European languages. For example, 'English literature' as a term quite often has the meaning 'literature in English' rather than 'the literature of the English people'. In certain contexts it more often than not even refers to Commonwealth and American literature rather than to British and American literature.

The case for African literature in European languages today largely rests on wider readership and wider currency. African writers speak to larger audiences today when they write in a modern European language rather than in an African local language. On the other hand, without the existence of such literature, it would be impossible to see the vigorous and diverse literary richness of the new dialects of the various modern European languages developing in the various African settings.

Although the great emphasis should now be on African literature in local languages, it would seem that the case for African literature in modern European languages remains strong. The two factors given above – wider readership and the development of new literary dialects – will continue to exist. Still more important, the example set by and the experience gained from literary attempts in European languages provide invaluable background and information on the rich possibilities and potentialities of the African scene for literary expression. The continued use of European languages for recording African literature is bound to establish useful contacts between the African and the world literary traditions, contacts that are bound to open new opportunities and directions in the development of African literature in the local African languages. Thus the continued development of African literature in modern European languages provides not only a catalyst but also an accompanying agent of enrichment in the rise, growth and ensuing fruitfulness of African literature in indigenous African languages.

Conclusion

Language and literature are so intricately interwoven that any full consideration of one in relation to any given community – say, an African country – inevitably leads to a discussion of the other. Furthermore, examination of either language or literature or of both is bound to lead one into cultural issues which touch upon political, social and religious questions. Thus a discussion of language and literature in Africa inevitably covers educational, political, social, economic, philosophical, scientific and religious matters. Indeed the issues of language and literature have such far-reaching consequences for the present and future development of Africa that they deserve the same urgent and serious attention as economic and technological problems demand. What is often lost sight of is that the success and effectiveness of political, economic and technological programmes in Africa will be decisively affected by policies concerning language and literature.

Notes

1   Edward Sapir, *Language: an introduction to the study of speech,* pp. 15-16

2   Raymond Cowell, *The critical enterprise: English studies in higher education,* London, Allen & Unwin, 1975, pp. 19ff

3   Peter D. Strevens, 'Pronunciation of the English language in West Africa', in *Papers in language and language teaching*, Oxford University Press, 1965, p. 112

4   *Ibid.,* p. 111

Questions for discussion

1 How is language related to literature, and how are both language and literature related to politics and religion in your own country?

2 How wise or feasible is it to pursue a policy of 'one country, one language' in Africa today? Is it reasonable to expect that the African continent can be served by only one language?

3 Is the making of indigenous African languages the centre of the educational and literary development of Africa a way of preventing Africa from emerging as a modern continent with an orientation towards science and technology?

4 How important is language in the life of any given individual person or community? How does this importance explain the African political scene today?

5 List as many African literary texts as you can, and indicate how far each presents African traditional societies and/or contemporary African communities with ethical and cultural diffusion, conflict or confusion.

Suggestions for further reading

Abercombie, David. *Problems and principles in language study,* 2nd ed., London, Longman, 1964

Alexandre, Pierre. *Introduction to languages and language in Africa,* London, Heinemann Educational Books, 1972

Cowell, Raymond. *The Critical enterprise: English studies in higher education,* London, Allen & Unwin, 1975

Dathorne, O. R. *The black mind: a history of African literature,* University of Minnesota Press, 1974

Fishman, Joshua A. (ed.) *Advances in language planning,* New York, Mouton, 1974. Contributions to the sociology of language, ser. 5

Goody, Jack. *Literacy in traditional societies,* Cambridge University Press, 1975

Greenberg, Joseph H. *Languages of Africa,* 3rd ed., Indiana University Research Center for Language Sciences, 1970

Klima, V., and others. *Black Africa: literature and language,* Dordrecht, Reidal, 1976

Larson, Charles. *The emergence of African fiction,* Indiana University Press, 1972

Pride, J. B. *The social meaning of language,* Oxford University Press, 1971

Sapir, Edward. *Language: an introduction to the study of speech,* St Albans, Hart-Davis, MacGibbon, 1973

Wauthier, Claude René. *The literature and thought of modern Africa,* Westport, Connecticut, Greenwood Press, 1975

Welmers, William E. *African language structures,* Berkeley, University of California Press, 1974

11　African views of the universe*

John S. Mbiti

Accumulation of ideas about the universe

As they went through life, African peoples observed the world around them and reflected upon it. They looked at the sky above with its stars, moon, sun and meteorites; with its clouds, rain, rainbows and the movement of the winds. Below they saw the earth with its myriad of life forms, animals, insects, and plants, and its rivers and lakes, rocks and mountains. They saw the limits of man's powers and knowledge, and the shortnesss of human life. They experienced and witnessed the processes of birth, growth, procreation and death; they felt the agonies of the body and mind, hunger and thirst, the emotions of joy, fear, and love. All their five major senses (of hearing, seeing, feeling, tasting and smelling) were open gates through which all kinds of experiences came upon them. These experiences stimulated them to reflect upon their life and the universe in which they lived. The result was a gradual building up of African views or ideas about the world and the universe at large.

No thinking person can live without forming some views about life and the world. Some of the ideas developed by individual reflection eventually spread among other people, through discussion, artistic expression and so on. These other people were stimulated to reflect further, extending old ideas, abandoning some of them, acquiring new ones and translating others into practical realities. And so the process gained momentum, people's ideas about the universe accumulated and definite views and systems of thought began to emerge. There can be no end to the development of people's views about the universe, as this process is a continuing one.

Obviously many ideas about the world have emerged among African peoples. It would be impossible to cover them all in detail, but in this chapter we can give a broad summary of them in order to make us familiar with their general content. These views are expressed in myths, legends, proverbs, rituals, symbols, beliefs, and wise sayings. There is no formal or systematised view of the universe, but when these various ideas are put together, a picture emerges. There are many mysteries in the universe, and whenever possible people try to find an explanation for them, whether or not the explanation is final.

* Reprinted from John S. Mbiti, *Introduction to African religion,* Heinemann, 1975, pp. 31-39. We are grateful to the author and the publishers for permission to reproduce it here.

A created universe

It is generally believed all over Africa that the universe was created. The Creator of the universe is God. There is no agreement, however, on how the creation of the universe took place. But it seems impossible that the universe could simply have come into existence on its own. God is, therefore, the explanation for the origin of the universe, which consists of both visible and invisible realities. People often say that 'God created all things'. In many African languages, the name for God means 'Creator'; even when there is another name, He is often called 'the Creator' as well.

The belief in God is found everywhere in Africa. When people explain the universe as having been created by God, they are automatically looking at the universe in a religious way. We can say, therefore, that the African view of the universe is profoundly religious. Africans see it as a religious universe, and treat it as such.

While there are many different accounts of the creation of the universe, it is commonly agreed that man has been put at its centre. We shall see that of all created things man is the most important and the most privileged. In some accounts of creation it is told that God made the heavenly part of the universe first, and then, standing on it, he created the earth. In other myths the order is reversed. Some accounts say that the entire universe was created in one act. It is also a widespread view among African peoples that God continues to create. Thus, the creation of the universe did not stop in the distant past: it is an ongoing process which will probably never end.

The nature of the universe

In many African societies it is believed that the universe is divisible into two. These are the visible and the invisible parts, or the heavens (or sky) and the earth. Some people, however, hold that the universe is in the form of a three-tier creation, namely: the heavens, the earth and the underworld, which lies below it. African peoples do not think of these divisions as separate but see them as linked together.

The heavenly part of the universe is the home of the stars, sun, moon, meteorites, sky, the wind and the rain with all the phenomena connected with them such as thunder and lightning, storms, eclipses of the sun and the moon, 'falling stars', and so on. It is also thought to be the home of God, although people cannot quite locate where he dwells, other than saying that he lives 'in the sky', 'in heaven', or 'beyond the clouds', or they simply say that 'God does not live on the earth like men'. God is often believed to have other beings living with him or close to him. Some of these are in charge of different departments of the universe, others are his messengers and servants or ministers, and some are like his children. But there are other Africans who say that God dwells completely alone and does everything himself, since he is all-powerful.

It is generally held that the heavenly universe is not empty but that it has its own population. It is teeming with its own kinds of life in addition to the visible objects mentioned above. This means that it is more or less the counterpart of the earth, even though what goes on there is invisible to us.

The earth, too, is full of created things. Some African peoples regard it as a living being, and call it 'Mother Earth', 'the goddess earth' or 'the divinity of the earth'. Symbolically it is looked on as the mother of the universe, while the heavenly part is the father. In some societies rituals are performed to show respect to the earth. For example, in Zambia, when the rains start, people have to refrain from working on the ground in the fields for a few days. In some parts of Africa when a major calamity like an earthquake befalls people, sacrifices may be made to the divinity of the earth. On the earth itself many things, animate and inanimate, are held in great esteem for religious reasons, such as mountains, waterfalls, rocks, some forests and trees, birds, animals and insects.

Man, who lives on the earth, is the centre of the universe. He is also like the priest of the universe, linking the universe with God its Creator. Man awakens the universe, he speaks to it, he listens to it, he tries to create a harmony with the universe. It is man who turns parts of the universe into sacred objects, and who uses other things for sacrifices and offerings. These are constant reminders to people that they regard it as a religious universe.

In many African myths it is told that at one time in the distant past, the heavens (or sky) and the earth were united as one. This union is pictured as being like the place where the earth and sky seem to touch each other at the end of the horizon. Other myths say that the union was formed by a ladder or rope between the two. These accounts go on to say how the separation took place. According to some, animals bit the leather rope into two, so that one part went up to the sky and the other fell to the ground, thus severing the heavens from the earth. Some myths say that it was through man's fault or error that the two parts of the universe were divided up. These are simply attempts to explain the fact that the universe is divided into two parts, as it appears to be to the ordinary person; and also to explain the fact that God and man are separated.

The universe is considered to be unending in terms of both space and time. Nobody can reach the edge of the universe since it has no known edge or rim. Just as there is no edge of the earth, so there is no edge to the universe. In terms of time, it makes sense for people to believe that there was a beginning for the universe, even though they do not know when it was. But nobody thinks that there will ever be an end to it. They say, 'The world will never end.' African ideas of time concern mainly the present and the past, and have little to say about the future, which in any case is expected to go on without end. Events come and go in the form of minor and major rhythms. The minor rhythms are found in the lives of the living things of this earth (such as man, animals and plants), in their birth, growth, procreation and death. These rhythms are thought to occur in the lives of everybody and everything that has physical life. The major rhythms of time are events like day and night, the months (reckoned on the basis of the phases of the moon), the seasons of rain and of dry weather, and the events of nature which come and go at greater intervals (such as the flowing of certain plants, the migration of certain birds and insects, famines, and movement of certain heavenly bodies). All these rhythms of time suggest that the universe will never come to a halt, whatever changes there may be.

In many places, circles are used as symbols of the continuity of the universe. They are the symbols of eternity, of unendings, of continuity. The circles may be used in rituals, in art, in rock paintings, as decorations on stools and domestic utensils, and so on. In other places this unendingness is symbolised by drawings of a snake curled round, sometimes with its tail in its mouth. The same idea is celebrated in rituals which re-enact birth, death and re-birth, showing that life is stronger than death. This can also be interpreted to mean that continuity on a large scale is more important than change in small details. People are aware that the laws of nature do not normally change, and so there is no ground for imagining that this entire universe might suddenly come to an end. Thus, the universe is considered to be permanent, eternal and unending.

In the African view, the universe is both visible and invisible, unending and without limits. Since it was created by God it is subsequently dependent on him for its continuity. God is the sustainer, the keeper and upholder of the universe. Man, on the other hand, is at the very centre of the universe.

Order and power in the universe

It is considered that the universe is orderly. As long as this order is not upset there is harmony. Order in the universe is seen as operating at several levels.

First, there is order in the laws of nature. These function everywhere, and give a sense of security and certainty to the universe. If they were completely unpredictable and changed at random, there would be chaos in the world which would endanger the existence of both life and the universe itself.

Secondly, there is moral order at work among people. It is believed by African peoples that God gave moral order to people so that they might live happily and in harmony with one another. Through this moral order, customs and institutions have arisen in all societies, to safeguard the life of the individual and the community of which he is part. Moral order helps men to work out and know among themselves what is good and evil, right and wrong, truthful and false, and beautiful and ugly, and what people's rights and duties are. Each society is able to formulate its values because there is moral order in the universe. These values deal with relationships among people, and between people and God and other spiritual beings; and man's relationship with the world of nature.

Thirdly, there is religious order in the universe. We saw earlier on in the chapter that Africans look at the universe in a religious way. Because of their basic belief that the universe is created and sustained by God, they interpret their life's experiences from that starting-point. The laws of nature are regarded as being controlled by God directly or through his servants. The morals and institutions of society are thought to have been given by God, or to be sanctioned ultimately by him. Therefore any breach of such morals is an offence against the departed members of the family, and against God or the spirits, even if it is the people themselves who may suffer from such a breach and who may take action to punish the offender.

There are, therefore, taboos which strengthen the keeping of the moral and religious order. There may be taboos over any aspect of life: words, foods, dress, relations among people, marriage, burial, social ostracism, misfortune, and even death. If people do not punish the offender, then the invisible world will punish him. This view arises from the belief in the religious order of the universe, in which God and other invisible beings are thought to be actively engaged in the world of men.

Fourthly, there is a mystical order governing the universe. The belief in this order is shown clearly in the practice of traditional medicine, magic, witchcraft, and sorcery. It is held in all African societies that there is power in the universe, and that it comes from God. It is a mystical power, in the sense that it is hidden and mysterious. This power is available to spirits and to certain human beings. People who have access to it are sometimes able to see the departed, visions, communicate at a distance without using physical means, receive premonitions of coming events, foretell certain things before they happen, communicate with the invisible world, and perform 'wonders' and 'miracles' which other people may not ordinarily be able to do.

It is the knowledge of this mystical power which is used to help other people (especially in healing, rain-making, finding the cause of misfortunes and troubles, detecting theives, and so on), or to harm them. When it is used harmfully, it is regarded as evil magic, witchcraft or sorcery; and it may also be used in curses. The ordinary people do not know much about this mystical power. It may take a long time for someone to be trained in the knowledge and use of mystical power; and such knowledge is often safeguarded and kept secret. In some cases the ability to use this mystical power is simply inherited or passed on without the conscious intention of those concerned. Once a person has discovered that he has some of this power, he may then proceed to undertake further training in using it, or he may just neglect it.

Man at the centre of the universe

As the Creator of the universe, God is outside and beyond it. At the same time, since he is also its sustainer and upholder, he is very close to the universe. But in African myths of creation, man puts himself at the centre of the universe.

Because man thinks of himself as being at the centre, he consequently sees the universe from that perspective. It is as if the whole world exists for man's sake. Therefore African peoples look for the usefulness (or otherwise) of the universe to man. This means both what the world can do for man, and how man can use the world for his own good. This attitude towards the universe is deeply engrained in African peoples.

For that reason many people, for example, have divided animals into those which man can eat and those which he cannot eat. Others look at plants in terms of what can be eaten by people, what can be used for curatives or medical purposes, what can be used for building, fire, and so on. Certain things have physical uses; some have religious uses (for ceremonies, rituals, and symbols); and other things are used for medicinal and magical purposes.

African peoples regard inanimate objects and natural phenomena as being inhibited by living beings, or having a mystical life. In religious language we speak of these beings as divinities and spirits. The idea behind this belief is to give man the ability to use or control some of these things and phenomena. For example, if people believe that there is a spirit or divinity of their local lake they will, through sacrifices, offerings or prayers, ask for the help of the divinity when fishing in the lake or crossing it in a canoe. This gives them a feeling of confidence and security, a feeling that they are in harmony with the lake (and with the life-agent personified by the lake or occupying that lake). In some societies it is believed that lightning and thunder are caused by a spirit; therefore people endeavour to be in harmony with that spirit, for fear that it might strike them dead or set their houses on fire.

We may say, therefore, that African people consider man to be at the centre of the universe. Being in that position he tries to use the universe or derive some use from it in physical, mystical and supernatural ways. He sees the universe in terms of himself, and endeavours to live in harmony with it. Even where there is no biological life in an object, African peoples attribute (mystical) life to it, in order to establish a more direct relationship with the world around them. In this way the visible and invisible parts of the universe are at man's disposal through physical, mystical and religious means. Man is not the master in the universe; he is only the centre, the friend, the beneficiary, the user. For that reason he has to live in harmony and the universe, obeying the laws of natural, moral and mystical order. If these are unduly disturbed, it is man who suffers most. African peoples have come to these conclusions through long experience, observation and reflection.

Questions for discussion*

1   Discuss the place of man in African cosmology.
2   'Order in the universe is seen as operating at several levels.' Discuss.
3   In what ways is the keeping of the moral and religious order assured?

* Prepared by the editor.

Suggestions for further reading

Forde, Daryll (ed.) *African worlds: studies in the cosmological ideas and social values of African peoples,* Oxford University Press, 1968

Horton, Robin. 'African traditional thought and Western science', *Africa,* 37 (1-2), (1967), 50-71, 155-87

Jahn, Janheinz, *Muntu: an outline of the new African culture,* New York, Grove Press, 1961

Mbiti, John S. *Introduction to African religion,* London, Heinemann, 1975

————. *African religions and philosophy,* New York, Praeger, 1970

Parrinder, E. G. *African traditional religion,* London, Sheldon, 1974 ed.

Ray, Benjamin, *African religions: symbol, ritual and community,* Englewood Cliffs, N. J., Prentice-Hall, 1976

Wiredu, K. 'How not to compare African traditional thought with Western thought,' *Ch'Indaba,* I (2) July/Dec. 1976

12 Art in traditional African culture

J. R. O. Ojo

Art: form and function

In considering the place of art in African culture, it must be stressed that the objects we now refer to as art were not originally destined to be displayed in our homes or museums for aesthetic contemplation like drawings, paintings and other products of modern European art.

While the meaning of the word 'art' is too varied to permit the formulation of a clear-cut definition that can be universally acceptable, it is nevertheless used for a variety of things all of which, it is assumed, have something in common. Thus the objects classified as 'African art' have affinities with objects which are described as art in English language.

'Art' is a category word which originated in Western cultural tradition, expressing an exclusively Western idea. Therefore, much as it is desirable that a definition of art should not be restricted to one civilisation, the word 'art' may not necessarily be suitable for describing objects from other cultures. Even if the word is used for purposes of expediency, it is misleading, as we shall soon see, to apply it to such things as African masquerade headpieces (so-called masks).

When European explorers collected man-made objects such as weapons, tools, pots, musical instruments, furnishings, masks, cult statues and other 'magical' implements, they were labelled 'artefacts' because at that time they were not considered as belonging to the category of art.[1]

Around 1900, however, European artists saw that the pieces in the ethnographic galleries of museums belonged to the same category as the works they were producing. Consequently, the first outside recognition of these artefacts (man-made objects) was with reference to Western values and not the traditions from which they originated. Thereafter, in museum displays and writings, anthropomorphic and zoomorphic representations, as well as artefacts which show ornamental patterns – in short, objects which correspond to the Western idea of an art object – were put under the heading 'art'.

As Macquet has pointed out, in Western societies, pictures that hang on walls of museums, galleries and homes were purposely painted to be used as decoration. They are art objects by destination. He went on to say that in the Western world, any object can become an art object if displayed in art framework. A typical example is Picasso's combination of a bicycle seat and handlebar which he called 'Bull's Head'. When African artefacts are thus displayed, they become art objects by metamorphosis, a process whereby 'mask and figurines become art'. Although they partake of the qualities that characterise art objects in Western societies, the 'mask and figurines' were originally carved for ritual purposes. This reminds one of the cartoon in an English humorous magazine which showed a foreigh visitor to Britain bringing an animal into a museum and seeking permission from the guard to sacrifice the animal to one of the objects on display. Presumably it was the image of one of the deities of the visitor's country.

There is also the story of the incident at a police check-point here in Nigeria. All passengers in a taxi were asked to identify their luggage. The duty policeman insisted on seeing the contents of a large, awkwardly-shaped sack. When the contents were brought out, a female passenger uttered a cry of amazement, knelt down before it, paying homage and addressing praise songs to the carving. It was a carved masquerade headpiece stolen from the woman's home town a few days earlier.

African artefacts, whether originally produced for ritual purposes or decorative use, have been converted to art objects by their Western beholders. And to them, whether art is by destination or by metamorphosis, the idea is to produce a visual effect. In Africa, however, this is not always the case. For example, according to Robin Horton, little attention is paid to visibility in Kalabari sculpture.[2] There are no relief doors or carved verandah posts, intricately worked tools or decorated wooden utensils. It is only in the shrines that we have an abundance of carved figures and other objects. Even then, because the sculptures are not kept for their visual impact, visibility inside the shrines is low. In addition, the shrines are so small that most people can neither enter nor peep into their badly-lit interiors.

Now, when objects from Africa are put into foreign museums, Europeans make art objects out of those which display 'aesthetic quality'. As Macquet has remarked, these foreigners have no alternative because the objects are out of context. They therefore take for granted that what they call art is art itself. They take art in its contemporary European meaning which implies exclusive visual function based on aesthetic qualities and the notion of art for art's sake. There is no doubt that those of the artefacts labelled art have non-instrumental functions which raise them to the level of aesthetic objects, but the users do not see them that way.

Indeed, some African writers such as Alioune Diop have reacted against the assimilation by Europeans of African religious and political implements into European art categories. They are not art objects, although there are also other objects with an exclusive visual function in African culture. Examples are cups carved in the shape of human heads by Kuba craftsmen for the nobility; and the bowls supported on animal and human forms found among the Yoruba. Furthermore, as among the Yoruba, some of the forms and motifs of the decorative objects (doors and houseposts) are the same as the ritual objects (cult statues and masquerade headpieces). Some of these motifs are horse riders and mothers with children. Even then, art objects by destination do not constitute the most visible part of 'art' production in Africa. For those which we have described as art objects by metamorphosis, the ephemeral character of some 'masks' and statues does not allow them to survive their primary functions, let alone be collected and 'transformed into art'. Masks and symbols of secret societies are not always available for public gaze; those that are, are available only for specific periods. When not in use, it may be mandatory for them to be destroyed, and if not, climate, insects and vegetation take over. For example, Igbo Mbari houses, which are not primarily built as the result of an aesthetic impulse but through an upsurge of religious zeal, are left to fall into decay in as much time as it took to build them.

There are other forms which cannot be collected and put in museums. For example, in New Guinea, people decorate themselves with beautiful feathers, animal furs, paint, leaves, and grasses during colourful ceremonies. Although the tangible elements of this self-decoration can be collected, these objects will be out of context because they are meant to be seen in relation to the human body and the paint applied to it. Like Nuba personal art, New Guinea self-decorations, in spite of their aesthetic appeal, cannot outlast the occasions for which they were assumed.[3] In many parts of Africa, especially West Africa, body scarification and cicatrisation are practised, and these can only last the lifetime of the individual on whose body we admire these ornaments.

From the foregoing, we can see that some of the objects classified as art by foreigners are not so regarded by their users and makers. Indeed, to them, the word 'art' refers to drawing and painting associated with Western-type educational institutions. Consequently, in any consideration of the study of 'African art', the European concept is inadequate. Other societies have concepts determined by their own culture and expressed in linguistic conventions familiar to members of that culture. The translation of these concepts into a foreign language may pose problems which can only be solved by familiarity with the world of thought expressed.

For instance, the word 'art' cannot be translated in a straightforward manner into the Yoruba language. To the Yoruba educated in the Western tradition, the word 'art' is associated with two-dimensional art – that is, drawing and painting. Translated into Yoruba it is *àwòrán*, a word which includes photography. In Yoruba usage, it is not normally associated with objects in three dimensions and other objects of indigenous craftsmanship such as carvings in wood (*ère*, images), stone and ivory; metal smithing and leather working.

In wood working, one can distinguish between those who carve wooden implements such as mortars, pestles and wooden trays and bowls; these are *gbégigbégi*, 'carvers of wood', and those who carve objects of aesthetic appeal. These are *gbénàgbénà,* meaning literally 'carvers of ornament'. They are also known as *agbégilére,* 'carvers of wooden images'.

The use of the word *onà*, 'ornament' in the English sense, in referring to the Yoruba artist shows that foreign terms can sometimes be inappropriate in describing other art forms; and conversely, that indigenous linguistic terms can lead to confusion if they are translated out of context to English or any other language. The Yoruba idea of ornament refers to decorative and figurative motifs on a flat surface such as the reliefs on door panels, three-dimensional statues and combinations of these. We see then that the **European** distinction between two-dimensional art (ornament), and three-dimensional art (images), is, for the Yoruba, rather arbitrary both conceptually and practically.

Furthermore, among the Igbo, the word *omenka* is used for carved figures, door panels and slit drums, the last of which are not normally supplemented with ornamentation. In addition, apart from being ranked with priests and diviners, some Igbo carvers are also priests, diviners and herbalists. They belong to a special class of people who understand the language of spirits and come into contact with them.[4]

It is not the intention here to enter into the nature of artistic creativity. It is enough to say that when the artist has mastered his techniques, he produces representations of the forms his eye sees. These are forms which make the objects represented 'visible'. These forms can have an aesthetic effect on the beholder. In other words, they can be appreciated for their beauty. But in the context of traditional African culture, there is more to carving than disinterested aesthetic appreciation. They have a content – that is, meaning and significance for the users. For example, the Igbo *ikenga* figure, as we shall see later, is the symbol of a man's right hand and whatever success he achieves in life. Also, the large, carved masquerade headpieces from northeast Yorubaland are displayed for less than ten days each year or alternate years and are tied up with religious symbolism especially with regard to plentiful issue, good health, peace and spirital well-being.

The separation of form from content is purely conceptual. In most cases, it is impossible to separate the two, especially when the objects under study are associated with indigenous rituals. In such cases, the form and content of the object constitute an organic whole which cannot be separated because a knowledge of the content is necessary in order to understand its form.[5]

It is the form that attracts the attention of foreigners, who then pay no attention to meaning and significance either through ignorance, but more because they are not interested in the content. Indeed, for some foreigners the knowledge of the content can distract them from their appreciation of the form. They then approach African art in isolation, admiring its formal organisation because they have no desire, or are unable, to know the meaning in the society that produces and uses the objects. Some even feel that knowledge of the meaning would distract them from direct appreciation. Redfield gave the example of the American lad who found them 'horrid'.[6] But then, even scholars and museum curators use value-loaded words similar to that which this museum visitor used. Two of these are 'curious' and 'weird', not to mention 'primitive', the descriptive adjective used for all 'art' objects from Africa. Redfield advised visitors to read about the uses and functions of 'art' objects so that they can respond to them both as works of art and as signs and symbols of another society.

On the other hand, to some foreigners, such knowledge will hinder their appreciation especially if, as Raymond Firth has pointed out, they see the objects as products of 'heathen savages', and therefore morally reprehensible. This is the point at which, for foreigners and Africans alike, Christian or Islamic religious prejudice creeps in.[7]

Whereas foreigners see these objects as art, to the users they are icons – representations of, and stimulus for religious and cosmological ideas, with immanent and transcendent meanings.[8] Such carved objects may, for the sake of compromise, be considered as both art and icon; but as we shall see later, there are objects which are more icons than art. Considered as art, foreigners use analogies which they have learnt in their own culture, and expressions derived from their own experience, when describing these African objects.

Indigenous African art can be considered from many points of view: aesthetic, economic, political, religious and historical. Whereas it is best to consider them together, these aspects are often separated for certain reasons. Aesthetic judgement deals with the formal qualities of an object such as arrangement of lines, mass, colour, and the individual's reactions to them. But aesthetic judgements have no universal validity; each person making an appraisal believes himself to be recognising an objective value binding at least for himself.[9]

This is not to argue that the indigenous craftsman and his patron are not aesthetically motivated. There are objects which serve purely decorative ends. Some of the ritual objects display characteristics of form that go beyond the functional. Because artefacts are meant to operate in certain contexts, they are so made that they fulfil the functions for which they are intended. However, the maker may go beyond the minimal functional requirements so that the objects exhibit non-instrumental functions which disclose aesthetic quality. For example, kings' sceptres range from shafts shaped like an ordinary rod to elaborately decorated gold objects which raise these items to the level of aesthetic objects, but not in the sense of art for art's sake. Again, verandah posts will support the eaves whether or not they are shaped in the form of equestrian figures. The point is that craftsmen go beyond the forms required for the use of implements either in secular or ritual domain.

Apart from the aesthetic point of view, art should be considered in its economic, political and religious aspects – in short, its total social context. If in certain objects we see technical perfection, an aesthetic impulse and the retroactive influence of art on other social institutions, it is still imperative that we consider this art in its total social context, and that the artistic forms be explained through the discovery of relationships between artistic and other social activities. The African art object (either by destination or metamorphosis), then, must be examined as it enters economic, political and other spheres as something deriving its significance and meaning from its place in a living culture and not in the glass cases of museums.

The forms and especially the functions of what we may now refer to as African art are different from those of European art. In Christian Europe up to the fifteenth century, European art forms included buildings (especially churches), statues, illuminated manuscripts, liturgical garments, ceremonial implements in metal, all of which functioned exclusively in the service of Christian liturgy. However, increasingly from the Renaissance onwards, and definitely by the nineteenth century, emphasis shifted to painting, sculpture, secular building and other arts which functioned in a secular domain. It is the use of 'artistic' products for non-artistic ends that marks off traditional African art from European art.

204

A work of art in its own particular society has a different value from its possible meaning to a stranger. It evokes associations which are determined by the culture to which it belongs. We have mentioned the case of the woman who paid homage to a stolen image at a police check point. But on a more serious note, the man who stole that piece (*Épà* masquerade headpiece) knows that it will be bought (illegally, according to Nigeria's antiquities law) as a work of art. It will, then, like other pieces, be seen in isolation, a way in which it was not meant to be seen. It has been separated from its social context. In its social setting, like other masquerade headpieces, it is a public object only for a few days or even a few hours each year, or in some cases, every other year, after which it is hidden away. Such carved headpieces are part of masquerade costumes, but because they share formal characteristics with what foreigners regard as art, they are avidly bought by collectors from illegal vendors.

There are myriads of other masquerade costumes without carved headpieces, or with headpieces of other materials such as animal skulls and ephemeral vegetable materials which are rejected by art collectors. But to the users, the absence of durable and 'artistic' headpieces on such masquerade costumes does not make the rituals performed by the masquerades less efficacious to the community.

We can now see that traditional African art objects reflect other aspects of culture; there are profound links between religion, social organisations and political institutions on the one hand and artistic creativity on the other. There is interaction between economic demands, religious and secular ceremonials, and artistic endeavours. We can see, then, that art has social implications in that artistic activity is a cultural ingredient which colours and gives meaning to other social dimensions. Because of this, it is imperative that we give some account of the use and meaning of art objects in the lives of the people who make and use them. If art is produced and used in a social setting, it has a cultural content. In order to understand this content, art must be studied in specific cultural terms at given periods of time because the art of a people can be best understood only against the background of the culture of the people. This will make it easier to understand the form, and, more important, the content or meaning of the form.

The forms and functions (content) of art vary from one African society to another. At a mundane level, decoration is used in the embellishment of domestic objects, for example, in stools. Art also serves as a means and index of social prestige. This touches on the political aspect in that highly decorated artefacts can be symbols of an individual or a royal court. The bulk of the examples of Ife and Benin art seem to be connected with royalty. Art has a religious dimension in that it gives material expression, in visible and tangible form, to superhuman entities. In this way, the artist gives material expression to religious ideas. This is not peculiar to Africa. Medieval European art was almost entirely in the service of religion. Art also has an historical dimension in that art objects serve as concrete evidence of the development of a people's civilisation. Examples are African rock art, the terra-cotta objects from Nok, and the bronze and brass objects from Igbo Ukwu, Ife and Benin.

Art in Africa

In this section, we shall discuss briefly the art of selected periods, peoples and areas. We shall divide our case studies into two groups: ancient and recent. In the first group, we shall examine rock art, Nok terra-cottas, Ife, Igbo-Ukwu and Benin bronzes, as well as a group of bronzes from Jebba and Tada. In the second group, we shall discuss Ekpu figures from Oron, Igbo Mbari houses and Ikenga carvings, Yoruba masquerade headpieces, and Lega artefacts from Central Africa.

Our division into ancient and recent is in some respects arbitrary. Paintings and engravings on rock surfaces have been executed in comparatively recent times in some parts of Southern Africa. In Nigeria, Benin art is unique in that, unlike Igbo Ukwu and Ife, production has continued till the present day. Tada bronzes are still used in annual ceremonies connected with the culture hero of the Nupe people. In the case of recent art, there is evidence that art objects in this category were produced and used alongside objects which have survived from antiquity. It must be noted, however, that what we refer to as ancient art is made in non-perishable materials which, unlike some of the ephemeral materials used for 'recent' art, have survived the ravages of time.

Ancient art

African rock art

Paintings and engravings on rock surfaces are found in North Africa, especially in the Saharan region, the Libyan Desert, the Nile valley, in the Sudan, West and Central Africa, and East and South Africa. Rock shelters in the mountainous areas of the Sahara contain pictures of elephants, lions, antelopes and birds as well as human beings armed with bows and arrows. Some of the animals depicted are now extinct, thus reflecting climatic changes which have taken place in the Sahara.

The Tassili region, 2 000 square miles of high mountains and dried-up river beds, is very rich in rock art. Several thousand years ago, when the Sahara was humid, the area was covered with forests and traversed by rivers.[10] There were giraffes, elephants, antelopes, rhinoceroses, goats and bulls on the plateau. The inhabitants decorated their rock shelters with representations of the animals they hunted, their ceremonies, their gods and everyday happenings. These scenes of family groups, hunts, battles and ceremonies serve as testimony to the artistic genius of the African.

Attempts have been made to date these pictures. It is suggested that the Tassili was occupied by the sixth millennium B.C., and that artistic creativity started soon after. On the basis of actual pictures, we are given four periods. Pictures of the earliest period show hunters of buffaloes, elephants, rhinoceroses (one of which is 26½ feet long), giraffes and ostriches. In one of the hunting scenes, one human being is represented as 11 feet high. The hunters use clubs, throwing sticks, axes, bows and arrows. The next period is known as the cattle period. Dated about 4000 B.C., it may have overlapped with the hunter period. The third period, dating from about 1200 B.C., is the horse period, the pictures showing horse-drawn chariots, riders and horses and (presumably after about 700

B.C.) camels together. The fourth and most recent period shows camels, horses and other animals which are still to be found in the Sahara today. These are antelopes, oryx, gazelles, ostriches and goats. An examination of weapons has also been used to indicate time dimension in Saharan rock art. Those depicted are stone axes, throwing stickes, bows and arrows, javelins, swords and firearms.

In Ethiopia, apart from the representation of elephants and lions, rock art reflects the pastoral origins of the present-day inhabitants. In Tanzania, modern rock art exists side by side with older examples showing human figures with hunting gear and figures wearing elaborate ornaments.

Examples of rock art abound in Zambia, Mozambique, Zimbabwe, South Africa, Swaziland, Lesotho, Botswana and Namibia. A site may contain one or as many as over a hundred pictures. These may contain single figures or animals; animals and figures may be combined in compositions which depict recognisable activities. The subject matter is everyday life – walking, running, hunting, dancing, feasting and fighting. It is difficult to date these works. Archaeological deposits found in association with some examples have been dated to 7 000 years ago, but using the subject matter of the pictures, scenes of combat with Zulus have been dated to about A.D. 1800. There are also scenes of Europeans with rifles and horses.

Nok Art

Terra-cotta (or baked clay) figures associated with the Nok culture were found during tin-mining activities in the plateau region around Jos in northern Nigeria. The first object came from the town of Nok, but other terra cottas have been found in various places on the River Kaduna, and at Katsina Ala, south of the River Benue. These represent at present the westernmost and easternmost limits of the Nok culture. Similar terra cottas have also been found around Zaria to the north and Abuja to the south. The finds include naturalistic and non-naturalistic figures and heads, some with elongated ears. Found in association with them are stone and iron axes similar to those depicted on the figures. There are also ornaments and pottery. From Zaria, the northern marginal area of Nok culture, come surface finds of heads, torso, hands and feet in association with potsherds.

Dated to between 900 B.C. and A.D. 200 (some place the earliest point at 500 B.C.), Nok art is regarded by some scholars as the precursor of Ife art. It is not the intention here to argue about the merits and demerits of this suggestion. It must be pointed out that the corpus of Ife art includes not only terra cottas, but also bronzes, stone carvings and beads. In postulating relationships on iconographical grounds between art forms, one must exercise great caution, especially where considerable distances of time and space are involved. Resemblances of form must be accompanied by a corresponding resemblance in the meaning of form in order to buttress any theory that contacts have taken place.

Ife art

As indicated above, the corpus of Ife art consists of bronzes, terra cottas, stone carvings and beads. Among other things, there are also bead-making crucibles, fragments of metal-smelting furnaces, and potsherd pavements (pavements paved with broken pottery, the pieces stuck in the ground with the edges up). Just as the high degree of naturalism of the art objects has attracted scholars, so has the source of the technology that produced the form baffled them. It has been suggested that the whole corpus was produced around the thirteenth and fourteenth centuries A.D.

The bronzes consist of portrait heads of (probably) kings and queens, with half- and full-length figures of the king; all produced by the lost-wax method. The terra cottas, of which there are infinitely more than the bronzes, depict human heads, animal heads such as rams, sheep and elephants, full-length figures and seated figures on stone stools. There are carvings in quartz of stone stools, of which there are also representations in terra cotta and bronze. One of the latter is in the form of a figure coiled round a vessel placed on a stone stool. This is an indication that the production of art forms in bronze, terra cotta and stone were contemporaneous. There are also granite stone carvings of figures and monoliths, the largest of which is the staff of Oranmiyan. Other staffs, such as those on Okemogun where the king of Ife celebrates the Olojo festival annually, still feature in ceremonials.

Representations of human figures in bronze and terra cotta indicate a lavish use of beaded decoration. It is therefore not surprising to find bead-making crucibles. The facial striations on some of the figures have also been found on representations of animal heads. Other forms of striation have been found on terra-cotta figures. They could have served decorative functions. Potsherd pavements can be found all over present Ife, including places not yet swallowed up in urban development but which in the past were presumably occupied by houses or were the sites of sacred groves and shrines.

One gets the impression that the art of Ife was produced for the king and his hierarchy of chiefs and priests. In this connection, it may be mentioned that there have been surface finds, and that there are plenty of potsherd pavements around the residence of Obalufe, the second in rank to the king of Ife. The art was probably an embellishment of secular and religious ceremonial, still a prominent feature of Ife today.

Benin art

A persistent tradition, accepted by some scholars but disputed by others, tells us that bronze-casting (that is, by the lost-wax method) was introduced to Benin from Ife at the request of a Benin king. In any case, Benin developed a characteristic art of her own and a wider range of subject matter than Ife. Remains of potsherds pavements in Benin have been dated to the thirteenth and fourteenth centuries. There is evidence of the artistic use of copper by the thirteenth century, although this was smithing rather than casting. Now, if there was a distinctive culture by the fifteenth century and the peak of cultural excellence was in the

Fig. 12.1   *An Ife terra-cotta head, produced by the lost-wax method, from the 12th–15th century*

sixteenth and seventeenth centuries, it has been suggested that there must have been some centuries of development before these three centuries.

Attempts have been made to divide the art of Benin into periods. The first, from about 1300, witnessed the supposed introduction of bronze casting from Ife to Benin. The second period is from 1485, and marked the coming of the Portuguese whose arrival was a catalyst to Benin art in that they provided a more plentiful supply of copper as well as additional subject matter for the artist. This period was the high water mark of Benin culture. The third period was marked by civil war and a consequent lull in artistic activities. The fourth and last period was marked by a revival in the eighteenth century, but following the decline of royal power, there was artistic decadence, and with the death of King Adolo in 1888 the last royal bronze heads were cast. Yet the production of Benin art has survived there until the present day. This survival, in contrast to the position of Ife art, is explicable by the fact that the city of Benin seems to have been occupied continuously from early times, whereas the site of Ife has been abandoned on more than one occasion on account of invasions.

Art objects from Benin include bronze heads, simple at first (if Fagg's periodisation is accepted) but becoming more and more elaborate and heavy as (presumably) the supply of metal increased. Some of the heads with large holes on the top supported large, carved ivory tusks, and were placed on ancestral shrines with other objects. There were very many plaques (flat bronze reliefs), showing the king supported by attendants, warriors, hunters and the Portuguese. These plaques may have been nailed to wooden pillars in the king's palace. There were hip masks, bronze bells and stools, animal figures such as leopards and cocks, compositions with animals and human figures; ivory gongs, trumpets and bracelets. Benin mythology and folklore feature in the representations. Such representations include those of elephants whose trunks end in human hands.

Essentially an adjunct of the royal court, art in Benin was a prerogative of the king. Only the king could use bronze objects. This may be one of the reasons why bronze stools supported by snakes are associated with the king, and wooden stools showing the same iconographic motifs are associated with chiefs.[11] The various craft guilds − weavers, wood and ivory carvers, smiths in various metals − supplied the king's needs by way of art objects which provided an impressive background to court ceremonial.[12]

Igbo Ukwu art

The objects which were excavated here consist mainly of bronzes and highly decorated pottery as well as objects used in personal decoration. Apart from earthenware pots, there is a representation in bronze of a roped (presumably earthenware) pot. Other objects in bronze include snake ornaments, ornamental bronze scabbards and hilts, bronze bowls shaped like calabashes and snail shells, and pendants in the form of animal and human heads. There are also beaded armlets, copper fan holders, anklets, and elephant tusks. Some of these objects may have been the regalia of an important chief, and others the grave property of a royal burial.

Cast by the lost-wax method, these bronze objects have been dated to between 700 and 1000 A.D. In looking for parallels between archaeological finds and surviving analogues in the area, it was found that some excavated objects have traits in common with what is known about the present-day peoples in the area, leading to the conclusion that the objects are probably connected with the institution of the Eze Nri, a priest king in Igboland.[13]

210

Fig. 12.2   *A decorated Igbo 'cooler' pot, purchased in the Enugu market*

Remarks on bronze

At this point, it will be apposite to make a distinction between bronze and brass objects. Objects in the three case studies above have been referred to as bronze in conformity with previous practice. They are in fact not all bronzes. Igbo Ukwu objects are heavily leaded bronze with up to 12 per cent tin and 16 per cent lead. Other objects are of pure copper.

Bronze is an alloy of 90 per cent copper and 10 per cent tin, whilst brass is an alloy of 70 per cent copper and 30 per cent tin. Copper in its pure state is easily worked, but bronze and brass are much harder; the former can be smithed, and the latter is used for casting in its molten state.

211

Benin objects are made of brass with a high percentage of zinc, and of the Ife objects analysed so far, five are of almost pure copper, while twelve are of leaded brass. In passing, it may be mentioned that copper and its alloys were in use before the advent of Europeans but became plentiful only with European importation.

Nupe bronzes

These are also known as the Tsoede bronzes, Tsoede being the legendary hero and founder of the Nupe kingdom. Here we have perhaps an articulate link between art objects and a nation's history. The bronzes are located in Tada and Jebba. They are described by tradition as part of the relics of Tsoede, who is reputed to have been born to an Attah of Igala in (or about) the fifteenth century when the Nupe people were subject to the Attah. After his death Tsoede is said to have bequeathed the insignia of his rule to the Nupe people. Brass chains and bangles associated with him are still found today in most Nupe towns.[14]

The bronzes consist of three figures in Jebba, with strong iconographic and stylistic affinities to Benin works, and other figures in Tada, the latter including a seated male with striking stylistic resemblance to Ife work. All the bronzes are sacred objects which feature in ceremonies throughout the year.

Because of their stylistic heterogeneity, it seems that these Nupe bronzes come from different sources.

Recent art

Ekpu figures

There are at least six hundred figures in the museum at Oron in Nigeria. Such figures are no longer carved, nor does anyone remember having seen them carved. Like other objects, they were not originally conceived as works of art for art's sake. Although they have great aesthetic merit, they now serve essentially as records of Oron's history, a storehouse of vanished customs and habits such as the wearing of long beards, the possession of ivory horns and other symbols of authority and wealth. Their purpose seems to have been to perpetuate the ancestors of lineage groups, since they are kept in special shrines where sacrifices were made to them, and in carving them the hardest wood was used to ensure durability.[15]

Mbari houses

Perhaps the best example of the association of art with social life is the Mbari (houses of images), built by the Igbo of Nigeria in response to major crises such as famine, plague, warfare and other calamities which were regarded as signs of divine displeasure.[16] Some of the deities depicted are Amadioha, god of thunder, who is now represented in European clothes to show the march of progress; and Otamiri and Ekwunoche, river goddess and providers of large families.

The erection of an Mbari is a communal project in which each family in a town nominates men and women who will stay on the site until the project, which may take more than a year, is finished. In the past, an Mbari was built with local material such as mats, but nowadays corrugated iron sheets are used for the roofing. It is larger than a normal dwelling house, and falls to pieces in as many years as it took to build it. During the construction, there are sacrifices, dancing, singing, and body painting – all forming an integral part of the building activities. Those working on the site are led by a professional artist, but the finished product is regarded as communal work.

Inside the Mbari is represented every aspect of life from birth to death, and even beyond. The building may contain from thirty-five to over a hundred figures depicting things which are beautiful, good, terrifying, forbidden or humorous. There are representations of family wealth and productivity, traditional and modern diurnal activities as well as terrifying images from mythology and nature and the underworld of spirits. The central figure is that of the deity to whom the Mbari is built; there may be other deities, representation of myths and typical scenes such as the ideal mother represented by a goddess, and with the advent of the white man there are representations of him too.

Images of both the Igbo and the white man change with time to incorporate the latest advances in housing, clothing and technology. Thus, Mbari houses mirror changes in the social environment. In an Mbari house dedicated to Ala in Owerri are representations of Amadioha; Ekwunoche with a large family; Mammy Water, a capricious creature which can bestow wealth or insanity; leopards and pythons, which in dreams and in reality are regarded as a threat to man. Forbidden things are also represented. These include masquerades which can be inspected by women and children at close quarters, a thing that can never happen in real life; also erotic and sexual imagery, whereas in ordinary daily life overt reference to sexual matters is forbidden.

Ikenga

Ikenga (personal shrine) sculptures among the Igbo vary from schematised (outlined, semi-abstract) to naturalistic human figures with a pair of horns on the head. Some are simply blocks of wood terminating with horns or schematised heads with a pair of horns. More elaborately carved ikenga are in the form of horned human figures holding a staff in one hand and a severed human head in the other. Sometimes the horns are carved to represent those of a ram. Whatever the type or degree of complexity, all ikenga have horns.

For the Igbo, if an individual derives his *chi* (accompanying soul) from Chuku or Chineke (God), it is the ikenga that serves as intermediary between him and his chi. Because the chi may either be good or bad, to chi is attributed good or bad luck. Success or failure is caused by chi which operates through ikenga, the symbol of an individual's progress and achievement.

It has been suggested that the word 'ikenga' is a combination of three Igbo works, *'ike mu ga'* (my power), which has been shortened to two words, *'ikem ga'* and eventually one word 'ikemga' and pronounced 'ikenga'. It is therefore not surprising that it is the abstract concept of the power of the individual. [17]

Every Igbo man looks forward to the day when he will have his own ikenga, simple at first, but becoming more elaborate as the owner's status improves. In annual ikenga feasts, the owner reviews his achievements during the previous year, and when he dies, the ikenga is brought out and the owner's achievements recounted. Sacrifices are offered to ikenga after every successful venture, the end of the yearly yam harvest, the attainment of high social status, escape from danger or illness.

As objects, ikenga are never carved unless commissioned. They are carved from trees which are believed to have special powers. Offerings are made before the carving begins, and when it is delivered, the owner also makes more offerings. The decorative and other features of ikenga are significant for the Igbo. The *ichi* scarifications on some ikenga are symbols of a titled man, while the horns refer to the role they play in the animal world. The raised matchet in the right hand is associated with success in farming, formerly the main occupation. But in a wider context, ikenga is associated with a man's right hand which controls the 'spirit force' of ikenga, and without which there can be no success in farming, fishing, hunting, war, trade, title taking – in short, in all aspects of a man's endeavour.

Masks and masquerades

Masks are headpieces used by masqueraders in association with costumes which cover the rest of the body. Because they function in particular social contexts, it is apposite to treat at some length some of the great variety of masks which are encountered in Africa.

Leach has pointed out that the arts are integral adjuncts to public festivity, and on such occasions, music, dancing, poetry and the plastic arts come together in a single complex. [18] This is particularly true of masquerades. He went on to say that it is fatuous to comment on such works as if they were intended to decorate the corner of a room, pointing out that masks are nearly always intended to be seen by a crowd of people at a distance. [19] In what follows we will summarise information on the use of masks in their social context.

In Malawi[20] the carving of masks is governed by the religious tradition of the Nyau, a men's society which occupied a central place in the life of the people. Because Nyau is connected with ancestors, the masks represent ancestors or spirits, and the performances take place during girls' ceremonies and funeral obsequies. Some masks are of animal skin over a wooden framework, while the more ephemeral ones are constructed with leaves and sticks, which are freshly made for each ceremony, used at night and then burnt.

In neighbouring Zambia, Mubitana[21] has recorded a performance of Wiko masquerades in connection with boys' initiation in modern Livingstone. Using costumes of dyed sisal and masks, some represent ancestors and are accompanied by lesser masquerades representing non-human supernatural entities. These masquerades come out towards the end of the three-to-six months' boys' initiation period.

Nyanga circumcision costumes consist of masks, hats and hoods made of antelope skin or bark cloth which are used with a variety of leaves and fibre costumes during circumcision ceremonies. Worn at different stages of the ceremony by different people, some are expressions of status and authority. They are not preserved after the ceremony.[22]

Tikar masks are 'crudely' carved[23] and used in annual dances to honour the ancestors; hence they are the common property of the community. The dancer's face and figure are concealed, and he speaks to the Supreme God through the ancestors.

Among the Bété of the south-west Ivory Coast, masked dancing is loaded with social, religious and psychological implications,[24] a remark which applied to the vast majority of African masking traditions. Of the three categories of Bété masks, the most important is the Great Mask, serving as intermediary between the world and the city of the dead. It is a face mask with a cloth hood attached,and the wearer's body is covered with raffia.

Generally, masking is associated primarily with men; some even claim that the object of masking is to frighten women. But among the Mende of Sierra Leone,the Sanda (or Bundu) society is a female initiation society in which women wear sculpted masks which are syntheses of Sande's ideals,[25] expressing, communicating and perpetuating some of the fundamental concepts of the society through the incorporation of standardised details. According to Richards, the lobes of fat around the neck, a striking feature of the masks, signify healthy and wealthy womanhood. Sanda women are expected to attain a state of spiritual and physical beauty, and to achieve this initiates use oils mixed with herbs, clay and other ingredients as skin tonics, as well as for protection against witchcraft. Similarly, the masks are rubbed with palm oil to give them a highly polished surface which, with the small mouth of the mask,is regarded as a mark of beauty.

The Nupe of Nigeria stage *elo* masked dances using long-sleeved costumes which have been compared with those of the Yoruba further south. As recorded by Stevens, one masker used a headpiece similar to Abeokuta (Egba–Yoruba) types. Nadel has suggested the elo is of foreign origin.[26]

In contrast to elo masquerades, *ndako gboya* is Nupe in origin, but has diffused into Yorubaland where it is acknowledged as being of Nupe origin. And as in Nupeland, their appearance in annual rituals is designed to discourage potential witches and to weaken the evil powers of witchcraft. In Nupeland, *ndaka gboyo* masquerades appear during the annual rites of *gunnu*, the most important religious ceremony. The maskers do not use carved wooded 'masks'. The costume as described by Nadel is a huge cylinder of cloth about 15 feet high hanging down from circular rings fixed on wooden pole. The masker representing the 'spirit' or ancestor *gboya* stands inside the costume, carrying in his hand the pole with which he regulates the height of the costume.[27]

John Picton has described masquerading as a central feature of Igbira ritual; performances are staged to prevent and control barrenness, illness, and death caused by witchcraft.[28] They also serve as the principal vehicle for entertainment. They appear during a two-and-a-half month period starting from late September or early October. Of the various species, Picton singles out three as being important. These are: *ekuoba*, which represents the individual decesaed elders, *ekuecici,* the servants of the world of the dead; and *ekurahu,* singing masquerades whose principal function is entertainment.

Among the Igala of Nigeria, masquerading is a national festival and an occasion for ancestral rituals to be performed throughout the kingdom. Of the various masquerades, *Egwu Afia* represents clan ancestors, and, according to Boston, is one of the three pivots of the ancestral cult. *Egwu Ata,* the royal masquerade, represents the king's ancestor during annual festivals.[29]

Ekpo ritual is a Bini village cult associated with the use of masks and performed to combat diseases and keep the town in a state of ritual purity; performers use face masks and cover their body with palm fronds. The maskers represent important persons, traditional, modern, and supernatural – herbalists (native doctors), chiefs, district officers, policemen, deified heroes, deities – and also animals such as the leopard, which is sacred in Bini ritual.[30]

Dead Mothers are the names of masquerades which commemorate titled women in Okpella (Ukpilla), a northern Edo people who are the southern neighbours of the Igbira. These masquerades appear with other masked figures in the annual ancestral festivals. In his detailed account, Bogarti has pointed out that although masking belongs to the male domain, certain Okpella titled women, known as Mothers of Spirits, can own masks, though they cannot dance with them. They can own and be commemorated by Dead Mother masquerades, just as titled men can be commemorated by Dead Fathers.[31]

The mask considered most appropriate to represent women of high status and economic standing is a wooden mask with a finely featured face and elaborate hair-style and superstructure. The masker is costumed in bright cloth with stockinged feet. Cloth wrappers, scarves, jewellery and other items of feminine dress are added to the costume before a performance.

There are various types of masquerades in the Niger Delta. Among the Abua, occupying thirty-five villages in the Niger Delta, the most important masquerade is Onwuema which, according to Eyo, is of 'spiritual significance for the Abua people', and Egbukele.[32] The former, representing the local water spirit, was said to have been found floating as a shapeless piece of wood; a cap mask was then carved to represent it. Each village has an Onwuema cap mask, while the masker's body is covered with cloth joined to the mask. The performance is intended to remove evil from the village and purify the community for the festival of Eyal. Egbukele is performed for general entertainment, but the leader of the Egbukele Society in each village must make a sacrifice before the performance. Unlike Onwuema, the masks are owned by individuals but are kept in a common place. In the past, reports of theft, violence, adultery and other offences were lodged with Egbukele members, who imposed fines, but they had no jurisdiction over serious crimes.

At Evwremi, a western Urhobo town, the Ohworu festival

commemorates a spirit of the same name. As recorded by Foss,[33] for two days 'works of art in wood and palm raffia become visual enactment of deep-seated beliefs in water- and forest-based spiritual forces'. During the festival, in which the leader dancer is also a master carver, Ohworu and her followers are summoned to receive praises. On the first day, eleven masquerades using face masks with white cloth attached to the edges and draped over the tight-fitting costume of the masker appear. The face masks, with swollen, exaggerated foreheads surmounted by a combination of animal and human motifs, are faces of the spirits and therefore they are not intended to appeal to humans as beautiful.

By far the majority of Delta masquerades are performed by the group of societies which, depending on locality, is known as Sekiapu or Ekine among the Ijo, Kalabari, Nembe, Ibani and Okrika.[34] It is a religious institution designed to solicit the help of water spirits through representation. All Delta masquerades are believed to have come from water spirits, so that several represent various fishes, as well as crocodiles and hippopotamus. There are also representations of the tortoise (*Ikhaki*) and monkey. While some masks are sculpted representations of spirits, fish or animals, others have a framework of bamboo covered with cloth or paper and decorated with coloured plumes. They are attached to the costume, and, when worn, the masks sit on top of the head in such a way that they are not clearly visible to the spectator, especially when plumes and other decorations are added.

Before undertaking his study of Afikpo Igbo masquerades, Ottenberg had made himself conversant with other aspects of Igbo culture. In his monumental book on the masked rituals of the Afikpo, he describes masquerading as one of the principal activities of all male secret societies.[35] In all, there are twelve types of Afikpo masks, one calabash form and two net types, the rest wooden. Older masks are preferred because they are considered more powerful; remnants of egg shells are often placed on them as offerings.

Okumkpa, the best attended masquerade, is performed in nine stages, in the first of which more than one hundred masquerades assemble. During the fourth and main stage, real people are satirised in songs and speeches. It is a 'secular display in which religious elements associated with the secret society spirit and instilled in the masked player give sanction to topical ridicule and commentary ...'

Njenji is a parade of boys and young men accompanied by costumed singers. Some of the maskers are dressed as Aro and re-enact the part of Aro slave traders from Okposi where a large slave market was once located. Before the advent of the Europeans, the Aro controlled routes leading into and out of the Afikpo region.

The masking rituals of western Nigeria are as varied as the ethnic groups. Some masquerades are found among several ethnic groups, while others are peculiar to one ethnic group only. Ancestral masquerades are found among the Oyo, Ibadan and Oshun Yoruba, as well as in areas which were subject to the suzerainty of Oyo and later to Ibadan. Masquerades have diffused to other places where they are found side by side with local types such as Gelede in Egbado, Epa in parts of north-east Yorubaland, and Agemo and other masquerades in the Remo area of Ijebuland.[36]

The diffusion of Oyo Yoruba masquerades is an example of the link between art forms and historial development. Such links are fairly easy to detect in north-east Yorubaland where, among other things, equestrian motifs are depicted on doors and verandah posts. These representations have been described by Carroll as records of invaders who overran the area in the past.[37] But equestrian motifs also occur profusely on masquerade headpieces used in ceremonies performed for the benefit of the community. Why should motifs of conquering invaders be used in rituals by people who were the victims of aggression? It has been suggested that this is a species of role reversal whereby the people identify themselves with the very forces that threaten them in order to enhance their own powers and to destroy those forces.[38] The Benin were active in north-east Yorubaland possibly as early as the fifteenth century, and came into contact with the Oyo army there in the sixteenth century. In subsequent years, Ilorin, Nupe and Ibadan armies were active in the area. And by 1840, Ibadan forces were ravaging north-east Yorubaland up to the border with Nupe-dominated territory where they came face to face with Nupe cavalry.

In the Yoruba masking ceremonies, headpieces are named *Jagunjagun* or *Ologun,* 'warrior', or more specifically *Ologun ba an ja* ('warrior fight them'). Other headpieces are named Ogun after the god of war. The warrior age-grades participate actively in ceremonies in which weapons of war, war songs, musical instruments and drum rhythms are special features. In addition, stories of foreign invaders are told as background to some of the masking ceremonies, thus providing a link between masking rituals and the history of the people.

Lega art

Art objects among the Lega, a Central African people, are found in the context of *bwami*, a closed body of people who share esoteric knowledge, seeking wisdom and moral excellence.[39] There is a special relationship between the bwami association and sculpture. The association patronises the arts, creating, using and explaining thousands of pieces of sculpture which consist of human and animal figures in wood, ivory, bone and clay. These and other paraphernalia, both natural and man-made, are tokens of membership and insignia of status. Senior members hold large ivory figures and masks which are regarded as the ultimate symbols of the unity, autonomy and solidarity of each community. Ivory and well-polished wood (equated with ivory), are associated with the highest grades of the bwami. These objects are valued as insignia of rank, and a persons's status is enhanced by the possession of them in large quantities.

The objects are inherited patrilineally − that is, along the male line in a family. Individual carvers of objects are not remembered unless they happen to be high-ranking members of the bwami. Carvings are traced through lines of inheritance and succession to grades in the bwami, the line ending with the name of real or alleged first owner and not the maker. These objects serve as links between the living and the dead, even when the original objects have been replaced with new ones.

All arts taken together − plastic (sculpture), theatrical,

choreographic, musical and oral (proverbs, aphorisms, paraphrases and other verbal utterances) − are essential to the understanding of bwami. Conversely, Lega art can only be understood within the context of bwami, which has exclusive ownership of art objects and dance paraphernalia. Bwami has charge of a body of specialised knowledge; this is condensed into proverbs and aphorisms which are interpreted by means of music, dance, dramatic performance and the display of the art objects.

Lega artefacts are made exclusively for the bwami whose members use and interpret them, and when not in use are, like ritual objects in other parts of Africa, secreted away. When the objects appear in rites, verbal utterances help to identify and interpret them. The artist does not know the precise meaning of the work unless he is a high-ranking member of bwami. In any case, the meaning of Lega sculpture can only be understood when analysed in the total context. Form alone does not convey meaning, but rather the activities that surround the form. The form and its details are the focal points of symbolism. The objects are iconic devices which play essential roles, singly or in groups, with other natural and manufactured objects.

Because bwami share common purposes which underlie the political, economic, religious, artistic and other aspects of the social life of the Lega people, the explanation of objects indicates what they are and their use, and relates them to the social system. The objects are storehouses of symbols which translate the essence of Lega thinking. Lega art objects in their social, ideological and ritual contexts stress relationship with oral literature, non-artistic objects and patterns of action.

Conclusion

From the case studies above, following Macquet, we have attempted to show that some of the objects labelled 'art' are not art by design but my metamorphosis.[40] They were not originally made for disinterested aesthetic contemplation. Like medieval European sculptures and Egyptian mortuary art, African ritual objects have been metamorphosed into art by those who are historically and geographically distant from the users and makers. This transformation was meant originally for Western eyes, but it carries the assumption that it is also art for the African. This assumption is based on the premises that art is a universal phenomenon and that the definition of art is so broad as to be able to accommodate African masks, carvings and similar objects.

In this way, artefacts are transformed into art objects. But the process can be arbitrary, depending upon the whims of the individual. As Schlesinger puts it, attempts to describe conditions necessary to raise an artefact to the level of a work of art have not always been successful. There is nothing common to all members of the concept labelled 'works of art'; nevertheless the items are held together by having some family resemblance or common denominator binding them together.[41]

The problem here is perhaps that the aesthetic sense of the word 'art' is quite recent.[42] The Greeks and Romans did not distinguish between art and craft, and what we now call art was regarded merely as a group of crafts. Viewed this way, perhaps we can label all the things we have described above as craft. But again, the question arises as to whether Africans regard them as crafts. For as Collingwood eloquently put if, if a people have no word for a certain kind of thing it may be that they are not aware of it as a distinct kind.[43]

This is all the more reason why cultures have to be studied in their own terms and not as assimilated by Europeans. In this chapter, therefore, we have been concerned more with art as a social category, as part of social reality, than as a philosophical notion.[44] Yet we find that in Africa art for art's sake does exist and much art exists for the sake of religion — that is, as accessories of religious cults.[45]

Art has varying forms and functions in different parts and in different epochs of Africa. Apart from its antiquity, rock art has social dimensions in that through it, we have a glimpse of the everyday life of the rock shelter dwellers. Like rock art, Nok, Ife, Benin and Igbo-Ukwu art serve as historical documents. They also have a social component in that there is evidence, slight in the case of Nok, that the products were used in the embellishment of some aspect or other of social life. In the case of Ife, Benin and Igbo Ukwu, there is little doubt that these objects were connected with the king, chiefs and priests.

When the more recent objects were examined in their social ramifications, we found that the historical dimension was not lacking. Ekpu figures are records of lineage history, Afikpo maskers representing Aro slave traders serve as a reminder of the nineteenth-century internal slave trade, while the representation of equestrian motifs in north-east Yoruba art reminds us in wider context of the turbulent history of Yorubaland.

As to masks in general, we find that some are made of impermanent material. Understandably, these are seldom collected by art connoisseurs, but they are just as useful in themselves (and to the scholar) as those which are carved in wood and avidly collected. In addition, there are many masquerades which do not make use of carved headpieces.

African art also reflects social change. Even Mbari houses, with their painted ephemeral sculptures, mirror changes in the social environment. The creators are aware of social change which they incorporate into the Mbari. The relation of art to the various aspects of culture is not fixed, therefore, and change in religious, economic, political and other aspects of social organisation is reflected in the arts.

Note: Even though for descriptive purposes the word 'art' has been stretched to cover diverse forms of artefacts, it has been impossible to treat such objects as basketry in various media, beadwork such as the type used as ornaments in Kenya and as royal regalia by the Yoruba of Nigeria; calabash engraving; cloth weaving such as the Kente of Ghana, Akwete in Nigeria, and the wood blankets of the Peul in Mali.

Notes

1 My arguments here are based largely on Jacques Macquet's *Introduction to aesthetic anthropology*, Reading, Massachusetts, Addison-Wesley, 1971

2 R. Horton, *Kalabari sculpture*, Lagos, Department of Antiquities, 1965

3 Andrew and Marilyn Strathern, *Self decoration in Mount Hagen,* London, Duckworth, 1971; J. C. Faris, *Nuba personal art,* London: Duckworth, 1972

4 A. O. O. Onwughalu, 'Ikenga sculptures in Igbo Ukwu', B. A. (Fine Arts) dissertation, University of Ife, 1979

5 J. R. O. Ojo, 'The symbolism and significance of Epa type masquerade headpieces', *Man,* 13, (3/4) 1978

6 R. Redfield, 'Art and icon', in *Anthropology and art: readings in cross cultural aesthetics,* C. M. Otten (ed.), New York, Natural History Press, 1971; also Leach, 'Aesthetics', in *Institutions of primitive society,* Oxford, Basil Blackwell, 1967, 32

7 R. Firth, *Elements of social organisation*, London, Watts, 1951, pp. 158-9

8 Redfield, 'Art and icon', *passim.* See also Denis Williams, *Icon and image,* London, Lane, 1974; and 'Iconology of the Yoruba Edan Ogboni', *Africa,* 2, 1964, for important statements on this topic

9 See, for example, W. E. Kennick's provocative essay, 'Does traditional aesthetics rest on a mistake?' in *Collected Papers on Aesthetics,* C. Barrett (ed.), Oxford, Basil Blackwell; and G. Schlesinger, 'Aesthetic experience and the definition of art', *British Journal of Aesthetics'* 19 (2), 1979

10 D. Masonowicz, 'Prehistoric rock paintings at Tassili', *African arts*, II(1), 1968; H. C. Woodhouse, 'Rock paintings of Southern Africa', *African Arts,* II (3), 1969

11 For references on these, see J. R. O. Ojo, 'A bronze stool collected at Ijebu-Ode', *African arts,* (ix) (1), 1975

12 There is an important chapter on 'The art of Benin through the eyes of the artist, the art historial, the ethnographer and the archaeologist', by Thurstan Shaw in M. Greenhalgh (ed.), *Art in Society*, London, Duckworth, 1978

13 T. Shaw, 'The Mystery of the buried bronzes' *Nigerian Magazine,* 92, 1962; and his *Unearthing Igbo Ukwu*, Oxford University Press, 1977

14 P. Eccles, 'Nupe bronzes', *Nigerian Magazine,* 73, 1962; Nadel, *A black Byzantium: the Kingdom of Nupe in Nigeria,* London, Oxford University Press, 1942, pp. 73-4

15 P. O. Nsugbe, 'Oron Ekpu figures', *Nigerian Magazine* 71, 1961

16 H. M. Cole, 'Mbari is life', *African Arts,* II (3), 1969; H. M. Cole, 'Mbari is a dance', *African Arts,* II (4), 1969; J. Opkarocha, *Mbari: art as sacrifice,* Ibadan, Daystar Press, 1976

17 A. O. O. Onwughalu, 'Ikenga sculptures'. For a comprehensive survey of Ikenga figures, see J. Boston, *Ikenga figures among the Northwest Igbo and the Igala,* London, Ethnographica, 1977

18 Leach, 'Aesthetics', p. 27

19 *Ibid.,* p. 35

20 B. Blackman and M. Schofeleers, 'Masks of Malawi', *African arts,* (4), 1972

21 K. Mubitana, 'Wiko masquerades', *African arts,* VI (3), 1974

22 D. Biebuyck, 'Nyanga circumcision masks and customs', *African arts,* VI (2), 1973

23 M. B. Joseph, 'Dance masks of the Tikar', *African arts,* VII (3), 1974

24 A. P. Rood, 'Bete masked dances', *African arts,* II (3), 1969

25 J. V. O. Richards, 'Sande masks', *African arts,* VII (2), 1974

26 P. Stevens, 'The Nupe Elo masquerade', *African arts,* VI (4), 1973; Nadel, *A black Byzantium,* p. 23; and his *Nupe religion,* London, Routledge and Kegan Paul, 1954, pp. 214-16

27 Nadel, 'Witchcraft and anti-witchcraft in Nupe society', *Africa,* VIII (4), 1935; and his *Nupe Religion,* pp. 189-90

28 J. Picton, 'Masks and the Igbira', *African Arts,* VII (2), 1974

29 Boston, *The Igala kingdom,* Oxford University Press, 1967, *passim*

30 P. Ben-Amos and O. Omoregie, 'Ekpo ritual in Avbiama', *African arts,* II, (4), 1969

31 J. M. Bogarti, 'Dead Mothers of Okpella', *African arts,* XII (4), 1979

32 E. Eyo, 'Abua masquerades', *Nigerian magazine,* 97, 1968; also in *African arts,* VII (2), 1974

33 P. Foss, 'Festival of Ohworu at Evwreni', *African arts,* VI (4), 1973

34 E. J. Alagoa, 'Delta masquerades', *Nigeria magazine,* 93, 1967; R. Horton, 'Kalabari Ekine society: a borderland of art and religion', *Africa,* 38, 1963; and 'Igbo: an ordeal for aristocrats', *Nigerian Magazine,* 90, 1966

35 S. Ottenberg, *Masked rituals of the Afikpo: the context of African Art,* Seattle, University of Washington Press, 1975

36 A lot has been written on Oyo Yoruba masquerades; the following, which contain up-to-date bibliographies are the latest: Oludate Olajubu and J. R. O. Ojo, 'Some aspects of Oyo Yoruba masquerades', *Africa,* 47 (3), 1977; and *African arts,* IX (3), devoted specially to Oyo Yoruba masquerades.

37 K. Carroll, *Yoruba religious carving,* London, Geoffrey Chapman, 1967, p. 79

38 Ojo, 'Symbolism and signifance'

39 D. Biebuyck, *Lega culture: art, initiation and moral philosophy among a Central African people,* Berkeley, University of California Press, 1973

40 J. Macquet, 'Art in metamorphosis', *African arts,* XII (4), 1979

41 G. Schlesinger, 'Aesthetic experience'

42 R. Collingwood, *Principles of art,* Oxford University Press, 1938, p. 5

43 *Ibid.,* pp. 6, 8-11

44 Macquet, 'Art and metamorphis', *passim*

45 Collingwood, *Principles of art,* p. 11

Questions for discussion

1 If there is a museum near you, visit it and make a list of the exhibits. Find out where applicable the historical and/or social background of the exhibits.

2 Watch some of the traditional ceremonies in which 'art' objects are used. List the objects and find out the reasons why they are used.

3 Find out about the masking rituals and types of 'masks' used in your area.

4 What are the art forms in your area?

5 Arising from 4 above, in what ways do the types of material available determine the art forms?

Suggestions for further reading

Allison, P. *The Cross River monoliths*, Lagos, Department of Antiquities, 1968

———. *African stone sculpture,* 1968

Bascom, W. R. *African art in cultural perspective*, New York, Norton, 1973

Fagg, W. *Nigerian images*, London, Lund Humphries, 1963

Fagg, W., and Plass, M. *African sculpture,* Dutton Vista, 1964

Horton, R. *Kalabari sculpture,* Lagos, Department of Antiquities, 1965

Shaw, T. *Unearthing Igbo Ukwu,* Ibadan, Oxford University Press, 1977

———. *Nigeria: its archaeology and early history,* London, Thames and Hudson, 1978

Stevens, Phillips. *The stone images of Esie, Nigeria,* Ibadan University Press and Federal Department of Antiquities, 1978

Willett, F. *Ife in the history of West African art,* London, Thames and Hudson, 1967

———. *African art,* London, Thames and Hudson, 1970

Williams, D. *Icon and image*, London, Allen Lane, 1974

13 Introduction to music in Africa

Akin Euba

There are some people who believe that African music has always remained the same as we know it today. First, not all the music practised in Africa today can be categorised as African music, for, in addition to the indigenous types of music, many new types have developed which are clearly foreign in origin. Secondly, even the indigenous types, which are usually described as traditional music and are often assumed to have been handed down intact through various generations of Africans, have been subject to change. One assumption that can be made with some certainty is that changes in the social structure of Africa, whether resulting from peaceful or violent causes, have usually been reflected in the music.

One element which almost inevitably produced changes in African music was the interaction between Africans and non-African peoples as well as that which occurred internally among the peoples of Africa. It would be a mistake to think that Africans did not make contact with one another before the advent of Europeans.

The two most important and best-documented sources of foreign influence in Africa are the Arabic and the European. Claims have also been made for a South-east Asian influence.[1] Africans have been in contact with Arabs for many centuries, and elements of Arabic music have become so well integrated into African traditional music that they no longer seem foreign. By contrast, the first contacts between Europe and Africa are comparatively recent, and consequently, European musical traits found in Africa stand out because they have not yet been integrated into the main musical culture.

One reason why African traditional music is assumed to have remained unaltered is that changes which occur in the music take place over long spans of time and are imperceptible except under the 'microscope' of the musical analyst. Another point that needs to be borne in mind is that different categories of music within the same African ethnic group are subject to different rates of change. For example, religious music is less likely to undergo change than secular music.

In this chapter we will examine the principal music of Africa, that is, traditional music, as well as other types of music which have developed in recent times.

It should be pointed out that, with respect to music, Africa is roughly divisible into two geographical zones – the area north of the Sahara and that south of the Sahara. The music of northern Africa has the same characteristics as Arabic music and is usually classified with Arabic musical culture, which extends well beyond the shores of Africa.

The discussion in this chapter will therefore be mainly concerned with black Africa.

Traditional music

Traditional music may be defined as the music which has been practised in Africa from pre-colonial times. It is the oldest type of music in Africa, and, in spite of the new musical types which developed during the colonial period and in post-colonial times, traditional music remains by far the most widespread and the most popular of all the various types of music existing in Africa today.

Africa is a multilingual society, and, partly because of this, African traditional music may be said to exist in several idioms. The number of idioms may be roughly categorised in terms of the number of ethnic groups and the number of speech languages. (More will be said later with regard to the relationship between music and speech.) The statement about the multiplicity of ethnic idioms should not be interpreted to mean that there is no underlying unity in the music of black Africa. African traditional music represents a fine balance between unity and diversity,[2] and there are enough unifying principles to enable us to speak of an African music in the same way in which we identify a European or Chinese music.

General characteristics

As far as is known, black Africans have no indigenous musical notation. Music is an oral tradition and, in order to gain musical knowledge, it is necessary in traditional practice for the student to be in physical contact with the originators of the music. Moreover, although the musicians can and do describe the structure and practice of their art when questioned, there exists no indigenous theoretical literature on music, a point that needs little emphasis since written literature of any kind is a recent development in black Africa. In view of the absence of a notational system, traditional music is largely performed from memory.

One characteristic of the traditional music which has been noted even by casual observers is its sophisticated rhythmic organisation. Yet while it is true that rhythm is a striking element, its importance is often exaggerated. The tonal structure of African music is equally important.

Drums are popularly regarded as being the most common musical instrument in Africa but, as Merriam[3] has shown, the most common form of instrumental accompaniment is in reality hand clapping, followed by percussive instruments of the class known as idiophones, while drums occupy third place. It should be acknowledged, however, that the overall traditional instrumental music is essentially percussive.

One of the most important characteristics of traditional music is its integration with other arts (to a degree which often approaches the concept of total art) and the realisation of the resultant multi-art complex within the framework of social events. In other words, music and other arts are often presented as an embellishment of events which are otherwise non-artistic. More will be said later about the social context of music and about the relationship between music and other arts.

Other characteristics of traditional African music that may be mentioned here are firstly the use of musical instruments to reproduce human speech and convey signals, and secondly a tendency to conceive of music as a combination of voices and instruments. This is not to imply that unaccompanied vocal music and purely instrumental music do not exist as separate entities, but that the majority of musical occasions are those in which voices and instruments[4] are integrated.

Musical instruments

Contrary to the belief that African musical instruments consist mostly of drums, there is a surprisingly large variety of instruments in Africa. First, all of the four categories which musicologists commonly use in the classification of the world's musical instruments are represented in Africa. Secondly, the instruments in each category are of many different types. The reason for such a profusion of instruments in Africa could be that while some instruments have a fairly wide distribution, there are others which are restricted to specific communities and sometimes even to specific social contexts within the same community.

Before discussing the instruments found in Africa, it would be well to define the four main categories commonly used in the classification of musical instruments from all over the world. These are idiophones, aerophones, chordophones and membranophones.[5]

(1) Idiophones are instruments in which unstretchable materials are made to produce sound (e.g., rhythm sticks).
(2) Aerophones are instruments in which sound is produced through the excitation of a column of air (e.g., flutes).
(3) In chordophones, sound is produced through the excitation of stretched strings (e.g., violins).
(4) Membrophones are instruments in which sound is produced when stretched membranes are excitated (e.g., membrane drums).

The following list gives examples of African instruments under the four categories:

Idiophones

Percussion idiophones

(a) Percussion beam — for instance, a log of wood placed on the ground and beaten with sticks;
(b) Percussion trough — an example is a log of wood hollowed out on one side and beaten with sticks;
(c) Xylophones — with either fixed or loose keys;
(d) Percussion sticks (rhythm sticks) — for example, Yoruba *apepe*;
(e) Percussion gourd and rod — and example is the hemispherical gourd placed inverted on the ground and beaten with sticks

226

among the Hausa of northern Nigeria. Also, found among the Tuaregs is a hemispherical gourd placed inverted inside an earthenware basin containing water and struck with sticks. The harder the striking, the greater the displacement of water and hence the higher the pitch.

(f) Percussion pots − these are sometimes filled with water for tuning. The *udu* of the Igbo of Nigeria is an example of the waterless percussion pot.

(g) Percussion reeds − examples of these are found among the Lango of Uganda. Lango boys who have no access to proper drums are able to practise drumming through the use of six reeds of different sizes (and pitches) which are stuck in the ground and struck with sticks.

(h) Slit drums − these are often erroneously referred to as slit gongs. Slit drums usually have one slit and two tones (as, for example, the *ikoro* of the Igbo of Nigeria), but are sometimes found with more than two slits, consequently producing more than two tones (as, for example, the five-tone slit drum of the Mande of Sierra Leone).

(i) Gourd on gourd − two halves of a gourd each sealed with membrane and containing two small pebbles. This instrument is used by Topoke girls of the Congo region.

(j) Stamping tubes − these are tubular objects struck on the ground to produce sound. The Badouma of Equatorial Africa use bamboo tubes of different sizes with their joint membranes removed (except at the ends which are struck on the ground) and having different tones according to their lengths and diameters. The tone of a tube is sometimes modulated by holding a hand over the opening at the top.

(k) Bells − these are often erroneously called gongs. There are three main varieties, namely (i) natural bells (such as seed shells of the *borassus* palm used by the Amba and the Karamoja of Uganda and tortoise shells with clappers made from twigs, found among the Gishu and Karamoja of Uganda); (ii) wooden bells (the Konjo of Uganda carve wooden bells with two clappers made of bone); and (iii) forged bells (made of iron and either having clappers inside them or beaten with sticks) − those beaten with sticks exist as single or double bells; sets of bells tuned to different tones are also found.

Rattles

(a) Gourd rattles with narrow necks and no openings, having seeds inside; (b) gourd rattles externally strung with seeds or beads; (c) rattling objects attached to the bodies of dancers; (d) concussion rattles − for instance, two *oncoba* fruit shells filled with dry seeds and joined together by a chain; this instrument is found in Uganda where it is restricted to girls.

Plucked idiophones

These consist mainly of the *sanza* or *mbira* (which are popularly described as 'hand pianos' and whose Nigerian varieties include the Igbo *ubo,* the Yoruba *agidigbo* and the *ogumh* of the Igede of Benue State). *Sanzas* are found with gourd or wooden resonators and with keys made of iron or strips of bamboo. Large *sanzas* can have up to seventeen keys, and there are some instruments with two manuals . . . that is, having the keys arranged on two levels.

Friction idiophones

Examples of these are found in Uganda, and include:
  (a) a gourd rubbed against a board or stone;
  (b) a stick rubbed against a board; and
  (c) a stick rubbed against a box whose opening is placed in contact with the ground; pitch can be varied through changes in the pressure of rubbing.

Aerophones
  (a) Flutes – these may be either end-blown or side-blown and with an open or closed end. They could either be straight or globular. In addition to single flutes, sets of flutes (pan-pipes) are also found.
  (b) Trumpets – these may be defined as instruments having flared ends and in which sound is produced through lip vibration. By this definition, horns of animals are classified as trumpets. There are other trumpets which are made of metal. Like the flutes, trumpets are either end-blown or side-blown.
  (c) Bull roarers – these consist of flat pieces of wood of varying lengths to which are attached strings by which they are whirled round and round in the air. Bull roarers are described as 'free aerophones' because the column of air involved in the production of sound is the open air.
  (d) Reed aerophones – these are instruments whose sound resembles that of the European oboe. An example is the *algaita* of the Hausa of Nigeria.

Chordophones
  (a) Musical bows – these are ordinary archers' bows which are made to produce sounds through the striking of their strings. They are found either with or without resonators. Typical resonators are the mouth or gourds. In resonating by mouth the strings are held between but without touching the open lips of the player; such bows are sometimes called 'mouth bows'.
  (b) Zithers — these have either single strings or multiple strings. Varieties of the African zither include:
        (i) Raft zither – shaped like a raft (for example, the *molo* of the Hausa of Nigeria);
        (ii) Board zither – having a rectangular board as its resonator;

(iii) Trough zither − with a trough-shaped resonator;

(iv) Flat bar zither − with the bar mounted on a gourd resonator;

(v) Tube zither − with a tubular object as its resonator (an example of the tube zither is the *valiha* of Malagasy).

(c) Harps.

(d) Lyres.

(e) Fiddles − the single-string fiddle, which probably came from Arabia, is very common in Africa. It consists of a gourd resonator covered with skin (as, for example, the *goge* of the Hausa of Nigeria). Fiddles are either bowed or plucked.

Membranophones

Membrane drums are either single-headed (with one membrane) or double-headed (with two membranes). A single-headed drum is either open or closed at the other end. Some drums have tuning pegs while others are braced. There are drums which are stood on the ground when played and others which are held. Also, drums are either played with sticks, or with hands or with a combination of stick and hand. Varieties of drum sticks include straight sticks, curved sticks, spoon-shaped sticks, leather sticks and angular sticks.

Some drums have fixed tones while others have variable tones. The typical variable-tone drum is the tension drum whose tone can be altered through the application of pressure to strings which are connected to the drum heads. The tension drum has an hour-glass shape, and most examples of this drum have two heads. There are some, however, with single heads, such as the *kósó* of the Yoruba and the *kotso* of the Hausa. In the case of the double-head *bàtá* of Nigeria, the two heads are of different sizes and consequently produce different tones.

Even when a drum has a single fixed tone, this basic tone can be altered through muting (that is, the application of pressure to the head with the hand or stick).

Membrane drums can be further categorised by virtue of the kinds of resonators which they have. Although most resonators are made of wood, others consist of earthenware pots or gourds.

There is a certain kind of drum, the friction drum, whose sound is produced in a way other than by the beating of its head. In the friction drum, a stick is affixed to the underside of the head, inside the resonator, and sound is produced when this stick is rubbed between the palms of the hands.

Stylistic elements

In this section it is necessary first to make some observations concerning rhythmic and tonal organisation in African traditional music.

Rhythm

Rhythm in traditional music may be broadly classified under two categories, namely (1) free rhythm, and (2) strict rhythm.

Free rhythm may be described as rhythm which has no regular metre and is 'non-danceable'. This kind of rhythm is usually found in chanting with no instrumental accompaniment. In strict rhythm there is a regular metre which enables one to move or dance easily to the rhythm.

African instrumental music is often described as having complex rhythms. Rhythmic complexity arises from the use of the principle of polyrhythms simultaneously.

Tonal organisation

With respect to tonal organisation, many writers have attempted to define the scales used in African music. If the concept of the scale implies a predetermined order to precisely measured tones, then this concept is probably irrelevant in African music, except perhaps in regard to individual instruments (or instrumental ensembles) with multiple fixed pitches.

Whenever Africans sing in multiple parts, Europeans often assume that this is a result of the influence of their music. This is not necessarily true, since Africans have an indigenous vocal polyphony (part-singing) which is distinct from European polyphony. It is likely that, except for Islamised areas which are characterised by choral music in unison (as is typical of Arabic music), African choral music is essentially polyphonic. One of the most sophisticated styles of vocal polyphony is to be found in Central Africa.

Other notable elements of tonal organisation existing in Africa are *heterophony* and the *hocket* technique. Heterophony may be described as partial polyphony. In heterophony, the musicians perform in unison most of the time and only occasionally diverge into multiple parts. The hocket technique involves two or more musicians playing the same tune by sharing the notes of the tune. Each of the musicians on his own is able to supply only a fraction of the total number of notes required to produce the tune.

Repetition and variation

The basic style of African traditional music is characterised by a careful balance between repitition and variation. This principle is as applicable in vocal as in instrumental music and may be clearly observed in the so-called 'call-and-response' technique commonly used in vocal music all over Africa. This technique involves an alteration between a soloist and a chorus, in which the chorus part consists of a short phrase which is repeated over and over with little or no change, while the soloist's part changes. The following is the text of a Yoruba song which illustrates the call-and-response technique:

Solo: *Omo kí o yé jòwó o*
Chorus: *Omo jòwó*

Solo:	*Mo kúnlè mo bè ó o*
Chorus:	*Omo jòwó*
Solo:	*Mo fèkuru bè ó o*
Chorus:	*Omo jòwó*
Solo:	*Mo fàkàrà bè ó o*
Chorus:	*Omo jòwó*
Solo:	*Kí o yé jòwó o*
Chorus:	*Omo jòwó*
Solo:	*Kí o yé jòwó o*
Chorus:	*Omo jòwó*

A similar system of organisation is also found in ensemble instrumental music. Typically, it is the function of the leader of an orchestra to provide variation while each other member of the orchestra has a pattern which he repeats over and over again. Foreigners sometimes complain about the monotony of African traditional music and this is because, being unable to understand texts which the leading instrument plays, it is the repetitive structure of the secondary instruments that dominate their attention. For those who can understand the texts played by the leading instrument, the repetitive structure of the secondary instruments merely-serves as a background against which the textual-musical variation of the leading instrument stands out clearly.

Speech texts

The preceding statement leads naturally to a discussion of the importance of speech texts in traditional instrumental music. In most cultures of the world, the use of texts in vocal music only is assumed, but in Africa both vocal and instrumental music have a textual basis. This is what gave rise to the popular concept of the African talking drum, except that drums are not the only talking instruments. Any instrument that is able to produce multiple tones is potentially a talking instrument in Africa.

A musical instrument is able to talk by simulating the rhythm and intonation of ordinary speech. The element of intonation is so crucial that one is led to postulate that talking instruments are probably preponderant in African communities which use tone languages. Customarily, it is the leading instrument in an orchestra that does most of the talking. Since intonation has a semantic function in tone languages, it is important that a talking instrument is understood in the same way as ordinary speech. Consequently it is necessary for the talking instrument to observe the movement of speech tones, and, therefore, the musical patterns of the instrument arise from the natural contours of speech tones.

The speech tone principle is equally applicable in vocal music, and the structure of song melodies is usually conditioned by this principle. It should be noted, however, that whether in vocal or instrumental music, the principle is never followed dogmatically, and now and then departures are made from it either for emphasis or for better musicality.

Improvisation

It is sometimes believed that because African traditional music is performed without a notation, it is therefore entirely improvised. While improvisation forms a significant part of traditional musical practice, it should be emphasised that an equally significant proportion of what traditional musicians perform consists of previously learnt material.

The social context of music

Traditional music is usually realised within the context of social events. Although there are many occasions when music is performed purely for its own sake, the greater proportion of musical activity is that which takes place as part of social ceremonies.

From this point of view, the form which a given musical performance takes is determined by the structure of the social ceremony. As Nketia has observed in his discussion of vocal music in Ghana, form is derived partly from the context of a song and partly from verbal texts. Room is always left for improvisation and for the re-arrangement of the order of verses, and, therefore, the actual shape of a song depends on the particular situation in which it is sung. In view of this, a distinction should be made between the basic form, basic pattern and basic length of a song on the one hand and its resultant form, resultant pattern and the duration of a particular performance at a particular time, on the other hand.[6]

The various social events with which music is most usually associated include religious worship, war, therapy, magic, work, children's games, sports, installation of chiefs and kings, festivals and ceremonies pertaining to the life cycle (such as birth rites, infant rites, puberty rites, marriage and funeral rites).

Apart from embellishing social events, music has other important social functions. In a society which, as far as we know, had no written literature until recently, music has served as one of the most important means of documenting history. Moreover, day-to-day news and other items of information are often transmitted through music. Indeed, music is indispensable in traditional society in the acquisition of general education pertaining to customs, life style, philosophy and other aspects of culture.

Music also plays a major role in politics. Kings and important chiefs usually have personal musicians whose duties include image-making for their employers. Musicians are particularly gifted in the subtle use of praise texts designed to enhance the prestige of their clients while castigating the clients' opponents.

One of the most important aspects of the social context of music is that the community at large has ample opportunity to participate in music-making. While certain areas of music are extremely difficult and can only be executed by specially trained artists, there are others which are simple enough for the average member of the community to join in. One obvious example of collaboration between specialists and non-specialists is in the call-and-response type of song in which the solo part is performed by trained musicians while the choral part may be sung by any onlookers who care to join in.

Certain musical instruments are identified with specific social contexts or personalities, and since such instruments are in some cases never used outside these contexts, this partly accounts for the large number of musical instruments in Africa. For example, percussion sticks are used in circumcision rites in Uganda and in initiation rites among the Bantu. According to Merriam, drums are reserved for royalty among the Tutsi and, apart from the king, only the Queen Mother is allowed to keep a drum set.[7] Bull roarers are commonly reserved for initiation ceremonies or activities of cult groups. In general, trumpets are regarded as symbols of royalty while bells are sometimes played to indicate the presence of divinities. Finally, among the Yoruba of Nigeria, ìgbìn drums are identified with Obàtálá, the god of creation; àgèrè drums with Ògún, the god of warfare and or iron implements; and ìpèsè drums with Òrúnmìlà, the god of the Ifá divination.

The relationship between music and other arts

African traditional performing arts tend to exist as a multiple-arts complex, with music forming the core of this complex. In other words, whenever music is performed, one or more of the other performing arts is usually present and, conversely, the proper realisation of a performing art other than music is often dependent upon music.

First of all, dancing takes place on a great number of musical occasions. While music can and is often performed on its own, dance rarely occurs without music.

Secondly, the degree of integration that exists between music and poetry leads to the conclusion that music is almost synonymous with poetry in traditional African culture. This is manifested not only in the use of musical instruments as surrogates for speech in the performance of poetry but also in the typical use of a musical intonation when poetry is recited vocally.

Other examples of arts which are customarily performed in association with music are wrestling, acrobatics, story-telling and puppetry.

Above all, music forms the basis of traditional drama. The structure of African social ceremonies is patently dramatic, and these ceremonies should be regarded as constituting the indigenous drama of Africa. As we have already shown, music plays an important role in the enactment of traditional social ceremonies.

Apart from having strong links with other performing arts, music is also closely associated with the visual arts. For example, one is likely to see a display of the most splendid costumes on those important occasions when music is performed. Although some of these costumes are more elaborate versions of everyday attire, there are other types which are specially reserved for these occasions. Moreover, music is usually performed whenever masks are displayed.

The traditional social ceremony is a unifying force in African art for it tends to bring together within a common context as many of the arts as possible. Furthermore, religion serves as the most important source of inspiration for African artists, and religious ceremonies are pre-eminent as a means of integrating the arts, with music being the most common factor in these ceremonies. The traditional African social ceremony, therefore, may be regarded as a kind of 'total art' whose foundation is music.

New music

As was stated at the beginning of this chapter, many Arabic musical elements are present in black Africa but, because they have been absorbed into the mainstream of traditional music, these elements are no longer viewed as foreign and are often hardly perceptible. On the other hand, European musical traits are clearly identifiable as belonging outside the framework of African indigenous music.

Much of the new music practised in Africa today has developed as a result of influences from European and other Western sources. Some of this music has developed concurrently with the music of the African diaspora in the Americas, and these two new traditions of music have much in common. Moreover, the new music of the diaspora was developed by Africans forced by slavery to develop a culture in which African and Western elements were co-ordinated. The development of new music in the African homeland, on the other hand, has been much influenced by liberated slaves who returned to Africa after having been exposed to Western tradition.

Another major source of influence in the growth of the new music of Africa has come from Christian missionaries. At first relying on Western hymns translated into African languages and sung to their original Western tunes, African Christians eventually created a new religious music in which not only are the texts in African languages but also the tunes are modelled on African traditional musical idioms. These hymns are often performed with an accompaniment of African traditional musical instruments.

It is important to note that the performance context of church hymns allows for congregational participation, something that is very much akin to the customary practice of pre-Christian African music.

In addition to hymns, African composers for the church have produced works on a larger scale, including masses (for example, the *Missa Luba* and the *Missa Katanga*) which are also based on traditional African stylistic elements.

The best of the Christian religious compositions have originated from the non-orthodox denominations and, to a lesser extent, from the Catholic denomination.

Apart from religious compositions derived from traditional musical culture, another type of neo-traditional music has been created for secular use. To begin with, there is an increasing demand in contemporary Africa for traditional music to be presented in the Western concert format and away from its customary social contexts. In the new context, audience participation is restricted, and some structural modifications are necessary to make its transition from the village scene to the concert stage possible.

Then there are other types of concert music, based either wholly on the principles of Western art music or using a combination of African and Western resources. These types have been created by African musicians who have been trained in the classical music of the West.

It should also be mentioned that contemporary African playwrights (working in both African and European languages) are making much use of traditional music as part of their stylistic equipment. Indeed, the modern African theatre is essentially a music theatre.

Lastly, African musicians have been considerably active in the creation of that type of music typically heard in night clubs and described as 'pop' music. Two kinds of modern pop music have become widespread in Africa. There are idioms of pop music which are direct imitations of Western pop music and which contain few African characteristics. There are other idioms which represent a fairly balanced combination of Western and African musical elements.

The picture of the contemporary musical scene which has been presented in this essay shows that several types of music are co-existent in Africa today. This picture must be regarded as a healthy one since the new musical types have complemented and not obliterated the old indigenous types. The latter remain, as they have always been, the prime musical fare in Africa, whereas the new types of music serve to enrich the overall musical culture.

Notes

1   A. M. Jones, *Africa and Indonesia: the evidence of the xylophone and other musical and cultural factors,* Leiden, E. J. Brill, 1964

2   See, e.g., J. H. Kwabena Nketia, 'Unity and diversity in African music: a problem of synthesis', a paper presented at the First International Congress of Africanists in Accra, 1962

3   Alan P. Merriam, 'Introduction and notes', for *Africa south of the Sahara,* 12-inch LP record, Ethnic Folkways Library Album, No. FE 503, 1957, p. 2

4   The definition of 'instruments' here includes handclapping.

5   This system of classification was devised by Erich M. von Hornbostel and Curt Sachs. See Erich M. von Hornbostel and Curt Sachs, 'Classification of Musical Instruments', translated from the original German by Anthony Baines and Klaus P. Wachsmann, *The Galpin Society Journal*, XIV, 1961.

6   J. H. Kwabena Nketia, *African music in Ghana,* Evanston, Illinois, Northwestern University Press, 1963, p. 27

7   Alan P. Merriam, 'Introduction and notes', p. 8

Questions for discussion

1   Using the four main categories discussed in the essay, classify traditional musical instruments found in your area.

2   Discuss the social context of African traditional music.

3   Discuss new musical types which have developed in Africa as a result of Western influence.

4   Radio, television and the phonograph have made a considerable impact on the musical culture of Africa. Discuss.

5   Music and other arts are interrelated in African traditional culture. Discuss.

6   Give a critical appraisal of modern African pop music.

Suggestions for further reading

Beby, Francis. *African Music: a people's art,* New York, Lawrence Hill, 1975

Jones, A. M. *Studies in African music,* Oxford University Press, 1959, 2 vols

Merriam, Alan P. 'African music', in *Continuity and change in African cultures,* William Bascom and Melville Herskovitz (eds.), pp. 49-86, University of Chicago Press, 1958

Nketia, J. H. Kwabena, *African music in Ghana,* Evanston, Illinois, Northwestern University Press, 1963

————. *The music of Africa,* New York, Norton, 1974

Nketia, J. H. Kwabena *et al. African music,* Proceedings of a UNESCO meeting in Yaounde, 23-27 Feb. 1970, Paris, La Revue Musicale, 1972

Wachsmann, Klaus P. (ed.) *Essays on music and history in Africa,* Evanston, Illinois, Northwestern University Press, 1971

14 Theatre in African traditional culture: survival patterns

Wole Soyinka

Even where other resources of pre-colonial society are unevenly shared, culture tends to suggest a comparatively even-handed distribution or – perhaps more simply – mass appropriation. This may help to explain why it is always a primary target of assault by an invading force. As an instrument of self-definition, its destruction or successful attrition reaches into the reserves of racial/national will on a comprehensive scale. Conversely, the commencement of resistance and self-liberation by the suppressed people is not infrequently linked with the survival strategies of key cultural patterns, manifested through various art forms. The experience of West Africa has been no different. The history of West African theatre in the colonial period reveals itself therefore as largely a history of cultural resistance and survival. Confronted by the hostility of both Islamic and Christian values, in addition to the destructive imperatives of colonialism, it has continued until today to vitalise contemporary theatrical forms both in the tradition of 'folk opera' and in the works of those playwrights and directors commonly regarded as 'Westernised'.

We must not lose sight of the fact that drama, like any other art form, is created and executed within a specific physical environment. It naturally interacts with that environment, is influenced by it, influences that environment in turn and acts together with the environment in the larger and far more complex history of society. The history of a dramatic pattern or its evolution is therefore very much the history of other art forms of society. And when we consider art forms from the point of view of survival strategies, the dynamics of cultural interaction with society become even more aesthetically challenging and fulfilling. We discover, for instance, that under certain conditions some art forms are transformed into others – simply to assure the survival of the threatened forms. Drama may give way to poetry and song in order to disseminate dangerous sentiments under the watchful eye of the oppressor, the latter forms being more easily communicable. On the other hand, drama may become more manifestly invigorated in order to counteract the effect of alienating an environment.

Nigeria offers a valuable example of the dual process of cultural attenuation and resurgence. For example, theatrical professionalism was synonymous by the middle nineteenth century with the artistic proficiency and organisation of a particular theatrical form which had emerged from the burial rituals associated with the Oyo monarchy, the *egungun*. The question of when a performed event became theatre as such, in its own formalistic right, as opposed to religious or cultic ritualism is of course a vexed one that we need not bother about in this context. It is, however, commonly agreed that what started out — probably — as a ritualistic ruse to effect the funeral obsequies of an Oyo king had, by the mid-century, evolved into a theatrical form in substance and practice. From an annual celebration rite of the smuggling-in of the corpse of that king and its burial, the *egungun* ancestral play became, firstly, a court re-enactment, then a secular form of performance which was next appropriated by the artists themselves. Its techniques were perfected by family guilds and township cults. About this time, however, Islam had begun its push southwards. The Oyo empire, already in dis-integration from internal rivalries and other stresses, found itself under increasing military pressure from the Hausa-Fulani in the north, a situation which came on the heels of a rebellion of tributary states to the south. The fall of Oyo took down with it the security which the theatrical art had enjoyed under its patronage. The Muslims, victorious in northern Yorubaland, banned most forms of theatrical performance as contrary to the spirit of Islam. The *Agbegijo, Alarinjo* and allied genres, with their dramatic use of the paraphernalia of carved masks and other repre-sentations of ancestral spirits, came most readily under religious dis-approval. It did not matter that, by now, they had lost most of their pretence to the mysterious or numinous.

Southern Nigeria and its neighbouring territories were, however, only temporary beneficiaries from this disruption of political life in the old Oyo empire. The Christian missionaries had also begun their northward drive, usually only a few steps ahead of the colonial forces. The philistine task begun by the Moslems was rounded out by the Christians' ban on the activities of suspect cults. The Christians went further. They did not content themselves with banning just the dramatic performances; they placed their veto also on indigenous musical instruments — *bata, gangan, dundun* and so on — the very backbone of traditional theatre. It was into this vacuum that the returned slaves stepped with their Western (and therefore Christian) instruments, their definitely Christian dramatic themes and their Western forms.

Another historical factor aided the temporary eclipse of indigenous theatre forms: the slave trade and its supply which involved inter-state wars, raids and casual kidnappings. The missionary compounds often offered the securest havens from these perennial hazards, just as did (in West Africa) submission to the protective spheres of the Muslim overlords. It is difficult to imagine a group of refugees from the old Oyo empire encouraged by their Muslim or Christian protectors to revert to the ways of their 'pagan art'. The records do not reveal any such acts of disinterested artistic patronage. Artistic forms might be appropriated, but only in the cause of religious promotion; thus, for example, the appropriation of musical forms by the nineteenth-century Christian missionaries in Buganda for hymns. This, however, was only a later re-finement, a sensible strategy for rendering the patently alien words and sentiments less abrasive to the indigenes by coating them in traditional harmonies.

It is difficult to trace, at present, the effect of the Oyo *egungun* dispersal on the development of theatrical forms in neighbouring areas. This is always the case with any situation of artistic hiatus — a period, that is, when a particular form of art goes underground or disappears temporarily, especially under the pressures of a dominant political and artistic ethos. The records simply ignore them, or treat them merely as isolated nuisances. The substitution of new forms belonging to the dominant culture takes pride of place in records, and this is the situation we encounter in the development of Western 'concerts' and variety shows in the colonised territories of West Africa.

At this point, therefore, let us clarify in our minds what theatre is. That this is more than a merely academic exercise is easily grasped if we refer to a sister art, sculpture, an achievement which the missionary-coloniser pioneers found convenient to deny to the African. The redressing assessment was made by other Europeans – the artists themselves, notably the Expressionists; they had no overriding reasons to deny the obvious, to ignore what was even a potential source of inspiration to their own creative endeavours. The vexed question of what constitutes drama and what is merely ritual, ceremony, festival and so on, while it continues to be legitimately argued, must always be posed against an awareness of early prejudiced reading of the manifestations encountered by culture denigrators, definitions which today still form the language of orthodox theatre criticism. To assist our own definition we need look only at any one cultural event within which diversified forms are found, forms which – through their visual impact – tend towards the creation of differing categories for a comparative description. In other words if, within one performance or cluster of performances (say, a festival or a celebration) in any given community, we discover consciously differing qualitative enactments, we are obliged to rummage around in our artistic vocabulary for categories that reflect such differences. Thus we find that, sooner or later, we arrive at the moment when only the expression 'drama' or 'theatre' seems apposite, and then the search is over. We will take an example from the Afikpo masquerades south-east Nigeria.

A contrast between the *okumkpa* event and the *oje ogwu*, both being components of this Afikpo festival, actually furnishes us with the basic definition we need. This masquerade, which is the professional handiwork of a male initiation society, varies, we discover, from basically balletic sequences as contained in the oje ogwu to the *mimetic* as contained in the okumkpa. The latter is indeed performed as a climax to what appears to be the prominent oje ogwu turn by the masqueraders. Both are basically audience-oriented – in other words, we are not really concerned here with the complication of a *ritual* definition but one of performance and reception. The audience plays a prominent appreciative role in this outdoor performance, judging, booing or approving on purely aesthetic grounds. Whatever symbolism may be contained in the actual movement of the oje ogwu is of no significance in the actual judgement. What the audience looks for and judges are the finer points of leaps, turns, control and general spatial domination. The poorer performers are soon banished to the group sessions – which demonstrates the importance given to individual technical mastery.

The okumkpa event, by contrast, consists of satirical mimesis. Masks are also used but the *action* forms the basis of performance. This action consists of a satirical rendition of actual events both in neighbouring settlements and in the village itself. Personalities are ridiculed, the events in which they were involved are re-enacted. In short, events are transformed artistically both for audience delectation and for the imparting of moral principles. Additionally, however, one standard repertoire consists of the taking of female roles by the young male initiates, this role being of a rather derogatory character. The satirised female is invariably what we might call 'the reluctant bride'. As the young actor minces and prances around, sung dialogues accompany him, built around the same theme: 'How much longer are you going to reject all suitors on the grounds that they are not sufficiently handsome/ strong/industrious etc, etc?' Competition is keen among the initiates for the honour of playing this central female role, and the audience judges the performance by the skill of the female impersonator. The various sketches in this vein are rounded off in the end by a massed parade of the various actors in the *njenji* where the less accomplished actors have their own hour of glory and the entire female world is satirically lectured on the unkindness of keeping the male rooster waiting too long.

We will not examine the sociological motivation of this kind of drama except to point out that this example is actually more rewarding, in our search for an explanation of man's motives in *dramatising*, than, for instance, the theory of the origin of the Oyo masquerade. Clearly, in the Afikpo masquerade we encounter a male-prejudiced device. It ensures man's claim to social superiority and creates guilt in the woman for not fulfilling on demand man's need for female companionship. It is of no more mystifying an order of things than, for instance, the disparagement by male undergraduates in their press of female undergraduates who have not submitted to their own desires – except, of course, that traditional society imposed heavy penalties on libellous fabrication (which is, by the way, a reliable indication of artistic barrenness). What we obtain from one, therefore, is genuine art; from their modern progeny, alas, only dirty pictures and fevered fantasies. The okumkpa provides us with drama – variety, satire. We are left with no other definition when we contrast it with its consciously differentiated companion piece – the oje ogwu.

Similarly, festivals such as the Ogun or Osun (River) festivals in Yorubaland provide us with multi-media and multi-formal experiences within which it is not at all difficult to find unambiguous examples of dramatic enactments. The high point of the festival of the Yoruba hero –deity Obatala is, for instance, undoubted drama, consisting of all the elements that act on the emotions, the expectations of conflict and resolution and the human appreciation of spectacle. We begin to understand now why dating the origin of African drama, locating it in a specific event, time and place is an impossible task – indeed, a meaningless one. In the study of art forms, it is clearly more appealing to look into extant material for what may be deduced as primitive or early forms of the particular art, noting along the way what factors have contributed to their survival in the specific forms. Festivals, comprising as they do such a variety of forms, from the most spectacular to the most secretive and emotionally charged, offer the most familiar hunting-ground. What is more, they constitute in themselves *pure theatre* at its most prodigal and resourceful. In short, the persistent habit of dismissing festivals as belonging to a 'spontaneous' inartistic expression of communities demands re-examination. The level of organisation involved, the integration of the sublime with the mundane, the endowment of the familiar with properties of the unique (and this, spread over days) all indicate that it is into the heart of many African festivals that we should look for the most stirring expressions of man's instinct and need for drama at its most comprehensive and community-involving. Herbert M. Cole renders this point of view in penetrating terms:

> A festival is a relatively rare climactic event in the life of any com-
> munity. It is bounded by a definite beginning and end, and is unified
> thereby, as well as being set apart from the above daily life. Its
> structure is built on a core or armature of ritual. The festival brings
> about a suspension of ordinary time, a transformation of ordinary
> space, a formaliser of ordinary behaviour. It is as if a community
> becomes a stage set and its people actors with a battery of seldom-seen
> props and costumes. Meals become feasts, and greetings, normally
> simple become ceremonies. Although dependent upon life-sustaining
> rituals, the festival is an elaborated and stylised phenomenon which
> far surpasses ritual necessity. It often becomes the social, ritual and
> political apotheosis of community life in a year. At festival time one
> level of reality − the common and everyday − gives way to another, a
> more intense, symbolic and expressive level of reality.[1]

What this implies is that instead of considering festivals from one point of view only − that of providing, in a primitive form, the ingredients of drama, we may even begin examining the opposite point of view: that contemporary drama, as we experience it today, is a contraction of drama, necessitated by the productive order of society in other directions. That is, drama undergoes parallel changes with other structuring mechanisms of society. As communities outgrow certain patterns of producing what they require to sustain themselves or of transforming what exists around them, the structures which sustain the arts are affected in parallel ways, affecting in turn the very forms of the arts. That the earlier forms are not necessarily more 'primitive' or 'crude' is borne out by the fact that more and more of the highly developed societies are turning to the so-called 'primitive' forms of drama as representing the significant dramatic forms for contemporary society. These societies, which vary from such ideologically disparate countries as the United States and East European countries, are re-introducing on stage, in both formal theatre structures and improvised spaces, dramatic forms such as we have described, from the macro-conceptual (as represented in festivals) to the micro-conceptual, as ritual may be held to epitomise.

In this vein, what are we to make of the famous Return-to-the Village Festival of the Koumina canton in Bobo-Dioulasso, Upper Volta? Here we encounter a people who, like many others in West Africa, have experienced the culturally disrupting influences of Muslim and Christian cultures. The traders came first, the Mande traders, in the early sixteenth century. In their next significant migration, the mid-eighteenth century, they were accompanied by Muslim clerics, with the cultural results with which we are by now familiar. By 1775 proselytisation had become so successful that an Imamate had been established by the famous Saghnughu family of scholars. The late nineteenth century saw the take-over by colonial administrators and Christian missionaries. Yet under this double assault, Bobo traditional arts have survived until today, and nowhere is it given more vital expression than in the 'Tagaho' season festival which marks the return of the Bobo to their village after their seasonal migrations to their farmsteads. The festival, which has for its core the funeral ceremonies for those who died during the period of farmland migration, has a far more important function for the living: the re-installation of the cohering, communal spirit and existential reality. Costumes are elaborately prepared, formal patterns both of 'ritual' and 'pageant' worked out and rehearsed, individual events enacted by masked figures for a delayed participation by the community as one entity. It is all of course a conscious performance, informed and controlled by aesthetic ideas, by the competitive desire also of 'showing off' dramatic skills. Simultaneously it is an affirmation of social solidarity. Can this form of theatre, considered in its most fundamental purpose and orientation, be viewed much differently from the theatre of 'happenings' which began in America and Europe in the sixties and is still encountered in parts of those societies today? To be sure, the former is more disciplined, formal and community-inspired, which are all attributes that we experience from unalienating forms of theatre.

At this point, it may be useful to consider instances where an art form evolves into another art form in one geographical/cultural area but fails to do so in another. The heroic tradition is one that is common to most parts of Africa (and, indeed, to most societies). Within this tradition may be grouped, at any level of its development, the epic, saga, praise-chants, ballads and so on, but here we are concerned with the performance aspect from which dramatisation most naturally evolves. East, Central and South Africa are particularly rich in the tradition of the heroic recitative. Among the Luo of Kenya and Uganda, for instance, we may note the form known as the *pakrouk*, a kind of virtue-boasting which takes place at ceremonial gatherings, usually to the accompaniment of a harp. The individual performer emerges from the group, utters praises of his own person and his achievements, and is replaced or contended with by another. Similar manifestations are found among the Ankole tribes, while further south, among the Sotho and the Zulu, sustained lyrical recitations on important historical events have become highly developed.

Among the Ijaw people of south-eastern Nigeria, however, the same tradition has actually developed dramatic variants, has moved beyond the merely recited to the enacted, a *tour de force* sustained by a principal actor for over three days. The saga of *Ozidi*, the principal source for J. P. Clark's play of the same name, is an example. By contrast, the history of the performance arts in Central and Southern Africa reveals a tendency towards virtual stasis of the putative dramatic elements. even the dramatic potential of such rituals as the *Nyasi-iye*, the boat-building and launching ceremonies of the Luo, with its symbolic 'cutting of the umbilical cord' as the boat is freed from its moorings, even the abundant parallelisms with nuptial rites, have somehow failed to move towards a truly dramatic rendering of the significance and life-intertwining role of

242

the boats in the daily pre-occupations of the Luo. One need only contrast this with the various rites and festivals of the coastal and riverine peoples of West Africa, where both religious observances and economic practicalities of the same activity have taken on, over the centuries, a distinctly dramatic ordering. One may speculate at length on the reasons for this contrast; the reality remains, however, that drama as an integral phenomenon in the lives of the peoples of Central and Southern Africa has followed a comparatively meagre development.

Well then, let us, using one of our early examples follow how traditional theatre forms adjusted or re-surfaced from the preliminary repressions of alien cultures. We find that the 'pagan' theatre ultimately withstood the onslaught, not only preserving its forms but turning itself consciously into a base of resistance against both dominating systems. We are able to witness the closing of a cycle of cultural substitution in a curious irony of this slavery–colonial experience. Having first broken up the cultural life of the people, the slave era, now in its dying phase in the first half of the nineteenth century, brought back the sons of the land with a new culture in place of the old. The returnees constituted a new elite: they possessed after all the cultural tools of the colonial masters. But − and now we emphasise the place of theatre among these cultural tools − even where they were fully assimilated into the cultural values of their erstwhile masters (or saviours), they found on their return company servants, civil servants, missionary converts who belonged in the same social class as themselves, but were culturally unalienated. These stay-at-homes had had what was more or less an equivalent colonial education, yet had also acquired a nationalist awareness which manifested itself in cultural attitudes. As the nineteenth century entered its last quarter, the stay-at-homes were able to provide a balancing development pattern to cultural life on the West coast which came predominantly under the creative influence of the returnee Christians, despite the latter's confidence in the superiority of their acquired arts and their eagerness to prove to the white population that the black man was capable not only of receiving but also of practising the refined arts of the European.

The cultural difference between the settlers of Liberia and Sierra Leone on the one hand, and the coastal societies of Ghana and Nigeria on the other can be translated in terms of the degree of cultural identification with, and adaptation of the authentic resources of the hinterland. To the former − mostly returnee slaves − the indigenous people remained savage, crude and barbaric, to be regarded only as material for missionary conversion and possible education. The converts who had remained at home, however, set off a process of schisms within social and religious institutions whose value-system was Eurocentric, delving again and again into the living resources of indigenous society. Naturally there were exceptions on both sides, but this dichotomy did hold in general. The direction of *new* forms of theatrical entertainment therefore followed an eastward pattern from the new returnee settlements; inevitably it received increasing native blood-transfusion as it moved further east away from the bastardised vaudeville of the 'Nova Scotians', so that by the time it arrived in Ghana, Dahomey (now Benin) and Nigeria, both in form and content, a distinct West African theatrical idiom had evolved.

'Academies', to begin with, were formed for the performance of concerts which were modelled on the Victorian music hall or the American vaudeville. The Christian churches organised their own concerts, schools were drawn into the concert rage — prize-giving days, visits of the District Officer, Queen Victoria's birthday and so on. The black missionaries refused to be outdone; Rev. Ajayi Crowther was a famous example, a black prelate who patronised and encouraged this form of the arts, while the Rev. James Johnson turned the famous Breadfruit church in Lagos into a springboard for theatrical performances. The Brazilian returnees added an exotic yet familiar flavour, their music finding a ready echo in the traditional melodies of the West Coast and the Congo whose urban suppression had not occurred long enough ago for such melodies to be totally forgotten. At the turn of the century and in the first decades of the twentieth century, Christmas and New Year saw the streets of the capital cities of Freetown and Lagos transformed by mini-pageants reminiscent of Latin fiestas, of which the 'caretta', a kind of satyr masquerade, appears to have been the most durable.

Cultural nationalism was, however, constantly at work against a total usurpation by imported forms. Once again religion and its institutions provided the base. Unable to accept the excesses of the Christian cultural imperialism, such as the embargo on African instruments and tunes in a 'universal' church, and the prohibition of drumming on tranquil Anglican Sundays, the breakaway movements began. The period 1888 to the early 1930s witnessed a proliferation of secessionist movements, mostly inspired by a need to worship God in the cultural mode of the forefathers. And now began also a unique 'operatic' tradition in West Africa, but especially Lagos, beginning with church cantatas which developed into dramatisations of biblical stories until it asserted its independence in secular stories and the development of professional touring troupes. The process, reminiscent of the evolution of the 'miracle' or 'mystery' plays of medieval Europe, is identical with the evolution of the Agbegijo theatre (then temporarily effaced) from the sacred funeral rites of the Alafin of Oyo to court entertainment and, thereafter, independent existence and geographical dispersion. From the genteel concerts of classical music and English folk songs by the 'Academy' of the 1880s to the historical play *King Elejigbo* of the Egbe Ife Church Dramatic Society in 1902, a transformation of thought and sensibility had recognisably taken place even among the Westernised elite of southern Nigeria. The Church did not take kindly to it. They closed their churchyards and schools to the evolving art. Alas, they only succeeded in accelerating the defiant erection of theatre halls, specifically designed for the performing arts. It was in reality a tussle between groups of colonial elite, fairly balanced in the matter of resources. By 1912 the secularisation of theatrical entertainment in southern Nigeria was sufficiently advanced for the colonial government to gazette a 'Theatre and Public Performance Regulations Ordinance', which required that performing groups obtain a licence before going before the public. In the climate of cultural nationalism which obtained in Lagos at that time, it is doubtful whether this disguised attempt at political censorship would have worked; it is significant that the ordinance was never made into law.

Ironically, yet another breakaway church, the Cherubim and Seraphim movement, swung the pendulum back towards a rejection of traditional forms and was followed shortly by other emulators in the Christian re-consecration of theatrical forms. The furthest these churches would go in the use of musical instruments was the tambourine; local instruments which had created a new tonality in the operettas now touring the West Coast – sekere, dundun, gangan, and so on – were damned as instruments of the Devil. Secular stories, even of historic personages and events, were banned and the new theatre halls, church halls and schoolrooms echoed once more to the Passion of Christ, the anguish of Nebuchadnezzar, the trials of Job, and other dramatic passages from the Bible. The Aladura, Cherubim and Seraphim, and their adherents did not however stop there. These 'prophetist' cults spread rapidly along the West Coast waging a crusade against all 'pagan' worship and their sacred objects. Descending on the provinces of the established churches, they ignited bonfires with their hot-gospelling in which perished thousands of works of art, especially in Nigeria, Cameroons, Ghana and the Ivory Coast. The vision of a fifteen-year-old girl, Abiodun Akinsowon, about 1921 was to prove a costly dream for the cultural heritage of West Africa, the heaviest brunt of which was borne by Yoruba sculpture. This period may also be justly said to constitute the lowest ebb in the fortunes of traditional theatre, their participation in the cultural life even of the villages being subjected to lightning descents from the fanatical hordes of the prophetic sects. In the physiual confrontations that often took place, the position of authority was predictable. Embarrassed as they sometimes were by the excesses of the sectarians, the European missionaries and their black priests had no hesitation about their alliances – and their voice was weighty in the processes of imposing the colonial peace.

But the 'vaudeville' troupes prospered. Names of groups such as we encounter in 'Two Bobs and their Carolina Girl' tell us something of the inspiration of much of these. Master Yalley, a schoolteacher, is credited with having begun the tradition of the vaudeville variety act in Ghana. His pupil Bob Johnson and his 'Axim Trio' soon surpassed the master and became a familiar figure on Ghana's cultural landscape, also later in Nigeria. More important still, Bob Johnson's innovations must be credited with having given birth to the tradition of the 'concert party' of Ghana, groups which specialise in variety routine: songs, jokes, dances, impersonations, comic scenes. However, the most notable achievement in the sense of cultural continuity was their thrusting on to the fore-stage of contemporary repertoire a stock character from traditional lore, the wily trickster Anansi. This quickly developed into a vehicle for social and political commentary, apart from its popularity in comic situations.

The Jaguar Jokers, for example, transformed Anansi into the more urban character of Opia, while Efua Sutherland's more recent *The Marriage of Anansewa* takes this tradition into an even more tightly-knit and disciplined play format – the term 'disciplined' being employed here merely in the sense of reducing the areas of spontaneous improvisation, without however eliminating them. Those who saw this piece during Festac 77 will have observed how attractively the element of formal discipline and free improvisation blended together to encourage a controlled audience interaction. By the middle 1930s, Bob Johnson had become sufficiently established to take his brand of vaudeville to other West African cities. West Africa in this decade could boast of a repertoire of shows displaying the most bizarre products of eclectic art in the history of theatre. Even cinema, an infant art, had by then left its mark on West African theatre: some of Bob Johnson's acts were adaptations of Charlie Chaplin's escapades, not omitting his costume and celebrated shuffle. And the thought of Empire Day celebration concerts at which songs like 'Mini the Moocher' formed part of the evening musical recitals, side by side with 'God's Gospel is our Heritage' and vignettes from the life of a Liberian stevedore, stretches the contemporary imagination, distanced from the historical realities of colonial West Africa.

Again, another irony of colonial intentions: while Bob Johnson was preparing his first West African tour and Hubert Ogunde, later to become Nigeria's foremost 'concert party' leader, was undergoing his aesthetic formation from the vying forces of a clergyman father and a grandmother who was a priestess of the *osugbe* cult, a European educationist, Charles Beart in Senegal, was beginning to reverse the policy of European acculturation in a leading secondary school in Senegal. The extent of this development – including also an appreciation of the slow pace of such an evolution – will be better grasped by recalling the educational charter of assimilationism, spelt in diverse ways by the publications of such dedicated African Francophiles as the Abbé Boillat, Paul Holle and so on. Boillat, in spite of extensive sociological research (*Esquisses sénégalaises*),[2] the result of his examination of the culture and philosophy of the Bambara, Sarakole, Wolof, Serer, the Tukulor and Moorish groups in Senegal, found no lessons to be drawn from African society for modern cultural development, no future but to witness 'the fall of all those gross, if not dishonourable, ways known as the *custom of the country*'.[3] If his addresses to the metropolitan centre of the French world did not become the cornerstone of French assimilationist policies, they undoubtedly played a key role in their formulation. Against this background, and ensueing decades of such conservatism, the Ecole William Ponty was founded. A famous teachers' college, it served Francophone Africa in the same way as did Achimota College in the Anglophone West and Makerere College in East Africa. They were all designed to provide a basic European education for would-be teachers and low-echelon civil servants. Such humanistic education as came into the curriculum of the Ecole William Ponty was of necessity French – French plays, poetry, music, art, history. Charles Beart, during his principalship, embarked however on a new orientation of the students' cultural instructions. From 1930 onwards the students were encouraged to return to their own societies for cultural directions. Assignments were given which resulted in the students' exploration of both the form and the substance of indigenous art. Groups from every colonial territory represented at William Ponty were then expected to return from vacation armed with a theatrical presentation based on their researches, the entire direction being left in the hands of the students themselves. Since the new theatrical sociology did not confine itself to the usual audiences of European officials and 'educated' Africans nor to Senegal alone, its influence spread widely through different social strata of French-speaking Africa. Was it, however, a satisfying development of the culture from which it derived?

The answer must be in the negative, though the experiment was not without its instructive values. It would be too much to expect that, at that period, the classic model of French theatre could yield completely to the expression of traditional forms. The community represented by William Ponty was an artificial one. It was distanced from the society whose cultural hoards it rifled both in qualitative thought and material product. The situation was of course not peculiar to William Ponty since it also obtained in the other schools and institutions set up by the coloniser for the fulfilment of his own mission in Africa. Thus the theatre of William Ponty served the needs of exotic satisfaction for the community of French colonials. Even when it 'went to the people', and with their own material, it remained a curiosity that left the social life and authentic cultural awareness of the people untouched.

We will conclude with the 'new' theatre form which has proved the most durable; hybrid in its beginnings, the 'folk opera' has become the most expressive language of theatre in West Africa. What were the themes that mostly engaged the various groups spread along the Coast? The Nigerian Hubert Ogunde provides a convenient compendium since he does appear to be more consistently varied in his dramatic fare than any comparable group to date in West Africa. His repertoire ranges from outright fantasy through biblical dramatisations to social commentary and political protest, both in the colonial and post-colonial era. A comparative study of the repertoire of the Jaguar Jokers, the Axim Trio, or the current Anansekrom groups of Ghana for example would reveal that these concentrate almost exclusively on social commentary, mostly with a moralistic touch – the evils of witchcraft, maladjustment in the social status of the cash-crop *nouveaux riches*, generational problems, changing status of women in society, sexual mores and so on, all of which also preoccupy the pamphlet drama of the Onitsha market literateurs. Hubert Ogunde explored these themes in his plays and more. His biblical adaptations became in effect a vehicle for direct commentaries on contemporary society. Reference is hardly necessary to those plays which have earned him the ire of colonial and post-colonial governments: *Bread and hunger*, a play not merely on the famous Iva Valley strike by miners in eastern Nigeria but on the general inequity of labour exploitation; and *Yoruba Ronu*, an indictment of the corruption and repression of the government of the then Western Region. Both plays were proscribed by the affected governments. They have entered the lore of theatrical commitment in Nigeria.

And additionally, Hubert Ogunde exemplifies what we have referred to up until now as the survival patterns of traditional theatrical art. From the outset of his theatrical career, Ogunde's theatre belonged only partially to what we have described as the 'Nova Scotian' tradition. His musical instrumentation was all borrowed from the West, movement on stage was pure Western chorus-line, night-club variety. Nevertheless, the attachment to traditional musical forms (albeit with Western impurities) gradually became more assertive. Encouraged no doubt by the appearance of more tradition-grounded groups such as Kola Ogunmola and

Duro Ladipo, Hubert Ogunde in the early sixties began to employ traditional instruments in his performance, his music delved deeper into home melodies, and even his costumes began to eschew the purely fabricated, theatrically glossy, for recognisable local gear. Rituals appeared with greater frequency and masquerades became a frequent feature − often, it must be added, as gratuitous insertions. Ogunde's greatest contribution to West African drama − quite apart from his innovative energy and his commitment to a particular political line − lies in his as yet little appreciated musical 'recitative' style, one which he has made unique to himself. It has few imitators, but the success of his records in this genre of 'dramatic monologue' testifies to the responsive chord it elicits from his audience. Based in principle on the *rara* style of chanting, but in stricter rhythm, it is melodically a modernistic departure, flexibly manipulated to suit a variety of themes. Once again, we find that drama draws on other art forms for its own survival and extension. It is no exaggeration to claim that Hubert Ogunde's highest development of the chanted dramatic monologue can be fixed at the period of the political ban on his *Yoruba Ronu*. Evidently all art forms flow into one another, confirming, as earlier claimed, that the temporary historic obstacles to the flowering of a particular form sometimes lead to its transformation into other media of expression, or even the birth of totally different genres.

This survey stops at the emergence of the latest forms of traditional drama. The finest representatives of this to date have been the late Kola Ogunmola (comedy and satire) and Duro Ladipo (history and tragedy). Their contribution to contemporary drama and their innovations from indigenous forms require a far more detailed study, just as Moses Olaiya (Baba Sala) demands a chapter on his own iconoclastic brand of theatrical wit. The foregoing attempts to highlight ways in which artistic forms return to life again and again after their seeming demise, ways by which this process emphasises the fundamental unity of various art forms and the social environment that gives expression to them; how certain creative ideas are the very offspring of historic convulsions. Finally, while for purposes of demarcation we may speak of Nigerian, Ghanaian or perhaps Togolese drama, it must constantly be borne in mind that, like the economic intercourse of the people themselves, the various developments we have touched upon here in drama and the arts do not obey the laws of political boundaries though they might respond to the events within them. The various artistes we have mentioned had, and still enjoy, instant *rapport* with audiences far from their national and linguistic boundaries. Their art finds a ready response in most audiences since their themes are rooted in everyday experience, fleshed out in shared idioms of cultural adjustment.

Notes

1 Herbert M. Cole in *African arts*, VIII (3)
2 Abbé Boilatt, *Esquisses sénégalaises,* 1858
3 *Ibid.*

Questions for discussion

1 Cultural resistance to colonialism differs significantly from other forms of resistance – political, social, economic. Discuss.
2 Compare and contrast traditional African drama and modern African theatre.
3 What does the author mean by his expression 'unalienating forms of theatre'?
4 What is meant by the 'heroic tradition' in African drama?
5 Describe the new cultural responses which developed in opposition to 'Christian cultural imperialism' in West Africa in the nineteenth and early twentieth centuries.
6 What elements make Hubert Ogunde's theatre a prime example of contemporary 'folk opera'?

Suggestions for further reading

Banham, Martin, and Wake, Clive. *African theatre today,* London, Pitman, 1976

Echeruo, M. J. C. *Victorian Lagos*, London, Macmillan, 1977

Graham-White, Anthony. *The drama of black Africa,* New York, Samuel French, 1975

Jones, Eldred Durosimi (ed.) 'Drama in Africa', *African literature today,* 8, New York, Africana Publishing Co., 1976

Traore, Bakary, *The black African theatre and its social functions*, Ibadan University Press, 1972

Index